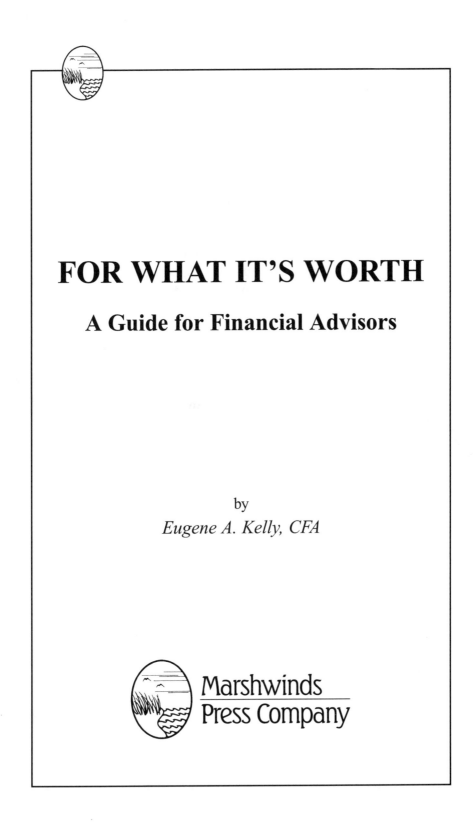

FOR WHAT IT'S WORTH

A Guide for Financial Advisors

by
Eugene A. Kelly, CFA

Marshwinds
Press Company

Copies of the book may be obtained by sending
$39.95 + $4.00 shipping to:

**Marshwinds Press Company
P.O. Box 21099
St. Simons Island, Georgia 31522**

Georgia residents add 6% sales tax

ISBN: 0-9614496-2-4

Library of Congress Control Number: 2001094827
First Edition
1   3   5   7   9   10   8   6   4   2

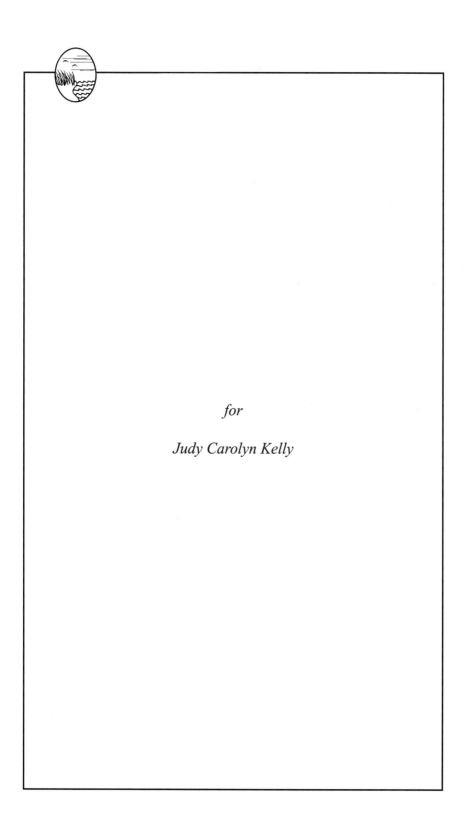

for

Judy Carolyn Kelly

Contents

BUILDING A BOOK

COMMUNICATING

Preface

There have been significant changes in the financial services business since 1985 when *For What It's Worth* was originally published. These changes are apparent in the title to the latest edition. The 1985 edition was a guide for new stockbrokers. This 2001 edition is a guide for financial advisors. You will also note this volume is twice as long as the first. There are plenty of reasons for the increased length besides my rambling.

The business is more complex and competitive. Clients are smarter and more demanding. A financial advisor must deliver exceptional service to build a practice today. With all of the complexity, the business is still based upon the bedrock of what is right for the clients' portfolios within the clients' risk tolerance.

The definition of a financial advisor has changed as well. Relationship managers at banks and trust departments as well as insurance professionals have joined the ranks of stockbrokers, investment counselors and financial planners providing services to institutions, small businesses, professionals and families. The principles and methods put forth in this book will work for all of these financial advisors.

I know the information in this book will help you be successful beyond your dreams. Not only did these FWIW's act as a blueprint for me, but they did it twice – once as a new stockbroker and then again as an investment counselor building a new business without the benefit of an established firm or track record.

The objective of this book is to assist other advisors in building a successful practice based upon ethical and professional standards. The first edition assisted tens of thousands of brokers to meet this objective. This book is the next step to evolving a financial services practice based upon helping clients be financially independent in the 21st century.

Special credit goes to Lisa Jackson, my assistant. More hours than she wants to remember went into transcribing my dictation and correcting my many errors. Her special skills in laying out the book and understanding how to use the computer have been invaluable to this project. Thank goodness for Lisa. Betty Snyder Bedell (Jacksonville, Florida) did the editing and we thank her for all the effort she put into the project.

Finally, my wife, Judy, has been with me through the writing of the original manuscript as well as this book. More importantly, she has been a vital part of building our business. Without her being at my side, neither the business nor this book would have come into being.

Eugene A. Kelly, CFA
Sea Island, Georgia

June 27, 2001

Preface – 1985 FWIW

I have wanted to write this book since 1968 when I first became interested in being a stockbroker. At that time I thought I could find a book which would give me an indication of what the job was about and how to enter the field. I was wrong.

There is very little written about the field, and what is written deals with "How" in a limited fashion but not "Why." This book tries to do both. Training classes will give mechanics; this book attempts to give understanding. Its size is the same as a "Holding Page" book. This was done on purpose.

The young stockbroker, now called a Financial Consultant, should use this book as a daily reference guide. Each FWIW is written assuming the reader is a new stockbroker.

Notice I said a reference guide, not an answer book. Our business is one where success comes in many individualistic ways. The reader of this book will quickly find a FWIW which he does not agree with. For that reader, my approach will not work. This is why I left the "MY WAY" column for notes. Each reader should use my approach as a starting point and adapt his own successful method to achieve his goal.

The overall objective of this book is to enhance the professionalism of our industry. Those of us who are fortunate enough to be in this business are truly blessed. We owe it to ourselves, our families, our clients, and our own personal GOD to bring to our career a level of professionalism which inspires those we come in contact with.

There are many who could have done a better job of writing this book – bigger producers and better managers – but they did not. I did. In sales nothing is original. Due to publication permission restrictions, I cannot recognize some of those who influenced some of the material.

If the book is a success, it will achieve my objective. If not, perhaps it will cause someone to write a better book. If so, my objective will also be achieved. Either way the public's interest is served.

Special credit needs to be given to Florence C. Smyth (Copywriter, Savannah, Georgia) who took the second draft of the manuscript and did an unbelievable job in correcting my use of the English language. Rencie gets the credit for the book being readable. Where poor grammar is used, it's my fault for not following her suggestions.

Finally, a word about my wife, Judy. Her contribution to this work is as great as mine. She encouraged me, she put up with my frustrations, and she typed and reviewed each of the drafts. Judy is my confidant and sounding board. There is no question this book would not have made it to publication without her assistance.

Eugene A. Kelly
Midway, Georgia

November 25, 1984

THE BIG PICTURE

FWIW # 1 .... *Is The Fat Lady Singing?*

Merrill Lynch set up Internet access for clients. Prudential Securities is advertising fee-based accounts. Charles Schwab is growing by leaps and bounds. Trades can be done on the Internet for $5.00. Research is available on the Internet for free. SEC filings are available on the Internet within minutes of their being filed with the government. Is the death of the highly compensated full-service broker rapidly approaching? No. Full service financial advisors will make more money than ever in the future. The challenge for currently active brokers will be the transition from the current system to the new one.

There have always been two kinds of highly compensated brokers. The first kind are excellent sales people. They have a knack for communicating with clients and are able to sell any investment their firm can create, especially the investments with high or ongoing commissions. These brokers thrive in the current environment of transactions and a transaction-based reward system. Their challenge is to transition from a commission oriented focus to a fee-based compensation program. While challenging, it can be done because these brokers have a strong ability to build relationships with clients. They recognize that being an investment manager, estate planner, or a financial planner is not their best attribute. They are strong at understanding what the client needs and going out and finding the right investment manager, estate planner, or financial planner to meet the client's requirements. These brokers turned financial advisors are excellent asset gatherers. Asset gathering is the key activity for any success as a financial advisor no matter what depth of knowledge will be subcontracted or learned and applied by the financial advisor. The transition is what will be challenging, but manageable, by this first type of broker. It starts with understanding what fee-based investments are available, merchandising the available securities and services, and understanding which clients have needs or wants for each of the investments or services.

The second kind of highly compensated brokers have always been financial advisors to their clients. By their nature, they have been able to communicate with the clients and their prospects. Their focus has been on matching the client's objectives and constraints with the right investment. If a high commission liquid investment fits, that's fine. If a low commission U.S. Treasury note fits, that's fine. The advisor's focus is on matching the right client with the right investment at the right time. Client portfolio growth has pushed this kind of highly compensated broker higher and higher up the economic ladder. Certainly, some of their clients will decide to go it alone and shift to a discount broker or the Internet. But, for everyone who does switch, there will be two new clients to take their place. Why? Four reasons: (1) demographics will substantially increase the number of people who have a rapidly increasing net worth through their own productive endeavors, (2) there is a generational change taking place where more money than ever in history is being transferred from one generation to another, (3) market volatility is increasing and the volatility will cause investors to seek a professional's help, and (4) investing is becoming more complex with more knowledge available to all investors.

The world operates on a fiat monetary system that requires greater and greater amounts of money in the system. Any monetary crisis is cured with the standard prescription of more money and lower interest rates. The end result is a slowly depreciating currency evidencing itself through higher salaries and higher asset values. The successful executive in a business today earns more than $100,000 a year when 25 years ago the same position might have paid $35,000. Almost all occupations in this country have some form of retirement account for the worker. An IRA, SEP, money purchase plan, 401(k), 403(b), or defined benefit plan are the vehicle for pouring hundreds of millions of dollars a year into the investment markets. While real estate investing receives a portion of this ever-growing retirement asset pool, the overwhelming percentage of the funds goes into stocks, bonds, and money market funds.

The generational transfer of assets is huge. The depression era generation is dying out, having kept their promise that they would never go through hunger and uncertainty again. Their children do not know the same fears. The huge amount of frugality will be passed on to those who don't know its value, but who all of a sudden know the responsibility and fragility of the new found wealth. Adding this gift from one generation to another to the assets accumulated by the younger family members brings on a concern about protecting and growing those assets. People who are confident about making investment decisions with what they regard as a small amount of money find themselves unable to make a decision when the asset base becomes larger than they can handle psychologically. What level of assets causes the indecision? That depends upon the investors. It should not matter to the professional financial advisor because the compensation structure on a fee-base business makes it worthwhile to work with all different levels of portfolios. The generational passing of assets is a major catalyst in triggering the younger generation's anxiety about preserving and growing their assets.This is a perfect situation for a professional financial advisor.

When the investment markets had a bias for rising, as they had during the period 1992-1999, the potential negative consequences of making investment decisions were not severe. Stick with quality and the rising market will drag most stocks upward. As the markets reached lofty levels and more decisions were made in anticipation of the future, the volatility increased significantly. Investors are finding that there is not a clear and strong connection between a company's fundamental financial factors and the share price. Investors begin to experience what is called "paralysis by analysis," a condition created by being overwhelmed through the accumulation of information from many sources, some contradicting others. What seemed from a distance to be a science, up close appears to be unscientific, and that disturbs many investors. The fact is, investing is an art, not a science. Volatility causes anxiety and anxiety causes investors to seek out a professional who can make sense of the huge amounts of information and alternatives available in the marketplace.

Even professionals can become challenged by the information overload. Not only do small investors have access to the raw data usually reserved in the past for professional analysts, but there is an explosion of opinions available to investors, for free. Taming and harnessing this raging river of facts and numbers and opinions is too much for the person who has to run a business, raise a family, and likes to have a life outside of their portfolio. These investors want to find someone who does understand how to filter the noise out and keep the important information in the decision making process. They want someone who can look at their unique family circumstances and build an approach to matching the correct investments so they can meet their objectives. They want someone who can supply stability and logic to their financial future. They want someone who can make adjustments to the program as the family life evolves. They want someone who will not disappear or become indecisive during the challenging investment times. In short, they want a financial advisor they can trust, a real person who understands them and tailors advice to fit. They are the clients of the future and they are searching right now for a professional financial advisor. The fat lady is not singing, she's not even on stage. The new era in financial services is just beginning and there will be untold riches for professional financial advisors.

FWIW # 2 ....*An Entrepreneur*

The Random House College Dictionary defines an entrepreneur as "a person who organizes, manages, and assumes responsibility for a business or other enterprise." Generally, an entrepreneur is thought to be someone who owns and operates a grocery store, wholesale business, small manufacturing business, or restaurant, and employs people. Financial advisors are thought of as employees, not employers, and never as entrepreneurs. But this is a misconception. A comparison of a small retail merchant and a financial advisor will illustrate the similarities between the two.

The merchant has gross sales from which cost of goods sold is deducted to obtain a gross margin. From the gross margin, selling and administrative expenses are deducted to arrive at profit before taxes. Generally, this figure is 7% to 15% of sales. After deducting income taxes, the merchant has net income after taxes, usually 4% to 10% of sales.

Now look at the financial advisor. The advisor has gross commissions or fees from dealings with the public which are the sales or revenues of the business. In essence, the advisor contracts with an investment brokerage firm for certain services or sets up an independent firm. The cost of the services, either contracted from an investment broker or part of the independent firm, will usually run 50% to 70% of the revenue of the advisor's business and include the selling and administrative costs. Therefore, the advisor's net before taxes can run up to 50% of revenues with the general norm being

35%. This is 100% to 200% more than that of a retail merchant or small businessman. (The reader can choose any business or industry but will find it hard to come up with one that has an operating income before taxes of 35%.)

One response to this analogy is that the advisor does not build net worth through retained earnings like the business owner does. While this is true, in some cases, it is by choice or ignorance and not by the nature of the business. Small businesses that are operated as Subchapter S corporations or partnerships do not retain earnings but flow them through to the individual owners and partners to be taxed only once at their individual level. Any business owner has the opportunity to draw a salary and to keep the difference between that salary and the net profits after tax as retained earnings. The financial advisor has the same choice. The advisor can spend all of the income or invest a portion as retained earnings. As a matter of fact, the retained earnings for the advisor have the advantage of being in the form of marketable securities which offer liquidity which is denied to a small business owner who reinvests the retained earnings in the business property, plant, and equipment as well as accounts receivable and inventory. The financial advisor, who is associated with an investment brokerage firm, usually has an additional benefit in the form of a paid retirement program as well as lower cost group medical insurance. Independent advisors do not have these benefits and have to provide them for themselves.

The best advantage the financial advisor has over the entrepreneur is the amount of capital it takes to begin a business. The fast food franchise requires $500,000 or more just to begin. A retail merchant's available capital for inventory and operating expenses directly determines the potential sales. A small manufacturer must finance an inventory and accounts receivable as well as plant facilities. On the other hand, the financial advisor needs very little capital. By associating with an established firm, the advisor is able to begin doing business without large amounts of invested cash, just "sweat equity." Personal efforts and integrity are the primary ingredients that are necessary to enter the financial advisory business.

Finally, few businesses offer men and women from every walk of life the opportunity to become one of the highest paid professionals in their local community as well as in the nation as a whole. The business of being a financial advisor does just that. The advisor only needs patience, persistence, and a desire to be successful, all of the attributes of an entrepreneur. Without the perspective and attitude of being a business owner, it will be hard for a financial advisor to succeed in the new age of investing. With the right perspective and discipline, an advisor has the potential to earn more than ever possible before. Let me make it even clearer. The new age of Internet investing and discount brokers makes being a professional financial advisor a more lucrative business than ever before.

FWIW # 3 .... *Equity Capital*

While a financial advisor does not have to have any capital other than "sweat equity," it's wise to go a step further by making some monetary contributions to the new enterprise. During the training period, an assessment is made of what is necessary to conduct business as a professional from the first day. Some, but not all, required tools of the trade are as follows:

> Clothes
>
> Club Membership
>
> Personal Computer
>
> Internet Access
>
> Subscriptions
>
> Cell Phone
>
> Day Planner/Client Relationship Organizer
>
> Technical Charts
>
> Support Help

Some unique locations have other requirements that can be added to this list as well. These expenditures are investments just as rent, inventory, and plant and equipment are for other businesses. If the advisor's business is going to be professional and successful, it must be conducted that way from day one. It is not only important for the public to perceive the service as professional, the advisor must know the firm is professionally conducted to have confidence in the business strategy during the tough times.

The question is how does the advisor get the money to invest when just starting out? The answer is by borrowing it. Every bank in the country and every major credit card company is willing to extend to individuals a personal line of credit. A locally owned bank is the best source of credit for two reasons. First, eventually the bank could be a source of referrals. Yes, they also might be competitors. But that does not preclude some members of the bank management or board of directors being clients. Just as important, the bank can be a source of reference for those clients who want to know someone who can attest to the advisor's character. Second, to get the loan, the advisor will have to submit a written business plan. The plan has to make sense to the bank loan officer. The act of creating the plan will help the advisor focus on what it takes to succeed. An alternative to bank credit is credit card debt which is more expensive and only to be used when a bank line of credit is not available. Research will help the advisor find the credit cards with the lowest interest rates. Forget the annual fee. Focus on the lowest interest rate. Find two cards with as high a line of credit as possible on both.

Spending borrowed money wisely for furthering a business makes sense. The key word is wisely. Owning an expensive car does not bring an advisor new business. Dressing professionally and being efficient builds prospective clients' confidence in the advisor. Investing in the resources that build knowledge of the business builds confidence in prospective clients when they talk to the advisor. Being part of organizations whose membership is prospective clients, builds business. Owning the resources that constantly improve knowledge of salesmanship and investments builds business. Equity investments are important, necessary, and votes of confidence by the advisor in the advisor's own future.

FWIW # 4 .... *No Free Lunch*

Can you imagine calling up a jewelry store and asking them to give you some jewels now because you may buy some from them in the future? How about calling a doctor and asking for a free diagnosis so you can decide whether or not to use that doctor in the future? Sure, it happens all the time, right? It never ceases to amaze me when brokers and brokerage firms give away the only valuable asset they have: their knowledge and experience.

When access to the markets was the product being sold, bragging about a firm's knowledge might, and only might, make sense. In this time of deep discount and online brokers, it's just plain stupid. You can't make your firm stop giving away the company's jewels, but you can make sure your clients appreciate and value your knowledge and experience. Start by realizing you are an important part of a successful investment program. As a financial advisor today, you need to know what you're talking about when it comes to growing your client's assets within their unique constraints. Read that sentence again. And again. Get it through your head that in the 21st century, you are going to make your client's richer or you are going to be out of the business. So now it becomes clear, step one is to find clients and step two is to grow the client's portfolio. Now stop and think: if your talents are to make your clients richer, why are you better off by giving your prospective clients your knowledge and experience hoping they will be kind enough to do business with you? If you are professional about your business and grow your clients' portfolio, your office will look like a Baskin-Robbins ice cream store on a hot July afternoon with people taking numbers and standing in line to talk with you about their portfolio. Besides, where is the logic of charging people who believe in you for your advice and guidance while giving your advice and guidance to people who don't believe in you? Doesn't make sense, does it? Investors are going to learn that there is no free lunch when it comes to using a knowledgeable, professional advisor.

You don't have a free lunch either. You had better know how to analyze a prospective client's unique situation and risk profile and match the right security and the right strategy to grow that portfolio. You had better know how to communicate this knowledge to that prospective client. You have to be able to convince enough investors that you are a knowledgeable, professional financial advisor who can help them build their net worth intelligently within the proper amount of risk. You have to know when someone will not make a good client for you no matter how much money they have. In short, you truly have to be a professional who projects the image and aura of a professional and backs it up with solid knowledge and experience.

FWIW # 5 .... *Clients Versus Customers*

In the 1980's marketing wizards who didn't know about the financial services business and its unique relationship between brokers and their clients found it chic to call securities "products" and clients "customers." Their perspective was to create special products, build in a lot of commission, and push it upon customers through the firm's brokers. Oh, by the way, the brokers were reduced to being "the distribution system." You know what all these wizards got themselves for their manufacturing perspective? Discount brokers who have evolved into Internet brokers.

Get it straight from the beginning. If you are a professional financial advisor, you have clients, not customers. You deal with investments and services that are tailored to make the client's portfolio grow within the client's constraints, not products.

FWIW # 6 .... *Time Investment*

Being a successful financial advisor is time consuming. It will take a minimum of sixty hours a week to build a successful business and more than that to maintain one at a high level of income for you. In the beginning, it's necessary to work hard. As the business grows and your experience grows, the working hard is leveraged with working smart. Notice, working smart enhances working hard, it does not replace it. Just working hard, however, is not the answer. There are a lot of people in this world who work hard but still fail. One of the misguided precepts of our society is that if a person tries hard enough, long enough, and often enough, success will come. Well, that's not true. ***There is no reward for trying, only for succeeding.*** The professional financial advisor must consciously cultivate habits which lead to success. Let's examine how to do just that.

First, when working out a daily schedule, the new professional advisor should plan the schedule as if their clientele was complete. Why? Because success comes from being good in all facets of the business. Every part of the business must be practiced every single day. Assuming a daily commute of less than 25 miles, the work week for a professional financial advisor should look something like this:

WEEKDAYS:

6:00 a.m. - 6:45 a.m. - Shower, dress, check market news for interest rate changes and your major stock holdings through business programs on television.

6:45 a.m. - 7:30 a.m. - Read local newspaper to be in touch with local news. Have breakfast.

7:30 a.m. - 8:00 a.m. - Travel to office and listen to motivational and salesmanship audio cassettes.

8:00 a.m. - 8:30 a.m. - Check news items on stock holdings and primary stock universe. Update technical analysis profile on your stock universe and holdings.

8:30 a.m. - 9:00 a.m.   -   Review status of administrative work with assistant, enter transactions if any for the day.

9:00 a.m. - 12:00 noon -   Appointments with clients and/or 300 Club members, a minimum of two.

12:00 noon - 1:00 p.m. -   Lunch with a client or a 300 Club member (FWIW # 40).

1:00 p.m. - 4:00 p.m.   -   Appointment with client and/or 300 Club member, minimum of two.

4:00 p.m. - 5:00 p.m.   -   Return to office, confirm the next day's appointments, meet with administrative assistant to review new items and what was to be done on this day.

5:00 p.m. - 6:00 p.m.   -   Appointments out of office or community service meetings.

6:00 p.m. - 6:30 p.m.   -   Travel home and listen to motivational and salesmanship audio cassettes.

6:30 p.m. - 9:00 p.m.   -   Spend time with the family, no work whatsoever.

9:00 p.m. - 10:00 p.m. -   Read material about portfolio management or information on managers in referral program.

10:00 p.m. - 11:00 p.m. -   Read material on salesmanship or develop action sales idea for next day.

SATURDAYS AND HOLIDAYS:

Spend two hours reviewing client portfolios for any adjustments that are necessary, prepare any trades that need to be made based upon market movement or new accounts during the last week.

Using this schedule, the professional financial advisor can build and maintain a well-organized business. There still, however, is time for family, sports, and exercise. All aspects of the business are part of the schedule. Special times emphasizing a closer focus on one facet of the business, such as education, can be incorporated in the schedule without major disruption. It's very important to understand the concept that every aspect of the business is practiced every week.

FWIW # 7 .... First Love?

Most people believe a financial advisor's profession is easy and stress free. Nothing is further from the truth. Dealing with clients' money is highly stressful. It's stressful because clients are counting on you to grow their net worth. It's stressful because nothing is as important to most clients as their money. It's stressful because decisions are made to buy and sell and are either right or wrong and the advisor's ego is on the line every single time. It's stressful because clients can and will leave because of bad investment decisions or because of some small clerical issue that makes them mad. Watch the small beads of sweat on the upper lip or forehead develop when an advisor starts thinking about losing clients and the fragile nature of the relationship.

Dealing with stress is a prerequisite of success in the financial services business. Stress is easily dealt with when you truly like what you are doing, when you like the challenge of finding investments, when you like the challenge of communicating with clients, when you like the challenge of competing with other advisors, when you like to watch clients' portfolios grow, when you like to operate in difficult market environments, and when you like working long hours to accomplish the tasks necessary to succeed. Without this total immersion, you can make a living, but you can't be successful. The business becomes a major part of your life fabric. Family becomes the other part. The greatest stress any financial advisor has is balancing the amount of time and intensity to be successful with the amount of time and focus that your spouse and family demand and expect. Your spouse wants a loving, attentive, and burden sharing soul mate. You want someone who understands the amount of focus it takes to be successful and, therefore, does not put pressure on you for your time and your emotions. Inevitably, the issues are framed in terms of who or what do you love the most. The career or me, your spouse will say. Oh, by the way, the question never comes up when it's time to take an expensive trip, buy a new car, or antique, or move to a nicer house in a nicer neighborhood.

There is a way to merge career and family and have a spouse and children focused on your career. Make them understand the connection between the hard work and long hours and the progress in the family's goals. The first step in accomplishing this all important task is to separate your efforts focused on your spouse from those efforts focused on the children. Stop and think for a minute. What makes you feel good in your career? Isn't it being rewarded for meeting goals or succeeding in growing your clients' portfolios thereby raising your revenue stream? Why don't you reward your spouse when you hit some personal goals each year? If your goals include monthly targets for assets under management or generating certain fee levels, decide you will give your spouse something special when the goals are met. Flowers, balloons, special presents, special time out with just the two of you. Whatever says to your spouse, "we did it, thanks for being a partner in the progress of our business." The only stipulation is to make sure the reward is uniquely for your spouse. If they want to share it, or it can be shared like a weekend away, make sure the trip is where your spouse wants to go and the activities are what your spouse wants to do. Make each reward a surprise, make sure each one comes at an irregular time frame so that it doesn't become something that is expected. Achieving the goal has to be a milestone, not a regular event. There must be a closer connection between the hard work and the sharing of responsibilities and the present that is just for them. Help your spouse know the reward is because you know how much their participation added to your achievement.

Clearly personal and totally unnecessary gifts to reinforce the bond between the career and the family work great with spouses. With children, the only real gift that counts is your time. Giving of time in a business that is usually unstructured, demanding, and time-consuming takes planning and flexibility on your part. Start by helping your children understand the importance of your career and their part in your career success. Let them see how you and your mate work together to make your career, and theirs, if it's a two career family, successful. Be an example for what it takes to be a success. Talk to them about what requirements there are for your career. If you show and demonstrate the importance to the family of the work you do, when you take time out to be with them during the workday, the value of your time will be understood. Find out at the beginning of the school year when parents' days, teacher conferences, assemblies, and sports events will take place. Almost 90% of these activities can be put on a calendar weeks or months ahead of time. Commit to these activities. Your career won't skip a beat if you turn each one of these family events into a business development experience. School activities are not singular activities. They, by their nature, involve other children, other parents, teachers and administrators. In today's world of professional client development, the more people you contact, the more opportunities you have. Do you know about your child's teacher's financial situation? The teacher might be inheriting substantial wealth at some point in life. Their spouse might have a high income and fat retirement plan. The sports coach is possibly an entrepreneur with a business earning hundreds of thousands of dollars a year. At the very least, they might be good friends with someone who has a great deal of money. Participating in family activities, interacting with other parents and families, is one of the best ways to add to the 300 Club. It will also make it easier for your children to understand when you can't be around. It lifts their self image when they know you consider them important enough to put them ahead of business. More than anything else, it teaches them to balance their work and play just as you are doing. There is an added benefit when you take time for your children. You instinctively work more efficiently and get more done in the time you have left in either that day or that week.

FWIW # 8 .... *Habit of Winning*

Two constantly uttered phrases are: "I can't believe they are so successful, they were so dumb in school," and, "they are so smart, so well read, yet so unsuccessful, how can you figure that?" The world is full of people who exceed their boundaries and others who fail miserably to live up to their potential. There doesn't seem to be any common denominator for these surprises, but there is. It's not working hard, it's not working smart. Plenty of people work hard and smart and get nowhere, they fail to meet their goals. If working hard and working smart isn't the secret, what is? Habit is the secret of success. Not just any habit. Vince Lombardi once said winning was a habit, and so was losing. Earl Nightingale gave a speech once that focused on success coming to ***people who make a habit of doing the things failures don't want to do.*** Think about that for a minute. What are the actions in the financial services business that separate the successful few from the rest? The extra client contact, the extra hours of preparation, reading the extra research report or annual reports, or the extra business development call, these are the things failures don't want to do in your business.

Succeeding as a financial advisor takes time. There is no short cut because the business is built on human relationships and human relationships are woven together slowly through personal contact and sharing of information. Relationship building is a process of confidence building. In our early lives, success came from achieving specific objectives where we could "cram" the night before a test and pass the test with high marks. That's not possible as a financial advisor. Persistence and repetition of the many tasks involved, from business development, to client relationship building, to portfolio management and research, all have to be done day in and day out even when you don't want to or when it appears no progress is being made. What keeps a person going when going on appears hopeless? An intangible desire to succeed called "the fire within." This impalpable quality is like a person's soul: it is there and it radiates heat and light yet it is invisible and indefinable. It is possible to neither create it nor to acquire it. Everyone is born with it, "the fire within," but society has decreed that it is uncivilized and dangerous and needs to be extinguished. And so most people spend their lives banking it in the ashes of conventional behavior so that they too will be deemed nice, polite, upright citizens who fit the mold of society.

What motivates a person is usually illogical and emotional, not logical and rational. Wanting to give a better family life to your children than you had. Wanting to travel in a different circle of friends than you do now. Wanting to be recognized by your peers as a leader. Wanting to be better than your (fill in the blank) did in their career. Wanting to restore the family's wealth and prestige. None of these wants are logical, but each one of them will cause somebody to get up earlier, work longer, read that extra text, sharpen their communication skills, or ask for the opportunity to serve more than the next person.

Just like an actual rekindled fire, the fire within the achiever burns hotter and brighter the more it is stoked. When you are alone in a quiet moment, think about what ignites the fire within you. Don't be afraid of admitting it. Cherish it and stoke it and commit to achieving it. Focus on it, but don't talk about it. Others, including in most cases, your spouse, will not understand. Your fire within is unique to you. It will make you a success, but no one else.

Finally, make a point to seek out other achievers who have the desire and drive like you do. A positive attitude, successful winning habits, drive and determination are all contagious. Be infected by these masters of their destiny no matter what their field. Seek out those who are the best of the best and you will be a part of that minority of leaders.

We are all taught at an early age not to judge a book by its cover, yet 95% of us do exactly that! Have you ever dismissed, in your mind, a shabbily dressed person as someone of no consequence? Even in this age of reverse chic dressing in t-shirts and slacks made popular in Silicon Valley, when it comes to important issues, most people want the professionals they deal with to project the right image. A doctor with unkempt hair, wrinkled clothes, dirty hands, and an unkempt office will not give you confidence in their diagnosis. It's important for a financial advisor to be appropriately dressed so that the client or prospective client has a neutral, positive impression of professionalism, not flashy, not disheveled. You want your client to focus on your work, not on your appearance.

The challenge comes in looking the way you are supposed to look because the right appearance varies from locale to locale. In a resort community, the appropriate dress code might be a sports shirt and slacks. In a small town, perhaps a sports jacket, shirt, tie, and slacks, or a dress, or a skirt and blouse. In a big city, both male and female advisors are appropriately dressed when in a business suit.

There is a simple way of determining how you should dress every day. Imagine you have a meeting this day with your best prospect and a board of directors who are looking to judge if you should be their financial professional. What would you wear? Now you know what you should wear every day. Simple, isn't it?

What about casual days at the office? Casual days are a dilemma. The regular business week is five days long. If one of those days is a casual day, it means 20% of the time is dress down time. Are you as effective in a casual setting as you are in a regular business setting? Isn't the point of dress down day to be casual and more relaxed? Does that include a more relaxed attitude about events and work during the day? Are you willing to interact with your best client on a casual day? Do you feel comfortable out of traditional business wear when discussing portfolios with a client? The concept of dress down is almost childish in that its purpose is to give employees some sort of relaxed camaraderie. A study of an organization's efficiency on dress down day would be interesting. In your case, do what makes sense for your business development and efficiency.

Quality counts. Whatever dress code is appropriate for your area, make sure you have quality in what you wear. Quality clothing shows and speaks volumes about the person wearing it. For your own financial sake, buy traditional cuts of clothing that will not go out of style quickly. High quality and traditional cut wardrobes make sense and can be systematically expanded and replenished by adding a new outfit to the collection every six months.

Hair styles and shoes are two crucial elements in looking professional. Neat hairstyles properly groomed make for a professional appearance. Polished shoes are a must. The total picture speaks for an intelligent, prepared, disciplined professional who takes pride in all aspects of work and who projects the image of taking care of clients' portfolios in the same way. Isn't that the kind of person you want to handle your investments?

FWIW # 10 .... *Who Are You?*

Ever since there has been a financial services industry, the debate over specializing in one area or being a generalist has been hotly contested. Interestingly, there are enough successful financial advisors on either side of the argument to insure that the debate will continue. When thinking about the issue from the client's perspective, the allure of being a specialist is attractive. It's human nature for us to want to do business with the expert or specialist in any field from medicine, to law, to retailing. As consumers, we are willing to pay a specialist a premium for their expertise. It's a way of distinguishing yourself from your peers. Two points are important to keep in mind.

First, a specialty should not be selected just because you want to operate in that area. You should take time to see if your primary market perceives a need for the specialty. This market survey comes through your prospecting and communicating with future clients. Second, the specialty should appeal to a broad section of investors, not just a small segment. For instance, commodity futures or option trading are great specialties in a city the size of New York or Los Angeles because the subgroup of investors using these markets is large. A financial advisor specializing in commodity futures or option trading will have a tough time staying in business in small towns or rural areas.

Self-confidence in the business skyrockets when you take the time to become especially knowledgeable about one particular area. This additional assurance translates into more business because the clients and prospective clients can see and feel your command of the issues.

Credentials are more important today than ever before as a way for the public to distinguish one advisor from the rest of the group. A college degree is necessary to be in the business. Clients should be aware of special educational milestones in addition to a regular college degree. A law degree or a CPA status will enhance your professionalism because both indicate special learning skills even though neither directly prepares you for being a successful financial advisor. Obtaining a CFP is the way to start immersing yourself in the business. This designation assists you in understanding the alternatives as well as the outside factors that influence investors' decisions. It elevates you above other advisors now, but eventually will become a necessary prerequisite just as a college degree has become.

As your career progresses, you will be faced with a monumental decision: are you going to focus primarily on business development and placing of client assets with other professionals who manage the assets or are you going to become the manager of the portfolio as well as the business development director? This is a major crossroads in your career when you face this decision. If you choose to participate in the management of the client's assets, a Chartered Financial Analyst designation, referred to as a CFA, is important. It is also difficult to achieve since it takes a minimum of three years and three six-hour examinations. Success in achieving the right to use the CFA will propel your career to new levels as you are able to not only communicate your firm's benefits to your clients, but also speak with the depth of knowledge that comes from fully understanding and practicing the art of portfolio management.

During the 1980's and the period of "manufactured securities," specialization had one meaning: being good at one area of investing such as tax shelters, limited partnerships, oil and gas investments, or municipal bonds. With the focus on stocks and their relatively low capital gains tax rate, a generalist will usually focus on general portfolio management while a specialist will focus on a particular type of stock investing such as growth or value or specialize in fixed income investing entirely. How do you choose whether to specialize or not? Let your instincts decide. First, don't make a decision for at least the first three years of your career. Be a generalist and see what success comes from what area of your business development and asset management. For those who have been in the business for a while, reviewing your client accounts and prioritizing them as to how much money they have made and how successful they have been will give you an inclination of the areas of the business that you find more appealing. For example, make a decision that you want to look seriously at specializing in one form of investing such as fixed income investing. Until you have some expertise, seek out ways to place the assets with your firm's professionals or outside managers and mutual funds who focus on this area. Talk to the professionals. Read everything you can about what they do and how they do it. Learn the terminology of the various securities and how they interact. Develop your skills in explaining the benefits of a sound fixed income portfolio in the client's overall financial picture. Compare and contrast fixed income investments with equity investments or specialized investments or real estate investments. Set goals for identifying and communicating with investors wanting or needing fixed income portfolios. As you progress in knowledge and experience, how comfortable are you with the process? Does learning the fixed income elements of investing come easy? Does the process and methods of generating above average returns delight you? Can you both help and benefit clients and build a good career for yourself? Repeat this in-depth immersion of yourself in each area of the business. Perhaps one area will hold your attention better than another. Perhaps not. If it does, you are a candidate to be a specialist. If you love it all and don't want to give up any part for another, you should remain a generalist. Either way, your ability to succeed will be enhanced by your efforts.

FWIW # 11 .... *Keys To Success*

Building a successful financial advisor practice isn't easy. There are no secret phrases you can utter or shortcuts you can take to develop a clientele who trust you. ***Motivation and knowledge*** are the keys to success. Something, or someone, or some drive has to make you work harder, longer, and smarter than your competition. We've already discussed what it takes to build winning habits (See FWIW # 8). Having the desire is only part of the process. You have to know what you're doing each step of the way. There are four parts to a successful practice. The first is business development. You have to understand your market and how your potential clients live in your community. Are country clubs an important gathering place? How about churches? Is a university or college a center of focus in the community? What charities are supported by the leaders in the community? What role do local politics play in your town? Is the city dominated by the political class, the medical community, the business community, or academic community? How strong is the Chamber of Commerce? You have to study your local community to understand where the potential clients work, socialize, and live. You have to put yourself directly in the middle of where the prospective clients are. Knowledge of your marketplace is a prerequisite to success.

Constantly upgrading your knowledge of how to communicate with clients and prospective clients helps you make the most of every potential business development opportunity. Communicating is selling and there is no such thing as a born salesman. Selling is an acquired skill. It is a product of your environment, not your heredity. A desire to succeed is an essential component of a successful person. Translating that desire into bringing benefits to your clients from the service that you offer is salesmanship and communication.

Salesmanship is part science and part art. Behavioral psychology has made great advances in intensifying and improving effective communication techniques. Unless the financial advisor has sharpened and polished communication skills, the wants and needs of their clients cannot be identified, much less met. There is a wealth of books and tapes available on developing selling and communication skills. Each and every day, therefore, the financial advisor should conscientiously work on the communication skills of presenting facts and features as advantages and benefits for the client. The language of salesmanship is just that: a separate language that has to be mastered.

Business schools use hypothetical case studies to teach future MBA's. You should construct several hypothetical situations and practice developing the type of sales presentation that assists the client in understanding what it takes to help grow the portfolio. It might be a widow who has just been left a $500,000 insurance policy and is afraid to invest the money. It might be a business person who has just sold their business after thirty years of building it and has a retirement portfolio as well as several million dollars in proceeds that has to be invested to take care of two generations of the family. Think about the various investment objectives, investment constraints, and investment strategies to meet those objectives within the constraints and how you communicate them to your client. What kinds of questions are needed to understand those objectives and to identify those constraints? How can those questions be constructed in a non-offensive way? Effective communication is a set of skills learned by practice, practice, and more practice. It doesn't come by accident.

Investment knowledge doesn't come by accident either. Going through a disciplined course of study, such as the CFP program or the CFA program, greatly speeds up the learning curve. Disciplined reading outside these programs is also necessary, particularly when the programs are over. Thinking about the investment process and relating it to the potential client is important. Investing for a tax-deferred retirement account is different than investing for a taxable client. All clients evolve in their life and their family over time which has the potential to change their objectives as they age and as their family changes its character. Periodic updating of what you know about a client through regular communication makes you aware of life cycle changes in the client's family. You can then relate the evolving changes in the client's life to the investment process.

The final key to success is knowledge of administering the business, knowing what it takes to operate the portfolio and keeping track of the investments as well as the checks and balances within the portfolio itself. The rapidly changing dynamics of technology in the business has to be mastered by the financial advisor if portfolio growth and growth in the number of portfolios are to be expected without quality service being strained. Working with a financial services firm that allows client access over the Internet certainly makes the job easier. When a new client is obtained, give them the software for accessing their account and help them understand your role as a financial advisor and the role of the Internet access as a way of monitoring the assets, ordering checks, moving assets from one account to another, and seeing if a dividend or interest payment has been received. Your clients are embracing the technology and so should you.

FWIW # 12 .... Nice to Know vs. Need to Know

A by-product of the Internet is an explosion of facts, figures, opinions, and just plain noise about every conceivable subject, especially investments. Next to sex, investment knowledge and ideas is probably the most sought after information on the web. Step one in making sense of this barrage of information is to begin to recognize the difference between ***nice to know*** and ***need to know*** information. Nice to know material is entertaining and generally is someone's opinion of a subject. At the very least, it's information that an advertising agency or a public relations department has put out for puffing up the profile of the company or managers or industry in question. There might be facts, but they are carefully selected one-sided facts or even worse, someone interpreting the facts. Unless you live with or shop with the interpreter of facts, what will you do if the interpretation is incorrect? What if you make a decision based upon that interpretation, the information is later found to be incorrect and another decision has to be made about the investment? Where is the opinion maker then? The challenge is that nice to know information is entertaining and easy to read. Need to know information is not.

Need to know information is usually facts or statements that factually describe a situation. For example, in an annual report the Letter to Shareholders is nice to know information. It's upbeat, even when results aren't. It addresses the fun and optimistic aspects of the company. It makes you feel good if you are a stockholder. On the other hand, the Management's Discussion and Analysis of Financial Condition and Results of Operation is factual. It has to be because it is required by law to be written in a factual manner. It also has to be truthful. It has to be complete or the management risks class action lawsuits. Financial statements and footnotes are factual. They are sometimes dull reading but they give a clear and undistorted picture of what's going on. This is need to know information.

Quickly being able to sift through the blizzard of data to gather the nuggets of wealth from need to know information comes with experience and knowledge.

Your most precious commodity is your time. Between family, business, and relaxation you don't have a minute to spare for people or things that don't improve your life or make you more efficient. In the past, the three primary office time wasters were the tape watchers, the quote machine, and mediocre brokers. The tape watchers are about gone since offices are being designed without moving stock price ticker tapes and seating for people to sit and watch the tape. As one time waster goes by the wayside, another more potent one takes its place: business news television and the Internet. Massive amounts of time are wasted watching the talking heads on television waiting for the real facts or news that can be used in the investment decision process. A large amount of the material on TV would have been illegal to broadcast years ago when there were industry rules against spreading unfounded rumors. Besides rumors, such silly but entertaining information about how much a CEO's net worth changed when the company's stock made a major move is nice to know, but utterly useless dribble for a professional financial advisor in the middle of a busy day.

Old-fashioned quote machines were an allure to brokers who spent untold minutes every hour pushing up the correct price of securities in portfolios. Now, most systems available to the financial advisor have monitoring screens that blink every time a security on the screen trades or the price changes. Green for up, red for down, white or blue for unchanged, the display is fascinating. Looks like a Christmas tree. Almost as big a time waster as the past quote machines, yet certainly more effective and less of a time waster because of how much more the data can be manipulated to provide really helpful information (See KEEPING IT ALL TOGETHER section).

Alas, there is not a substitute for the time wasting mediocre broker who does enough to keep a career going but not enough to be truly successful. Because these individuals have been in the business a while and do have some experience and knowledge, they are interesting as great debaters and analyzers of the latest financial report, market change, or any other nice to know tidbits about the business that they heard from the talking heads on business TV. None of this brings the focused financial advisor close to meeting the day's goals and objectives. What to do? You don't want to hurt anyone's feelings, particularly someone who is friendly and supportive when you are not performing on all cylinders, so the best way to handle the situation is to be clearly busy when the time waster comes up to your office or desk. If not, count to 100 silently and then make an excuse that you have to call a client or prospective client. Ask the broker, have you made your quota of business contacts today? That will usually send them running out of your office. If the problem persists, speak to your manager, who will then speak to the offending person quietly and put a stop to the distraction.

FWIW # 14 .... *Client vs. Prospect*

Prospecting is hard and getting harder. In the past, investors were not nearly as knowledgeable as they are now. Investing news saturates anyone who wants to know what the markets are doing. High quality clients do not just show up unannounced and without carefully repeated contacts and months of work. The courtship is something to behold, but it seems that when the prospect becomes a client, the marriage is less than successful because the financial advisor neglects the new client. The client is treated as a possession not a person who has freely selected the advisor to assist in the portfolio growth. Yet, when former clients are questioned about why they closed their accounts, they cite *too busy, indifferent, and no service* as major causes of their desertion. All of the time and effort devoted to winning the trust and confidence of the prospect is wasted because of the advisor's less than professional attitude, inexplicably, because the client is much more valuable than a prospect.

A client has already embraced the knowledge and experience of the financial advisor and is looking forward to working as a team to grow the portfolio. All of the long hours of developing the prospect's confidence are over. The hours of portfolio management activity, research activities, and administrative work are more efficient since there is another client who benefits. Even more important than efficiency, the power of compounding works for both the client and the financial advisor. Growing the client's assets steadily moves the client closer to the financial goals. With more clients, the financial advisor's assets under management grow. Since more and more advisors are compensated by fees based on the size of their clients' portfolio, more clients with growing portfolios means more fee-based assets without the difficulties and hard work of prospecting. Want a new $10 million account? Focus on $100 million of client assets and grow these assets 10%. Every day should be devoted to making sure your clients are delighted they are working with you. Every day you should make sure you can feel good about the attention you paid to improving your clients' portfolios.

FWIW # 15 .... *Six Month Blues/Boredom*

An outsider to the financial services business thinks the financial advisor's career is easy, glamorous and consists of reading the Wall Street Journal, watching business TV, answering a few calls from clients, taking a long lunch hour, and finishing off the day playing golf at a country club. Even new trainees have this same attitude. As their training progresses, the trainee's confidence builds and builds because no one at the firm has as much creativity and dedication. Within the artificial atmosphere of the training class, dynamite sure fire sales presentations and scripts are developed which will gather in the new accounts without fail. When the training is over, the real world intrudes. With the first week out of training comes the reality that prospects are not bowled over by the sales presentations nor the charm nor the hard work. Just like a battery, the energy level slowly drains away along with expectations of fast success. Doubts creep in. Doubts about the ability to succeed, doubts about the firm's research, doubts about the firm's operations area, and doubts about the career, since so many discount brokers and Internet sites are unfairly competing for investors. It becomes clear that success is 1% inspiration and 99% perspiration. All of this takes place in the first six months of being in the business and is called the six month blues. Anyone experiencing the six month blues only has to decide if the **want to** is there, then all of the preconceived ideas and illusions have to be discarded and the basic mechanics of the business, developing business, portfolio management, research, client relationship, and administrative skills have to be learned, practiced, and honed to a sharp edge.

Getting through the six month blues is the first test. Passing that test usually leads to a strong five or six years of good business development. The second test comes around the fifth year and it comes slowly, creeping out of the mist of self assurance. Without realizing it, boredom infects the advisor. Not the kind of boredom where a person realizes they are bored, the kind where a person seeks out distractions under the guise of business development. It makes sense to be involved with Rotary, the Chamber of Commerce, a church, the local college, the Salvation Army and the Cancer Society. It doesn't make sense to be involved with all of these activities at the same time. Business development activities become distractions instead of opportunities. Boredom with the nitty, gritty details of running a business leads the advisor to want to do those ego boosting activities that are part of the business. Discipline and a recognition of what is happening is a solution for this boredom. More dangerous is the boredom that leads to restlessness and unhappiness with the firm or the office manager. Frustrations build quickly when an advisor believes correctly or incorrectly that events at the office are keeping business development or a smooth administration of the business from being successful. Thoughts of going to another firm begin to appear. Rumors of huge amounts of up-front money start to appear attractive. More and more small issues become irritants. It's not fun anymore. It won't be this way at the other firm. The other manager supports the advisors. The other office has better research. The other advisors are more congenial. A career is at a turning point. Changing firms in the first five years sets the career back far more than the advisor realizes. Not as many clients make the transfer as believed because there is no benefit for the clients in the transfer and they know it. Just as important, without realizing it, the advisor has reverted to starting over again with an emphasis on rebuilding the clientele and ensuring the likelihood that boredom will set in again. There is the real danger a twenty-year career will be four five year careers and since a five year advisor doesn't make nearly as much as a twenty year advisor, that's a waste of time, talent and energy.

FWIW # 16 .... *Adaptability*

To accomplish anything, a financial advisor has to have the day planned from beginning to end. There's a reason why. At 9:00 a.m. a client is going to call, or an administrative problem will arise, or a major change in the market will require attention and the daily schedule will go out the window for a period of time. These kinds of schedule wrecking diversions are commonplace in the financial services business. This need for adaptability is one of the ingredients making the career lucrative. Without flexibility and the ease of shifting focus, the stress level will just be too much.

Without the rigid planning and discipline to stick with the plan, an advisor will constantly be stuck in a quicksand of frustration, being sucked into the abyss of inefficiency. By having a daily action plan in place, the advisor can adapt to unexpected events and quickly get back on track making progress accomplishing the important tasks of the day.

FWIW # 17 .... *Advisor/Manager Relationship*

It's commonly known in the business that 90% of the advisors who switch firms say they do so due to a poor relationship with the office manager. A precise study will probably find that 90% is a conservative estimate. Boredom is the root of the conflict in many cases. Clashing egos ranks second as a cause for the revolving door syndrome, particularly when the former trainee begins to blossom out and be a good advisor earning more than the office manager.

A lot of the blame in advisor/manager conflicts rests with the manager. Managers cause a significant amount of relationship problems because of their ego. How else could someone have the confidence to be good at this business? Mediocre managers make their advisors feel like cows whose only function is to bring in the milk. You are the manager's friend if you generate significant revenue, but not until then. Some managers resent the fact that the best advisors can make much more money than the manager while coming and dropping the problems of the day in the manager's lap without a thank-you or even a smile. That's the nature of the business. Those managers who were excellent producers and did not cause problems for their managers resent the whining advisor who can't run a smooth business with a minimum of problems.

What many advisors don't realize is just how effective a good working relationship with the manager is in running the advisor's business. With a little logic and less ego, the advisor can realize the manager holds the key to smoothing the inevitable problems, and more importantly, can go to bat for the advisor with the operations area, the regional management, and senior management. The secret to controlling the manager and using all of the influence and power of that position in building the advisor's business is to just give the manager what all managers want: substantial business in a professional and ethical manner with no compliance problems. Wait a minute. How can that be good for the manager? Substantial business (meaning substantial earnings to the advisor) in a professional and ethical manner (meaning doing what's in the client's best interest so the client will do more business and, therefore, give more earnings to the advisor) with no compliance problems (meaning the advisor has a long and productive career) is EXACTLY what the advisor wants. If both parties want the same thing, it's easy to see the manager and advisor working together to boost the advisor's business. Here's how.

Step one is to find out the kind of business that made the manager successful. How? Ask for the information. Have you ever seen a high ego person turn down the opportunity to talk about their accomplishments? Is the business the manager excels at the kind of business you want to do? If so, probe for more information and tips

43

on how to improve your skills.

Step two is to ask for advice on specific areas of your own business development. Make the question short and to the point covering just one situation. Some challenge that can be solved with the manager's guidance works best. That way, your success becomes the manager's success. The team concept is reinforced.

Step three is to use the manager effectively but sparingly to help obtain a client or reinforce special clients' commitments to your firm. Perhaps you want to go after a high profile family in the community. Ask the manager to go to lunch with you and the prospective client to reinforce with the client your firm's desire to have them as part of their clientele. The manager can reinforce the team concept and ensure the client that all the firms' resources are available to them. At other times, have a luncheon for five of your best clients and have the manager attend and give a 10 minute talk on your firm's position on the economy, the bond or stock market, or a particular industry sector. Don't ever underestimate the prestige and image your manager carries with your firm's clients. The manager can be an important business development tool for you to use in building your business.

FWIW # 18 .... *80/20 Rule*

Throughout all parts of business, not just financial services, the general rule is that 80% of the business comes from 20% of the clients. It's a chilling prospect because there are many factors beyond your control that can cause those 20% of your clients to disappear. They can die, the operations area can cause them to leave, your competition can offer more service, the stock market can fall, interest rates can go up, or they can get a divorce. The list can go on and on. There is a ray of sunshine on the horizon, however.

Being paid a fee based on assets under management defuses the 80/20 rule. The more uniform the portfolio sizes, the less dependent you will be on a small handful of clients. This thought alone should make an advisor set a target for the size of accounts that will be acceptable. Don't make a rigid rule and be flexible but firm. For instance, a $100,000 account from a neurosurgeon just out of medical school and still paying off student loans is better than a $500,000 account from a 65-year-old soon-to-be retired client who will be withdrawing all of the income for living expenses. On the other hand, a $100,000 account from someone who will not be able to add to the account and may need some of the assets to pay taxes next year or take a vacation is not someone you can help long term either. There are three rules to building a fee-based clientele. First and foremost, don't take an account with anyone that you cannot help. Second, have an understanding of the revenues that you want to receive from each client. And third, don't focus on a small number of large clients. Focus on a larger number of medium-sized clients. Banks and brokerage firms like to have many borrowers and clients. The diversification helps cushion the institution against a single bad loan or a client leaving. You should deliberately use the same diversification rule. Don't let the loss of one or a few clients put the survival of your business at risk.

FWIW # 19 .... *Lunchtime*

Lunchtime can be your most productive time of the day because you can accomplish two tasks at one time – if you do it right. Lunch should be taken in your office, or at the right restaurant with the right person.

A client or a prospective client is the only person you should have lunch with outside the office. If you are going out, besides eating, the objective should be either business development or client relationship building. What better way to have someone focus on you and your message than to be sitting across the table having an enjoyable meal. Clients who have been with you only a few months are ideal lunch partners since they need the bonding that comes with the time and attention you give them. By the way, you should always buy lunch when you are with a client or prospect. Lunch with a client or prospect is an excellent way to gather information that assists you in tailoring a portfolio to a family's unique situation or advise you of changes that will require a change in investment objectives, constraints, or the strategy you're using. Isn't it more congenial to ask the person about their children and grandchildren over a salad than it is sitting in an office where the questions come across as fact gathering rather than friendship building? The wealth of information people will share over a meal is astounding. By sharing that information with you, the client begins to bring you into their inner circle of friends. As they get to know you and facts about your life, there develops a small but real resistance to changing from you as their financial advisor. When your competition begins to solicit their business, you will be given a chance to compete rather than find the account is being moved without your knowing it.

Just as important as who you go to lunch with is where to go. You want to go where your prospects and clients eat lunch. If it's a chili joint, that's fine. If it's a white tablecloth restaurant, so be it. The business development objective is to be seen and to see. Everyone is curious who someone is, particularly when they see the same person over and over again. You develop a presence and become recognizable.

When you have lunch with a client or prospect, you are associated by others with that person. All of your luncheon partners' friends unconsciously accept you by your association with the client. Those who come over to speak to your dining guest are introduced to you. Whether or not your client endorses you verbally, you are endorsed by the client just because the two of you are together. The benefits of this form of luncheon prospecting are subtle and cumulative. The more you do it consistently, the more impact and reward it has. It's also not cheap.

Decide now how many days a week you want to use the lunchtime for business development (eating out of the office) and how many for administrative work (eating in the office). Plan the week or month ahead. Make these out-of-the-office lunches productive. Ideally, you can reserve the same table at the same time. Generous tipping, 20%-25%, ensures you will receive courteous and prompt service. After a while, the staff will call you by name and you will be a regular.

The really bad mistake you can make at lunchtime is to eat with another financial services professional, particularly one from your office. They cannot help you at all. If they are more successful, you aren't going to be taught how to be a better competitor. If they are less successful than you, they're looking for you to teach them and that's not your function.

Turn what is usually a non-productive time into one of the best career building times of the day.

FWIW # 20 .... *Community Service*

No one gives to charity out of the goodness of their heart. They give for important reasons. Many give to be recognized in the community. Don't ever underestimate that point. Recognition is the number one motivation for giving charity and community service. Others give because of a deep-seated belief in the organization. They are emotionally involved in the cause. Still more give to beat the IRS and that's okay, particularly if they are stroked over in the process. Finally, a number of people give to accrue the power brought by being a big donor. Board of trustees seats, positions of leadership, and the contacts made are able to be used to solidify or build a presence in the community. Participating in community service is (a) exceptionally rewarding to your career, (b) time and money consuming, and (c) slow-developing but highly effective the longer it's done.

There is a method to community service prospecting. You must do it right or it has the potential to turn into a career destroyer rather than being a source of good solid business (FWIW # 15). Here are the rules of the game. First, make a master list of the potential activities in your community, starting with United Way. Look at the agencies that United Way supports and add them to the list. Add your church. Add the service organizations like Rotary, Kiwanis, and Lions. Don't forget the museums and art associations such as the theater, symphony, and dance companies. Now add the charities. See which ones have gala affairs each year. Keep building the list no matter how obscure the organization. Did you add the Salvation Army, the number one recipient of charity giving in this country? Is there a college or private school in your community? Do any of them have foundations? Is there a community foundation? When the list is finished, begin by getting information about each organization's leadership. How many have a paid executive director? You can bet they have a long list of donors to sustain the group's infrastructure if they do. Who sits on the board? Who are the people sitting on more than one board? It won't take long to figure out which organizations are actively supported by serious segments of the money class in your community.

Second, prioritize the list by the amount of exposure and context it will give to you. Once done, look at each organization and see if it needs active volunteers each year. Some do and some don't. Some organizations only have boards where members are invited to participate. Now, the most crucial step is taking the top ten organizations on your list and deciding which ones you are interested in helping. Unless you have a sincere interest in the goals of an organization, you will not effectively embrace the organization and its fund-raising activities. In other words, your efforts will fail to bring you positive and professional recognition. The newer you are in the community, the more you should consider the United Way. It has the mechanisms in place for new participants to enter at the bottom of the ladder and work their way up. More importantly, the organization is constructed so everyone above any given level is aware of who the best people are below them. The organization also brings together people in different areas of the community so the number of contacts you will make are broad. Remember that list of people who are involved with charities that you made? Getting to know some of them through United Way is a shortcut to getting involved with these other organizations – if you do a good job for United Way.

Community service only works right when you make a commitment to the organization and cause. Community service is a disaster to your business unless you stand out as someone who brings professionalism, discipline, and goal-oriented success to the endeavor. People witness your success in helping the organization and they translate that success into your business endeavors. If you're good helping them, you build the esteem and support when they think of using someone for financial services.

Indirect prospecting is the main focus. But, there is a more direct benefit as well. More and more people are focused on leaving money to charities or gift-giving of appreciated stock. Organizations have a serious deficit of knowledge about making the process smooth. What better way for you to show off your skills as a financial services professional than by bringing in technical proficiency in handling the gift-giving and being knowledgeable in the various nuances of estate charitable giving.

You're no different than most. The recognition you receive by doing your community service can go to your head. The next step is to limit your activities to no more than two organizations at a time, perhaps United Way and the Cancer Society, or perhaps a university foundation and the Salvation Army. It all depends on your list, how you see your community, and your interests. More than two and your business will suffer or you won't do the top notch job that must be done to achieve professional recognition.

There is a way to leverage your time. Is your spouse active in community service? Perhaps your spouse can be active in groups that can help you as well. The same rules apply. Your spouse must do a top quality job to receive professional recognition and you can share part of the spotlight just as your spouse shares in yours. No matter what, you must limit the efforts so that a quality job is done each time.

Besides "sweat equity," money is what bonds most community

service organizations and their supporters. It will cost money to achieve the inner sanctum of the board of trustees. Being able to raise money is a plus, but you will also have to give some as well. How much depends on the social peer group in your chosen organization. Use as much leverage as possible in making the gift. For instance, buying at silent auction a $1,000 painting is not really as effective as paying for a $1,000 printing of the brochures and literature. Not only do you get a bigger tax deduction, but you change from being one of the outsiders having to get something for their money to an insider who is in the trenches making things happen. If you want to get in the club, that's how to get there faster.

Keep good records of who you serve with on a board or work with in an organization. Who is the leadership of the organization? Put them on your list. Make sure they know who you are. Make sure you keep track of where you served together and in what year. What was their position? What was yours? Did the organization reach their goals? Where did the person work? This is networking. Networking is not going to a cocktail social somewhere. Sharing interests and being meaningful in making the community work and helping those above you in the organization accomplish their goals and look good is the basis for networking. Do you think a person heading up a United Way division will forget the division volunteer who raised the most money? No way. They'll remember that person for a long time. They will also endorse that person's involvement in future organizations. Eventually, they will give that person an opportunity to professionally discuss business. That's all you want or need, the opportunity to present your abilities with the prospective client having an open mind.

Through community service you will begin to identify the real wealth and power in your community. Keep the list because it will hold future members of the 300 Club. Doing good for yourself by doing good for others makes good sense.

FWIW # 21 .... *Growth Investment*

If you own a retail store, you have to start over every year trying to entice customers to buy in your store. If you own a manufacturing plant, you have to convince customers to reorder your products every year. When you were a transaction-oriented broker, you had to entice investors or speculators to buy and sell assets to pay you a commission. Now as a fee-based financial advisor, whether you have discretion or not, you have one objective: ***assist the client in becoming wealthier each year.*** If the client has more assets and stays with you, your business will grow and you will prosper. If you have $50 million dollars under management today and compound it by 12.25% a year, in six years, without opening another account, you have $100 million dollars under management. The financial services business dynamics are outstanding for a professional and that's why it is so hard to succeed in the business. Someone who likes intellectual stimulation, wants a challenge every day, enjoys making a difference in people's lives, and likes to make money, will cherish the day they got their license to participate. Keeping that license is the challenge. Not only is the business hard, but there is a maze of rules and regulations that can cause a person to be outlawed from the business or even sent to prison. Understanding what is proper, ethical, and legal keeps the financial advisor within the CHALKLINES earning above average income and building net worth.

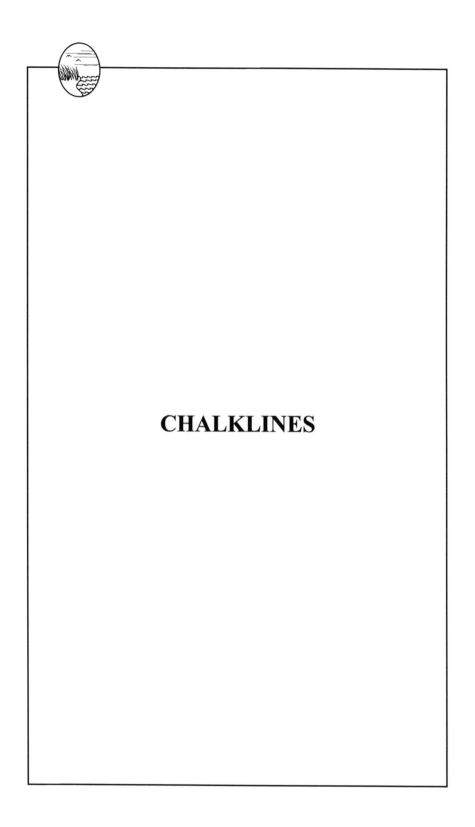

CHALKLINES

In every phase of life there are chalklines. Chalklines are the outer boundaries of ethical and legal conduct. How fast we go on the highway, how we conduct our relationship with our neighbor, and how we can conduct our business with our clients are all chalklines. Because we are dealing with people's money and because there have always been unscrupulous people willing to deceive and take advantage of gullible and greedy investors, the maze of regulations in the financial services business is astounding. It gets more complex every year. Chalklines are good if understood, a trap if not.

There are three kinds of people in the world. Some do not want to know the outer boundaries of what is acceptable. They are going to do what they want and reap the benefits as long as they can. Unfortunately, the regulatory activity reports indicate our profession has its share of these people. The faster they can be weeded out the better. The second type are those who are not going to the edge of the permissible playing field no matter where they know the chalklines are. They are going to stay in the safe and secure middle. They don't care that they limit their life and business. Safety is the most important issue. That's fine. Then there are those in life who want to enjoy and experience all of life and what it has to offer. These participants want to use all of the playing field. They like to go up to the edge but not over. They enjoy the thrill and satisfaction of making the most of their career but have the pride and ethical standards to stay within the boundaries of what is right for the client. Chalklines are best utilized by these advisors.

An advisor working for a major financial services firm has a compliance department which translates the rules and regulations into the firm's compliance policy. These watchdogs are the source of information as well as the last defense in catching any intentional or unintentional infraction of the rules. There are two ways you can view your firm's compliance department: (a) as a hindrance, or (b) as a tool. You had better decide right now the compliance department is your best friend, not your worst enemy. They know the rules and regulations. The compliance department can tell you where the edge is. More importantly, they can help you identify the difficult to understand situations and the challenging spots you get yourself into, and they can stand by you and defend you against unfair and wrong charges by clients. Making compliance issues an important part of your administrative work is the best way to make a lot of money in an ethical and professional manner. Failure to understand the nuances of the rules and regulations will keep you from increasing your business that small extra amount that makes a difference between being number one and number three.

FWIW # 23 .... *Client Chalklines*

When the business was transaction-oriented, there was fairly clear-cut evidence when a dispute arose between the client and the broker. Did the client authorize the trade? Did the client affirm the trade after the fact? Is the security suitable for the client? Fairly easy to define and understand questions and answers. If the client did not authorize the trade, is there a signed discretionary authority document? No? Well, bingo, the broker is at fault. If there is, did the client object to the trade after receiving the confirmation? No, well, tough luck for the client. Did the broker sell a highly speculative limited partnership to an 85-year-old who needs liquidity and current income? If so, give the client the money back. The era of fee-based financial advisors is not so clear and definable. Whenever you have a foggy area, you have lawyers who have the clarity of seeing through the rearview mirror and that spells trouble. Doubling the new risk is the move to more and more advisors having discretionary authority over their client's assets. Inexperience and blind faith in the investment wisdom of the day has ruined many portfolios constructed in good faith and with integrity. History is full of clear situations where changes outside of the advisor's control made good investments appear as bad investments or in the best interest of the advisor rather than the client. Doubt it? Well, remember these situations: (1) in the 1960's, the trend was to keep the client's portfolio fully invested and just sell a portion of assets to supply income. The theory was the portfolio would grow faster than the withdrawals and therefore the client's net worth would continue to grow while the client's income needs were met. Makes sense, doesn't it? Well, it did until Federal fiscal and monetary policy led to the 1970's higher interest rates, higher inflation, and a stock market that saw its value cut in half. From the viewpoint of the client, the attorney suing the broker, and a jury, who really benefitted from the idea of full investing? The client who ultimately lost half of the portfolio or the advisor-broker who benefitted from higher fees by keeping the portfolio in risky stocks?

(2) In the 1970's, the price of oil went from 25¢ per barrel to over $40 a barrel. Finding oil was a national obsession to keep the country out of the grips of OPEC. Oil and gas partnerships proliferated. Steady, tax-advantaged income was the focus along with wildly inflated gains from oil prices continuing to rise. Nothing was going to keep oil from going to $100 a barrel according to the analysts. No one was talking about the illiquidity of the partnerships and the turning of liquid capital into a high risk business venture. Oil prices didn't go to $100. They eventually went back to $7.50. A lot of money was lost in oil and gas ventures by people who could not afford it. When oil prices collapsed and the attorneys got involved, the clients who demanded to be in these risky partnerships were whimpering about how the advisor-broker duped them. How do you think the juries ruled?

An interested observer could go back in time and find a series of situations just like these two where good intentions and limited knowledge led to situations causing the advisor-broker to look greedy and unethical. There is a way to avoid most, if not all, of these rear-view-mirror disasters: written analysis and recommendations based upon written investment objectives, investment constraints, and a policy and strategy to meet those objectives within the known limitations. Having the client review and agree to these clearly stated facts and recommendations up front are a strong defense against hindsight. There is another reason for having these documents. In the late 1990's, trial lawyers and their friends in Congress began strengthening the *Know Your Client* rules. The tighter they make the requirements, the easier it is for you as an advisor to inadvertently fail to match a client and the proper portfolio mix. As more and more people make investing in liquid securities a focus of their net worth, the plaintiff attorneys will see a greater and greater opportunity for boosting their own net worth. You can't keep from being sued, but you can conduct your business in such a way that lawsuits will be discouraged and your defenses will remain strong. Here's how to do it.

Your firm probably has an arbitration dispute clause in your new account agreement. If you conduct your business ethically and in the client's best interest, that clause will work in your favor since people who understand the business will be deciding the merits in a controversy. An independent advisor should have a management agreement with every client. That management agreement spells out the rights of all parties and should identify investment objectives, investment constraints, and an investment policy and strategy to meet those objectives within the limitations. It should also define the fees to be paid and the discretionary authority and the limits to that authority. All of these sections, signed by the client before beginning, are based upon what you know about the client at that time. How do you prove what you know? Include a page that lists all of the facts that you know about the client on the date that the relationship began. The *WHAT WE KNOW* page is crucial to doing a good job for the client and protecting the advisor. If the client acknowledges with a signature the information on that page, a jury will have a harder time later finding the client is injured.

Don't hold back on the *WHAT WE KNOW* page. Tell it all and give the client the opportunity to add to the information. Ages and sexes of children and grandchildren, health issues, potential inheritances, income sources, debts, what the client wants from the portfolio, how the client expects to retire and at what age. Every single fact you can know about a client can help. Focus on the suitability of the investment objectives, help define the constraints, and help develop a clearly understood investment strategy.

Some financial services firms prefer not to have this information. You have to do what your firm wants done. How your firm operates is up to your compliance department, but it's in your best interest to know this information and to use it in your relationship with the client. Knowing the client's chalklines is just as important for you as for the client.

Warren Buffet once said that the best thing about working for oneself is you get to choose who you work with. Advisors have that same sweet privilege. It's hard when you are a new financial advisor with few clients to walk away from potential clients. However, sometimes that's the best approach. There are some people with money who are unattractive in the way they interact with financial advisors. You do not have to work with these people. You have a limited amount of capacity. Why fill it with people who make your life unhappy and are a potential source of conflict? Sure, you have to work harder to develop your clientele if you only accept certain ones, but you will enjoy your career more if you do.

FWIW # 25 .... *Wrong Number*

If you are successful and in the business long enough, you're going to have a difficult relationship with a client. You might be the cause, the client might feel slighted in some way, operations might really foul up the account. More likely, the markets go into a slump, the client loses money and is unhappy about it. Whatever the cause, when a relationship with a client turns difficult, it's important all communication be handled professionally and carefully. Some clients try to set you up by taping a phone conversation where there is a misleading or accusatory statement made. The natural instinct of the advisor is to ignore the comments or to stumble around and half-heartedly deny the comments. This is dangerous. The proper way to handle a phone call where you sense someone is saying things to lay the groundwork for an accusation is the following: clearly stop the caller, deny the accusations or false statements, and disengage from the call immediately. If a blatantly false comment is made, your response should be: "Mr(s). (_name_), you know that is not true. I recommend you come to the office and you and I will meet with my manager to discuss this subject." In that fashion, if the phone call is being taped, you have denied the accusation and you have offered the client a meeting with a higher authority.

If the client tries to set a certain time line, or progression of facts, your response should be: "Mr(s). (_name_), I do not agree with your interpretation of the facts. I recommend you come into the office and we will meet with my manager to discuss this issue." There are three key points to keep in mind when you sense a phone call has an ulterior motive: (a) don't get into a long conversation with an unhappy client on the phone, (b) clearly and emphatically deny or dispute any antagonistic or fabricated statement made by the client, and (c) recommend the client come into the office to see the manager about the issue as soon as possible. When you hang up the phone, close your office door and take time to write out a confidential memo to counsel about the phone call and everything you know about your relationship with that client up to that point.

By following these procedures, your action will reflect positively on the outcome of the dispute because you not only challenged the client's interpretation as soon as you heard it, but you immediately opened up for the client the proper channel of communication with the person who can resolve the issue before it gets out of hand.

FWIW # 26 .... *George Washington Defense*

Young George Washington said he could never tell a lie. You had better not either, particularly when dealing with your branch manager or the compliance department of your firm. Client disputes arise for a host of reasons, some fair and some not fair, some your fault, some the client's fault. Generally, the client will be satisfied by discussing the issue with the manager and being treated professionally and with respect. During most conflicts, the manager can propose a settlement of the issue that the client feels is fair. To handle the matter properly, the manager has to have all of the facts. If you are at fault, the manager has to know that right up front. Hell has no fury like a manager caught in a difficult position because the advisor shaded the truth or withheld material information. Not only will your standing go down, but the risk increases dramatically that attorneys will get involved, thereby raising the cost of the settlement to the firm.

None of us are truly blind sided by a dispute with a client. The relationship begins to deteriorate gradually. When you become aware of a change in your relationship, it's important to begin to construct a written record of your side of the story. Make the narrative detailed, clear, and complete as possible. When finished, mark the top and bottom of the page: *(Confidential Memo to Counsel)*. Keep a copy of your record, make a copy for your manager, and send the original to the compliance department. The document will be your guideline for refreshing your memory months or years from the incident when lawyers begin to ask you questions in a deposition.

The reason for marking the document (Confidential Memo to Counsel) is to keep the document out of your and the firm's records which are available to the client and the opposing legal team. Details, details, and more details are the key to a good document. Insignificant facts just might be the key to proving your side of the story or at least causing doubt about your client's version of the facts.

FWIW # 27 .... *Client Fantasies*

A person's character is revealed when they lose money, particularly large sums of money relative to their net worth. It will astound you how they turn from knowledgeable, sophisticated clients wanting on-the-edge, high risk, high reward investments into completely naive and manipulated uneducated pawns of a cruel and devious financial advisor focused on stealing their money. Good church-going people will lie with the fervor of a convert to the point that even you begin to believe their story.

Your blood pressure will soar, you will become emotional, you will feel betrayed, and you will feel threatened. It's your word against theirs and you are not necessarily going to be believed.

Fantasies, however, are easier to overcome if you have been professional in the conduct of your business. The first step is to remove the emotions from the situation when the client makes the accusation. If necessary, go somewhere and kick and scream to diffuse your anger. This is no time to be angry. This is no time to do anything except assemble the facts. Review the entire account from the day you first met the person. Write down anything you can think of about the relationship, even personal facts such as lunches, favors done, or social occasions. Any of these can be an affirmation of the type of business that had been conducted as well as present a friendship that indicates the current charges are false.

FWIW # 28 .... *Depositions*

There are three cardinal rules to giving a deposition:

(1) Tell the truth, the whole truth, and nothing but the truth.

(2) Answer questions in a short, precise manner.

(3) Have an attorney with you at all times.

Depositions are taken by lawyers when there is a dispute between a financial advisor and a client. A deposition is the process of a witness being interviewed with the interview being conducted under oath by an attorney representing the opposing side.

Besides trying to find out the facts about the disputed matter, the client's attorney will attempt to find out anything else about the advisor's temperament and ways of doing business which may be helpful to the client's case. If the broker is self-contradictory, nervous, hesitant, or evasive, the attorney will realize how this conduct will appear to a jury or a panel of arbitrators.

One tactic commonly used by attorneys is to ask the same questions several times during the deposition in different ways to see if the witness' story will hold up. In the pressure and tension of the proceeding, this probing is not always apparent. By telling the unvarnished truth, including *I don't remember,* the advisor will keep from being placed in a difficult position. If the testimony has to be repeated to a jury or arbitration panel, there will be no hesitation in telling the same story.

When a deposition is over, a transcript is provided. The advisor should go over the transcript carefully and make corrections to the testimony. This is the prime time for any unclear testimony to be clarified and the record set straight. After corrections, the testimony is certified as correct and it will be part of the record in determining the merits of the dispute.

No matter how comforting the evidence is, the advisor who is going through a deposition is bound to be nervous. The knowledge and confidence of testifying truthfully is about the only relaxing part of the process. Having a good attorney is important. Whenever in doubt about a complex question or answer, the automatic response should be to consult with the attorney. The firm is paying top dollars for the attorney's time so use every minute of it. Under all circumstances, follow the attorney's advice without question.

There is a silver lining in a deposition. Any advisor who goes through one doesn't cut corners in the future. Depositions are events in life that help you focus on the fact that you don't want to do that again. Following the rules professionally becomes the daily ritual.

FWIW # 29 ....*E-Mail and Diary*

Records are everywhere. Orders are time stamped when entered. Telephone calls are routinely logged by the phone company. Almost all communication an advisor has is part of the firm's record. The daily diary is personal to the advisor until a legal dispute arises. Appointments and special conversations should be recorded routinely. The method is up to you. The trend in client relationship management is to the computer and that's fine. There is a benefit to using electronic diaries. Since space on the computer is infinite, you have the luxury of expanding your comments. A well-kept diary is priceless. One that only has entries when there is a dispute is worthless. Make it part of your daily routine.

A word about e-mail. There is only one rule about e-mail: don't write anything you don't want your mother or your worst enemy to read. If you doubt this, speak to Bill Gates and any other person who has had a lawyer subpoena computer e-mail records.

FWIW # 30 .... *Monthly Reviews*

More clients leave an advisor for accounting problems than leave for lack of performance. This fact alone should tell the advisor to grab the monthly statements and go through every one of them the day and night (if necessary) the statements arrive. There is another more compelling reason: you'll make a lot more money by doing so. In this electronic age, paper statements are becoming rare, so the review has to be done on the computer. If so, get your paper and pencil, sit in a comfortable chair, and begin the process.

The new world order of financial services is integrating banks, insurance companies, and brokers to bring more services to the firm's clients. Bank accounting has been known for its high quality. Brokerage firm accounting has not been flawless. Think of all the time and effort expended to get a client and then to have their account fouled up by errors. Most of the time you can't stop the errors, but you can find them before the client does and initiate action to correct the mistakes. There are four types of entry on a statement that you should review. The easiest are the dividends and interest entries. Since these are generally automated now, very few mistakes are found. If anything, a dividend might be omitted since a position was bought right before ex-date or it might be put into the account because it was sold right before ex-date and did not settle. What does lend itself to error is the automatic dividend reinvestment process available at many brokerage firms. Seeing that the reinvestment takes place and the amount being reinvested matches the dividend paid is a simple process that does not take much time but saves a great deal of headache if an error is made and caught right away.

By far the most errors result from deposits or withdrawals to the account. Not only will you want to know the amount is correct, but you want to monitor any large deposits or withdrawals. Some firms print the name of the payee on the statement. Isn't it important to know your client wrote a check to your competition?

Buy and sell entries are checked when they happen so it is unusual for a problem to appear on the statement. Tender offers, buyouts, rights offerings, splits and mergers are not easily checked until the end of the period statement. Making sure they are correct and the fractional shares, if any, are sold, doesn't take much time and saves a lot of headache if there is an error.

Journal entries are the footprints of gremlins. A journal entry, by its nature, means human intervention was needed. Journal entries are usually done to adjust a dividend or interest payment, move a security or money from or to an account, or charge or credit a fee to the account. You need to know the who, what, and why of every entry because the client will want to know. Who made the entry, what did the entry do to the account, and why was it made are not easily acquired facts and therefore, getting this information before the client asks for it smooths the client's concern and bolsters their confidence in you.

There is a specific and proven way to turn an operational problem (a mistake on the statement) into a plus for you. CALL THE CLIENT BEFORE THE CLIENT CALLS YOU. Don't have your assistant call the client, you call them. They are your responsibility and you need to demonstrate your concern for their portfolio's accuracy and integrity. What you say is important. "*Mr(s). (name), in my regular audit and review of client portfolios, I noticed an entry that appeared incorrect. You will see it when you receive your statement. It is a (name the type of mistake) that appeared (or didn't appear) on the (date). My assistant is researching the issue and will call you back by*

3:00 p.m. on *(make the date four business days in the future)*. I'm sorry for the inconvenience and will have the situation resolved quickly."

What have you done with that phone call?

(1) You made a contact with a client where you were in complete command of the situation.

(2) You reinforced your active management of the client's portfolio.

(3) You impressed the client with the fact that you have a team approach to your business.

(4) You told the client not to call you about the issue until you have had four business days to handle the situation.

You are not going to get called by an upset client just when you are developing an analysis of a company, reviewing a portfolio, or conversing with a prospect or another client. You are controlling the situation. Attractive, isn't it?

Not nearly as attractive as the business ideas that the statement reviews generate. What stocks or bonds need to be sold for gains or tax losses? What cash reserves need to be invested? What shares have met their objectives? What gaps in the portfolio strategy need to be covered? What sectors are represented in the portfolio? What is the annual cash flow from dividends and interest? Portfolio reviews are important, fun, and productive to the professional financial advisor.

Every review should be done when the possibility of interference is small. So plan the time wisely. Evenings and weekends are good, but don't wait. Do the review as soon as possible. Have your assistant hold all calls. If the statements are on paper, or on the computer, have a notepad, pencil, or a micro cassette recorder handy. The recorder is used to dictate instructions to your assistant for handling some of the problems. The pencil and paper are for making notes that you will use in activating portfolio management decisions.

FWIW # 31 .... *Non-Orders*

"You are the expert. Do what you think is best."

"I'll leave it up to you."

"I'll be out of town. Do what you think is best."

"I'll trust your judgement."

"I value your opinion. Follow it and I'll go along with that."

What do all of these comments have in common? Every advisor hears them over and over again. They are non-orders. What are non-orders? Unless you have discretionary authority, non-orders are the fastest way to forced retirement. A non-order is a blank check handed to your client and drawn on you and your firm's net worth. It is a money-back guarantee that your client will not lose money. If the investment appreciates, the client will keep it. If it goes down, the client will say the trade was not authorized. A non-order is a trap.

When the client does not give discretionary authority, the client must specifically agree to buying or selling a specific amount of shares of a specific security. Even if there is only one security in the account, all of these elements must be discussed and agreed upon by the client before the trade is made or else it is a discretionary order. If a non-order is alluded to by the client, the proper response should be: *"Mr(s). (name), I appreciate the confidence you have in me. My recommendation is to (buy/sell) (quantity) of (stock or bond). With your permission I will enter an order now at (price). Does that meet with your approval?"* By responding in such a fashion, the advisor is exercising the good judgement the client praises. The client also has to answer yes or no.

Unless an order can be reduced to writing and entered at the time it is received, it is a non-order. Don't take them. An advisor has never been fired for not taking a non-order and plenty have been searching the want ads for a new career by believing the client meant what they did not say.

FWIW # 32 .... *Who's in Charge Here?*

Investors come in two packages. The first group wants an investment advisor to give advice and guidance but reserves the right to make decisions themselves. Your role is as an advisor. There are far more of these clients than the other type who want a decision-making portfolio manager to take over the reigns of the portfolio and make the account grow.

Giving advice and guidance but not having the ability to execute trades without prior approval of the client is called ***non-discretion***. The benefit of a non-discretionary account to the advisor is there is no responsibility for portfolio performance. The client makes the decisions. Since the portfolio is fee-based, there is no incentive for the transaction to be made other than maintaining the client relationship.

At this point, a word of advice: don't take any accounts under the old transaction-based structure. Compensation dependent upon transactions always has had the potential for conflicts of interest. Why is the trade being recommended? Is the advisor looking to generate income to pay his bills this month? These are nagging doubts clients have had for decades and have been unfair to the professional advisor for just as long. Leave these clients now to other advisors or to the Internet.

Non-discretionary clients are frustrating to a professional advisor. If the object of the business is to seek out the best potential return with the most controlled and defined risk then by definition the investment has to be somewhat controlled by investor FEAR. Your client is an investor and is experiencing the same degree of FEAR as everyone else. Asking the client to purchase shares in a company at that stage is usually met with a resounding, "I'll think about it." They won't tell you no and they won't tell you yes. Gradually, out of frustration or survival, you start recommending investments more in the spotlight just so the portfolio development can begin. Performance is mediocre and stays that way because the reward/risk relationship is out of balance. Too much of the reward is already in the price which adds to all of the other risks associated with the investment.

No one is overjoyed with the relationship. There is a way to improve the situation, however.

Through salesmanship, you can define and control the relationship of non-discretionary accounts in the same way you control discretionary portfolios. It's what's called *discretionary non-discretion portfolios*. The relationship has to be controlled every step of the way by the advisor. Here's how to do it:

(1) Assist the client in seeing the benefits of professional investment management where concrete investment objectives, constraints, and a strategy to meet those objectives are agreed to in advance. You and the client set clear guidelines within which to operate the portfolio.

(2) Explain to the client the interconnection between all of your recommendations. Show how each will eventually contribute to the long term goal of the portfolio's performance and how each recommendation will be part of the overall investment strategy.

(3) Explain to the client how you will never call with a recommendation unless you think it is the best fit for growing the portfolio at that point in time.

(4) Explain to the client you will accept responsibility for the portfolio's growth if your recommendations are followed. If the portfolio does not grow in line with a predetermined benchmark, you expect to be fired.

(5) Finally, after 1-4 have patiently and thoroughly been explained and understood, quietly explain to the client that if three of your

recommendations are rejected, you will no longer work with the client. Say it professionally, say it diplomatically, say it in a non-threatening way, but make it clear. When it comes time to make a recommendation, begin the process by reminding the client of the objectives and strategy of the portfolio. Then show how the recommendation you are about to make fits within the overall plan. Do this in such a way that rejecting the recommendation will almost be a rejection of the plan itself. After a year, if you have done your job as portfolio manager correctly, the portfolio will be growing and client resistance to your recommendations will be less frequent. If the client does turn down a recommendation, keep track of the impact on the portfolio. At review time, let the client know what the performance would have been if all of the ideas had been acted upon.

Discretionary accounts allow you to see how your knowledge and experience help your clients to meet their investment objectives. You are in charge. You are the portfolio manager. There is no one else to blame if performance is not up to par. There is no one to blame if the asset allocation is wrong. You are in line for the glory or the shame.

More important than any other aspect of your relationship is your total responsibility to the client for the matching of client objectives and constraints with the asset allocation and securities in the portfolio. You need to know what you are doing and you need to document what you are doing every step of the way. There was a time when discretionary accounts were incredibly risky to an advisor who is paid based upon the transactions in the portfolio. Now that fee-based portfolios are standard, the potential conflict of interest is removed. Only a misguided focus on seeking above average performance by taking too much risk in relation to the client's profile remains as the major danger to the advisor. Staying within the agreed objectives, constraints, and policy and strategy while updating the known information through client contact is the way to avoid this excess risk.

There are actually two types of discretion. The first is the limited right to make buy and sell decisions in the portfolio. This is the standard form of portfolio management used by most financial advisors in the U.S. It is all you need to do the job right. The second type is a full power of attorney where the advisor also has a right to direct client money out of the portfolio. The most common occurrence of this type of discretion is when the financial advisor is a trustee or executor of an account. The SEC considers a full power of attorney to be <u>constructive custody</u> of client funds. Most major financial services firms will not allow their employees to have full power of attorney. Independent advisors should avoid constructive custody because of the SEC's strong concern about these accounts. Full custody is steeped in high risk and generally the advisor receives no more of a fee for having constructive custody than they receive for the limited buy and sell trading authorization. Why take a higher risk for no more reward? It just doesn't make sense.

Non-discretion, discretionary non-discretion, and discretionary portfolios will all be part of the asset base of the successful professional financial advisor. Becoming successful within the CHALKLINES is dependent upon BUILDING A BOOK correctly. Let's see how it's done.

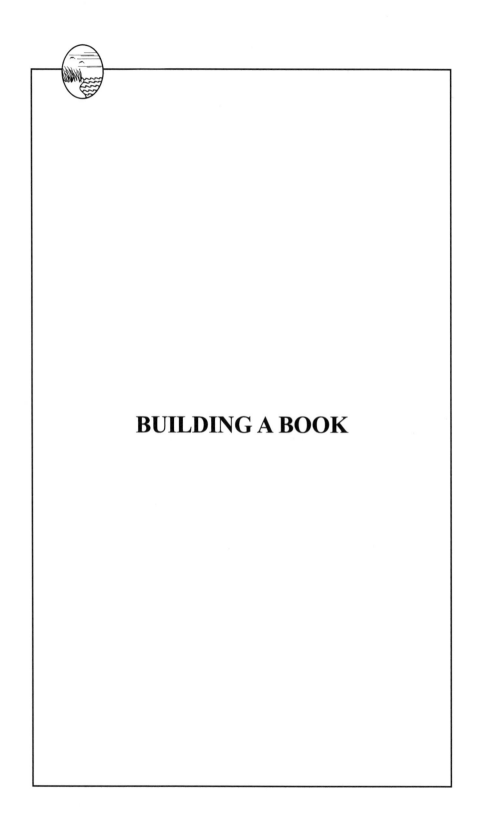

BUILDING A BOOK

The new financial services environment is giving all financial advisors an identity crisis. Am I a banker? A broker? A financial planner? How about a portfolio manager? Knowing what you are and clearly defining that role is crucial to helping clients and prospective clients understand you and the stability you bring to them in your business relationship.

Flexibility is a trait worth having except when it comes to projecting your image to your clients and your community. Serious investors seeking a financial advisor to guide them want to understand the stability of the firm and the individual advisor. There are many stories about bank trust departments where every time a client goes in to see their relationship officer, it is a new person. There is a reason the most successful bankers, advisors, and other financial professionals are usually older and represent a number of years in the business. Money is a serious subject to everyone, and the more they have the more serious they are.

In developing your role as a financial advisor, you must decide if you want to deal with clients on a discretionary or non-discretionary basis or a combination of the two. It seems like a small matter, but it's not. Non-discretionary business is much more time consuming than discretionary business. It is ten times easier to obtain a non-discretionary client, however. Easier to get more clients but less time to get them because of the difficulty of doing business when you have to call the client and get permission to do a trade. There are ways to make the process easier (FWIW #32). The question is not a small one. One strategy used successfully time after time is to seek out discretionary accounts but to take non-discretionary clients until your capacity for doing that kind of business is at its limit. At that point, only take discretionary accounts and give away your worst client for a new one that appears to be better than any that you have. Say that again. Give away your worst client when you find one better than any other non-discretionary clients you have in your business. Of course, take all of the discretionary clients available until you reach your capacity as long as they match your profile.

Capacity is not defined in terms of dollars under management. Capacity is defined in terms of the physical number of clients you can handle. You can probably handle 100 discretionary clients but only 50 non-discretionary clients if your role is on-going portfolio management as well as business development and relationship management. There is not enough time to call all of your clients and patiently explain why a particular investment is right for them. Even if each call took five minutes, a likely situation at least, then to call 50 clients will take over four hours if everyone agreed to the trade immediately. Usually, there is calling back and forth. Clients who do not need to be called before every trade are good but place substantial responsibility on your shoulders. There is a cardinal rule about discretionary accounts: *you should not take discretionary accounts where you are paid by the transaction.*

Transaction-oriented business is best done on the Internet for the lowest price possible. You should not have transaction-based clients. The focus with every client should be portfolio growth over defined and measured periods of time. Even if you are trying to transition from the commission generating business to financial advising and counseling for a fee, the absolutely only time you should be on commission is with a small handful of clients who are 100% fixed income investors. Bonds and preferred stocks are sold based upon the net yield to the client. Generally, a markup takes place rather than a separately computed and reported commission.

A fee-based compensation package removes any doubt in the client's mind about your selections for their account, be it discretionary or non-discretionary. It is far superior to transaction-based compensation from your perspective. Doing what is right for the client and not having anyone, the client nor your compliance manager, question your integrity in making the trade is a two-fold blessing. If you doubt this fact, just put a pencil to the steadily rising income you receive if you keep your money under management growing. A compounded asset base growth of 10% will cause your clients to double their assets in 7.2 years and you to do the same for your income.

Once you decide whether you will handle discretionary, non-discretionary, or a combination of the two types of clients and how you will be compensated, it's time to define the type of assets you will invest in for your clients. Will you be using only equities? What about bonds? Or a combination of the two? Don't laugh at the concept of only dealing with fixed income. There are many fabulously wealthy financial advisors who never look at the stock market. A well designed and run bond portfolio cannot match an equity portfolio for growth every year, but it can still grow at very competitive rates year in and year out without the risk associated with the stock market. There are many more people who are willing to invest in the bond market than in the stock market. Many financial advisors choose to be both an equity advisor and a fixed income advisor since most people do have a need for a balance between the two types of assets.

The next decision is whether or not you will be a growth oriented manager, a value manager, or just an income manager. This is the point when you have to be consistent in articulating a particular investment philosophy for the client. You can't be growth one day and value another day. Perhaps you will develop your own style. Fine. Just be able to clearly and logically articulate it to clients and prospects in three minutes or less. If you can't do that, your business will flounder.

Finally, you have to decide if you are going to be the portfolio manager and business development/relationship officer or just the business development/relationship officer. Anyone can be a portfolio manager with the proper educational background and experience. Not everyone can be successful as a business development and client relationship officer. It takes a special ability to communicate and care about people. The glamour is thought to be in the portfolio management, but the true satisfaction is in matching the right client with someone who can meet that client's objectives. Satisfaction comes in reviewing the portfolio objectives and adjusting them to meet the changing needs of the client over the years. Fulfilling the business development relationship and portfolio management roles will limit the number of clients that can be served properly. Knowing who you are, what works best for you, and defining the role you will play in the business is important to being the most efficient and productive financial advisor.

FWIW # 34 .... *Evangelist Versus Missionary*

Early in your career you have to learn the difference between being an evangelist and a missionary. A missionary preaches to the unconverted or disbelievers. These are individuals who do not understand nor want to understand the benefits of proper financial well-being. They live for the here and now. They are found in all socioeconomic groups. There are plenty of professionals making large sums of money who do not save or invest much if any of it. There are others who own their own business and are more comfortable investing any profits back into that business. Another group is distrustful of the investment markets and will not buy any securities other than bank CD's or U.S. Treasury Notes. Trying to convert these individuals into clients is a waste of time. At the very least, it is highly inefficient because if you are successful, they will only allocate a small amount for the investment program and call to discuss what is happening every week or every day. These are the kinds of clients you want your competitors to have.

You want to be an evangelist. You want to preach to the choir and the converted. All of your clients should understand and embrace the investment markets and your approach to the markets. When you show them the investment objectives, investment constraints, and the strategy to meet those objectives within those constraints, you want them to jump up and shout hallelujah. They understand how a stock and a bond work and how they will make money. Just being an evangelist, however, is not the whole story. You want to know who your converts are.

Catholic evangelists work best with Catholic converts. Baptist evangelists work best with Baptist converts. That doesn't mean the Catholic convert can't learn from and enjoy most of what the Baptist evangelist preaches. It just means the process is not totally in sync. It's the same way with your clients. If you are a value-oriented advisor, you can make money for a growth investor but that investor is not going to be as happy as if they were with a growth manager. The same goes for a value investor or a fixed income investor. Knowing who you can work with to be the most efficient and productive financial advisor is part of the maturing process. Wealthy prospective clients are everywhere. As a matter of fact, *high quality, knowledgeable financial advisors* will be scarce in the future and have more potential clients than the capacity to service them.

FWIW # 35 .... *Time Management*

Successful financial advisors have to be good at time management because they have no control over their time. Three unplanned events happen with astonishing regularity: (a) a client calls with an issue that has to be handled right then and now, (b) a potential client calls and responds to your inquiry and their interest is so strong it is important to follow through at that point, and (c) an unexpected event in the market requires immediate attention to portfolio adjustments. These regular irregular disruptions throw the best planned day out of focus. Without knowing what you wanted to accomplish, the likelihood of getting anything done before the sun goes down is slim. Let's examine how to be productive when schedule control is not always possible. FWIW #6 discussed how to allocate the daily time devoted to building a successful career. Overlay on that daily schedule a prioritized list of goals for the week. Only 80% of the weekly time should be allocated, recognizing that there will be slippage in the schedule. Once you have the weekly goals set, strive in the early days of the week to accomplish more than scheduled. Getting one day of focused effort completed will give flexibility to the rest of the week so that the inevitable interruption will not cause a complete breakdown on the road to success.

Finally, there are secrets of time management used by all successful people. First is an extremely focused period when everything, and I mean everything except the issue at hand is blocked out, completely blocked out, no distractions and 100% concentration. Save this exercise for those really critical situations when you must accomplish certain tasks within short time deadlines. After assuming this mode of activity and accomplishing the task that required it, find activities on your priority list that can be accomplished without intensity because you will need a change of pace in the stress level.

When all other time management techniques fail, use the ultimate weapon for getting things done: work longer hours. Don't laugh, it does work if you are committed to the other principles of time management. If you aren't, more time just raises the frustration level.

FWIW # 36 .... How Many Is Enough?

Since the beginning of the financial services business, the business model has been to gather in as many clients as possible. It made sense when the revenue flow was from transaction-based commissions. More clients led to more transactions and more commissions. More clients meant a diverse number of investment objectives so that there was the potential for having a transaction every day. Service and portfolio growth were not the focus of the relationship, access to the markets was the focus. Times are different now. Access to the markets has become a low-cost commodity. Mutual funds are for access to investment objective niches. Big cap, small cap, growth, growth and income, value, contrarian, and sector funds slice and dice the markets into every conceivable perspective imaginable. There are even funds of funds that boast of managing the managers. Many of these new mutual funds have little or no commissions for the financial service professional. What is your niche?

The same as it should always have been. The financial advisor's role is to identify the investment objectives and constraints of the client and create a portfolio policy and strategy to meet those objectives within the constraints. It takes time to do this function correctly. It takes time to be a partner with these clients in improving the net worth and adjusting objectives as the family and life evolves. Clients are not alike. Some require more service than others. Some only want partial service while others want close communications because of insecurity or an interest in the process.

Technology and the organizational structure of your practice will influence your decision about the number of clients you will manage. Efficiency and skills in the daily time management influences the number. The advisor's role in the total investment process influences the client population that can be handled efficiently. For those advisors with good technology skills and an efficient organizational structure and a desire to be the portfolio manager as well as business development officer, the number of clients can be as high as 150 if only about 40 are high maintenance clients. High maintenance is defined as a client who has contact with the portfolio manager once a week or more.

Transaction-based financial consultants are accustomed to having 1,000 or more clients and the thought of having only 100 to 150 is culture shock. Changing attitudes about the client relationship is the biggest adjustment senior experienced professionals in our business will have to make in the new marketplace. There is something in the successful financial consultant or broker that is comforted in having a large number of people validate their competence.

Those financial advisors who choose to act as an intermediary and place their client's assets with other professionals through mutual funds or wrap fee programs can handle more clients. Traditional trust departments and investment counseling firms usually only allocate 40 to 50 clients per relationship manager. So you can see the intensity of the client concentration really depends on the nature of the clients and the role that you play with those clients.

The concept today is to grow the client's assets and to earn the client's trust by being knowledgeable and having a genuine interest in the client's well-being. This approach is time consuming. Gone are the days when one transaction a year is done for a client. The compensation dynamics is changing as well. Portfolio values totaling $500 million can be achieved with 50 clients having an average of $10 million each or 500 clients having an average of $1 million each. Which do you want? Everyone wants to have 50 clients instead of 500 and that's why large clients have the lowest fee structure and the most people knocking on their doors. What's important for the professional financial advisor is to understand their own limits and build a practice accordingly. A client with $500,000 today can have $1 million in a few years and $2 million a few years after that. Focusing on growing the assets will go a long way toward balancing the time available with the right number of clients.

FWIW # 37 .... *Elephant Hunting*

It's human nature to want to do business with the most powerful and most respected people in your community. There is some intangible value for being the financial advisor to the society movers and shakers. Unfortunately, everyone wants to be their financial advisor. Consequently, the fees these clients pay are small. These large clients, known as elephants in the business, are usually demanding in their service and performance requirements. With so many advisors trying to get their business, they can be low revenue and high cost clients. Somewhere in the process of building your business you have to decide if you are going to be exclusively an elephant hunter.

One client with a $5 million portfolio will generate between $20,000 and $30,000 a year in fees. Ten clients with $500,000 portfolios will generate between $50,000 and $75,000 in fees. Do you have the technology and organizational skills to handle the ten smaller clients who might not be as demanding as the large client? Which profile of clients gives the practice the most stability? If you are successful in providing services and portfolio growth, which business practice will generate the most client loyalty over time?

Elephant hunting is not a time efficient experience. There should be no more than five in your 300 Club, enough to systemically work but not enough to monopolize your time. Your business development program should not be focused on elephants but on potential elephants. Here's what we mean. If you have a disciplined approach to the markets and if you have knowledge of the business you can find those people who are not actively solicited by your competitors, and develop a strong relationship with them, providing them service, getting a premium fee for that service, and growing them into quality clients.

FWIW # 38 .... *A Quality Client*

A quality client is ***someone who understands what you do, needs your expertise, and is willing to pay for it.*** If any one of these criteria is missing, the client is not a quality client. They might be satisfactory, but not quality clients.

Today, a client who wants someone to make a transaction is not a quality client. They are always wanting to pay you what they can pay an online broker or a discount broker. You want a client who recognizes the complexity of the investment markets, who understands markets do not always go up or down, who understands that with professional guidance portfolio growth can be enhanced and who has confidence that you have the skills and knowledge to give good unbiased advice to them.

You want a client who can see that your advice is tailored to them and their unique family circumstances. You want one who values your knowledge of the overall scope of financial and estate planning issues. You want one who materially and factually sees the benefit you bring to the relationship and recognizes that quality in any endeavor costs money. When you present your fee for service they are willing to pay the fee because they understand the service you provided.

Are there ideal clients like this out there? Millions of them. There is not now nor will there ever be enough quality financial advisors available to service all of the quality clients. If you reread the above definition, you can see that the financial advisor has a major role in shaping and creating the quality client. Helping a client includes showing the client the benefits they derive from dealing with you.

FWIW # 39 .... *Who? Where? How?*

Quality clients live within your community or the communities you serve. They are in all professions and walks of life. The nurse at the local hospital could have $500,000 in a 401(k). The bank office manager might have $1 million in bank stock. The school teacher could have inherited several millions of dollars. The factory worker who is retiring will have major assets to be rolled over into an IRA. You cannot exclude any walk of life from your prospecting program because of societal changes that have diffused money to more people. The depression-era generation is dying and leaving sixty years of cautious lifestyle wealth accumulation to their children and grandchildren. Significant increases in value of real estate and the stock market have swollen retirement assets to undreamed of amounts. Most people have a certain level of wealth they are comfortable handling on their own. When their net worth grows larger than that amount, or they see the prospect of not having as secure a job, people's anxiety over preserving and growing wealth multiplies quickly. The people described here are the potential quality clients today because they are not readily visible to all professional advisors.

While these potential clients are not readily visible, they have to live somewhere and that is where you start looking for them. A street map of your community is helpful. Identify, on the map, the attractive neighborhoods. Notice, I didn't say the most expensive neighborhoods. You do not want those people who have high incomes and high expenses. You want the clients who spend less than they make and place the extra in their portfolios. People with money are no different from other people in that they tend to congregate in groups. Therefore, the first focus is on neighborhoods. A city directory or a voter list will help identify who lives on what street in what neighborhood.

A country club membership list is a place to start, although it is a little awkward if you are a new member of the club. What is not awkward is getting a list of your local chamber of commerce members because they are business people and professionals who do have a sense of community and who usually have a successful business or practice. A third list that makes sense is that of donors to various charitable organizations in a community. When the master list is not available, one or two charities usually have a major ball or event during the year where sponsors and participants are listed in the program. The same type of approach can be used to garner names of the friends of your local symphony, ballet dance company, or theater group. Last, but not least, it's easy to identify those churches that have an affluent membership. All of these names can be tied back into a neighborhood through the city directory.

Once you have identified a list of potential clients it's time to find out who on the list has the profile of a prospective quality client. During the 1980's and the early 1990's the process was to simply pick up the phone and make a cold call. The influx of brokers and the emphasis on cold calling at dinnertime led to a number of states passing laws against unsolicited telephone canvassing. Besides, aggravating a potential client at mealtime does not seem to be the best way to begin a relationship. Cold calling does work but only with some forethought and planning. Even then, the efficiency of the exercise is low.

Another low efficiency method but reliable means of prospecting is direct mail. Evidently, extensive research has been done that indicates long multiple page letters or small paperback books are the most effective tools in direct mail solicitation for financial services. That is great for mass solicitation of an impersonal nature, but you are trying to establish a personal relationship where you bring special and valuable knowledge to the union. A combination of cold calling and direct mail solicitation works well when done properly. It impresses potential clients with the quality of the presentation and the focus of the solicitation. (See FWIW # 44).

Seminar prospecting is especially good when you can focus on an issue of importance to both clients and prospects. (See FWIW # 43). What's important with this type of prospecting is giving the attendees an opportunity to have quality one on one time with you either that evening or within three days after the seminar.

Community service with the right organization helps establish your presence in your city, gives you the opportunity to show your abilities, and builds a common interest with people who have money. A professional who wants to build a large practice in the community needs to participate in this indirect form of prospecting. Of all the ways to develop business, this reaching out and putting your skills on display carries the highest risk. If you do not work well as part of an organization or a team, your reputation will suffer. If there isn't a clear path from worker to leader in the organization, you should rethink participating in that particular group since you will not be able to show your leadership skills over a period of time. If there aren't any good prospects to be associated with, you should find an organization that does give you the opportunity to meet the right people in exchange for your services.

The best way to prospect is to receive referrals from existing clients. It is the highest compliment you can receive and, unfortunately, a rare occurrence. The best way to receive referrals is to offer your clients the opportunity to send your monthly newsletter to someone they think will find it interesting and helpful. The second best way to stimulate referrals is through seminars and allowing each client to bring a friend. However you do it, the most important factor is to treat the referral as the rare jewel it is.

FWIW # 40 .... *The 300 Club*

The 300 Club is not a religious organization. It is the most exclusive private club in town owned and operated by an entrepreneur – you. Membership qualifications should be strict. The prospective members should meet all of the criteria to become a quality client.

The club membership can be any number as long as it is over 200 and a fixed amount. Since the asset-based fee structure allows for larger revenues from fewer clients, the 300 Club can easily become the 200 Club. Many more than 300 becomes unruly and defeats the purpose altogether. Many firms tell new financial advisors to make lists of 1,000 or more prospects. This huge list of names is a method called shotgun prospecting, the random calling of strangers to solicit investment business. This superficial calling leads to the gathering of just the easy accounts. As with everything else in life, what comes easy is rarely worth having. The 300 Club is different.

The 300 Club begins, as always, with a suspect list of names. There is no other way to begin developing a group of people you want to do business with. The list might be from another division of your firm, or tax records, or voter's lists. The common denominator of this beginning list is that everyone is alive and everyone lives in an acceptable neighborhood. Qualifying the list is what is important and starts now.

Qualifying begins by communicating. Seminars, cold calls, referrals, introductory direct mail, or meeting through community service work takes over. Remember what makes a quality client: they know what you do, need your expertise, and are willing to pay for it. Now, it's naive to expect someone with all these characteristics to be sitting out there not using one of your competitors. Therefore, you need to be prepared to be patient and deliberate in gathering the information that will help the prospective client see that you are a professional. *It is important to realize that clients make financial decisions on their time, not your time.* Being around when they are ready to make a decision will give you an unusually strong beginning because the client has allowed circumstances to help them make the choice to do business with you. It might seem easy to the novice to get 300 qualified potential quality clients, but it's not. It takes persistence and hard work and time, a lot of time. Focusing on this aspect of business development will keep your business growing.

Once an individual is in the 300 Club, there are only three ways they can leave it. The first and best way is to become a client. This, of course, is the purpose of the whole system. The second way is if it becomes apparent that the individual is never going to do business under any circumstances. The clearest sign of this situation is when the prospect refuses to take your phone call or see you on a visit. If they will talk to you, you still have an opportunity to eventually do business. If they won't, you haven't spoken the right language.

The third way someone drops out of the 300 Club is when you find another person who is so clearly superior to the least qualified of the 300 members that you are compelled to replace them with the new prospect. Even then, before dropping someone from the 300 Club, you should spend at least one day intentionally trying to convert the person from the 300 Club into a client, or at the least, asking the prospect one last time to do business with you.

The purpose of the 300 Club is to bring order to your business development from its beginning. This step is crucial if your career is to take off from the start. Running randomly from one name to another wastes an awful lot of energy which could be channeled productively. Very few financial advisors have over 50 active prospects at any one time because they don't have a good system of working their business development. A financial advisor who develops a 300 Club will always be in the forefront of revenue generators.

In a transaction-based business the objective is to convince the prospects to accept your idea or allow you to assist in executing their idea. In any event, the commitment to do business is not nearly as great as it is in a fee-based business. A fee-based business relationship calls for the client to embrace you and your strategy for making the client's portfolio grow. This is not an easy leap of faith for most people so they have to get to know more about you and have faith that you are truly interested in them as people rather than just as an impersonal portfolio prospect.

Business development has always been like a pipeline. You put prospective clients in and eventually some of them come out the other end as clients. The more you put in, the more come out the other side. Because the business is changing with a greater commitment on the part of clients to allowing discretionary relationships, the pipeline is longer. A longer pipeline means it takes more time to get a client out the other end. This greater time lag is a larger risk for you if you don't have a full complement of members in the 300 Club. There isn't any excuse for failing to spend time on business development because if you aren't carefully nurturing the 300 Club members, you will experience a gap in new client development.

FWIW # 42 .... *Another's Client*

Quality prospective clients will usually respond to your initial solicitation with one of the following retorts:

"I have a financial advisor I'm happy with."

"My financial advisor is my brother-in-law."

"I'm completely satisfied with my present financial advisor."

"I'm not interested. I have a good financial advisor."

"I use on-line trading and save the money that I would pay you or someone like you."

When faced with definite rebuffs such as these, the average financial advisor usually moves on to someone else. That's a mistake because what each of these responses say is that the prospect knows what you do for a living, needs the expertise, and is paying someone for that expertise – just not you. Well, that's because they don't know who you are or what credentials you have and how you can meet their needs.

A response to one of these brush-offs:

"Thank you for your honesty. I am sure you are happy with your present financial advisor relationship. I respect that but perhaps over time I can assist you in ensuring that your financial objectives and constraints are being met by the investment strategy you are using. Are you mainly a growth investor or a value investor?" Then you take the conversation wherever it goes. Very few people will turn down an offer like that because it is focused on their needs, not yours. It also opens the door for a discussion of their investment objectives and constraints. Since very few clients have ever thought about these crucial parts of investing, you have a method of educating the prospect and gaining their confidence. Everyone wants to improve their financial well-being and will be willing and ready to discuss, with a professional, ways of enhancing their portfolio's total return. Your task is to discuss potential improvements without giving away your best asset for free – your knowledge.

FWIW # 43 .... *Seminars*

Seminars can be extremely effective if done right, but most of them are serious wastes of time and money because they are done wrong. The first mistake comes from the fear of no one showing up. This mortifying event of no one showing up is only surpassed by the dread of one or two people arriving and then broadcasting this disaster to everyone they know. To combat this career-threatening potential disaster, financial advisors advertise a seminar, mass mail invitations, and plan to serve breakfast, lunch, or wine and cheese in the evening, depending on the time of the seminar. The strategy is to offer food for the body to entice prospects to show up and hear the pitch. By the way, most seminar invitations do not go to clients. It absolutely makes no sense to exclude clients, but that's generally the case. If the location is attractive and the food is attractive, the seminar is usually well-attended by the targeted audience – people who want a free meal and entertainment for an hour. They have no interest or intention of doing business but would like some free advice or a chance to talk about their portfolio or the latest stock they bought. You waste your time and are led on a wild goose chase. Doing the seminar correctly is easier and much more productive. Let's examine how to do it professionally.

Step one is to limit the seminar to only sixteen people plus yourself. Never more than that. Step number two is to make eight of the sixteen invitees clients you already have on your books. Not new clients but those you have worked with and developed a portfolio for over an extended period of time and with whom you have a solid substantial working relationship. The kind of people who should be willing to give you a referral if they only thought about that sort of thing. Why preach to the choir by having clients at the seminar? Because they are friendly faces, they believe in you and your expertise, and they will be comfortable in beginning a dialogue when the Q&A session begins. You will make them look good in front of their friend because you look professional and knowledgeable and they were smart enough to pick you as their financial advisor.

The room should be adequate for the group and, if there is a choice, slightly large so no one feels cramped. Seating should be comfortable because the audience will be sitting for at least 45 minutes and you don't want them squirming in their seats distracting themselves and everyone else. If there is a room large enough at your office that is the best place for the event. If not, your office building, or your club, or a restaurant will have a conference room that will work.

Refreshments should not be mentioned in the invitation. You should have coffee, water, or iced tea as a matter of course. Cookies, nuts, or crackers can be available. You don't want people coming who expect to be fed. You want serious investors who have a specific interest and desire to learn something that can improve their financial situation. For instance, perhaps there is an early retirement seminar for an industrial business in town. Or, perhaps a seminar on rollover options or determining investment strategies to replace lost income. You want the people who are there to listen to you and your expertise. This is your chance to develop their confidence.

Invitations are sent out and responses required to get a ticket for admission. These tickets should be numbered and collected at the door. By requiring tickets, you can take care of two issues: (a) you have a list of everyone who has expressed an interest in the seminar, even those who, for whatever reason, don't show up and, (b) you know how many to expect and can send out more invitations if necessary. By the way, you don't want to sell anyone on attending. If you do, your chances of having a lot of last minute cancellations increase and it's probable they will not be productive attendees anyway.

In the invitations to your clients, tell them they have the opportunity to bring one friend to the seminar. You have to know who the friend is, and the friend's address, so you can send their ticket directly. Having a standard procedure will make it easier to handle matters without seeming to be intrusive. If all eight of your clients want to bring friends, your seminar list is complete. If they don't, go to your 300 Club and fill the open spots. If you go to the 300 Club, call the potential invitees, tell them the invitation is coming if they are interested, and get an affirmative indication of interest. Don't just make casual contact with these potential clients through the mail. Make every contact count as part of a long term relationship building process.

The seminar subject has to be timely, in-depth, and actionable. The timeliness is what will usually get the invitees to show up. In the first quarter of the year a seminar built around income taxes usually works well. In other quarters seminars about trusts, family limited partnerships, gifting, creating long term capital gains, strategies to replace income and other such subjects that help the invitees realize you are a reservoir of knowledge and expertise are appropriate.

Always have written material for the participants to take home with them. The written material should be in outline form with just enough key words to help them remember what you said but not enough for them to use independently of you. There should be a page at the end that raises the important questions about their investment program which should trigger the invitees' desire to get in touch with you to discuss specific situations. The key concept here is to assist the attendees in understanding a financial situation that impacts them, assists them in understanding that you have a firm grasp on the issue, and gives them an easy way to come to you for the solution to their unique circumstances. The written information should be in a folder, should be professional and printed clearly in a high quality manner.

You know how to follow-up with your clients who attended and the members of the 300 Club. The attendees invited by your clients are new to you. Do they have the potential to become clients immediately? How about being a candidate for the 300 Club? Following up and asking for a meeting to discuss how the seminar subject impacts them specifically will give you an indication of their intent. A top quality seminar ending with an actionable idea will help you take these referrals and turn them immediately into clients.

There is always a debate about having an "expert" speak at the seminars. You should be the expert. If your practice is placing money with investment managers, you should still be the expert who uses outside managers as tools to achieve the goals you and your clients set. If you manage the assets, you want the prospective clients to see how professional you are in your approach. If you work at a large firm, you will professionally give credit to the authors of the material used, but the focus will be on your skills in pulling all of the information together and translating it into an actionable plan for the client.

Seminars should be a standard form of prospecting. You should have one per quarter, every quarter, every year during your career. Your seminars should gradually build up a reputation for quality knowledge given in a way to improve and enhance the performance of the attendees' portfolio. This is a tall order. Reputation-building is not an easy process, but is certainly rewarding when it's done right.

FWIW # 44 .... *Reach Out and Touch*

Once the 300 Club is full, there should be enough referrals from seminars and contacts from community service to keep the club membership topped off. Until the club is full, the efforts have to be more intense and more active. Cold calling is a low productivity way of business development, so is direct mail. Put together, however, they become an acceptable means of introducing yourself to potential clients. Here's how to make an impression.

Start with the material in the direct mail. Go to an upscale stationery store. If necessary, get permission from your firm to purchase, at your expense, some of the finest stationery available in a size different from the standard 8½ x 11. Have your firm's letterhead and your name and title embossed on the page. Notice, I did not say printed. Have your name and address embossed on the back flap of the envelope. This is most effective when embossed without any ink. Use black ink on cream-colored paper. Thick, cotton fiber paper that looks and feels expensive and, unfortunately, is. Go to the post office and buy some special stamps, not the run-of-the-mill flag stamp, and for sure, not the postage meter at your office.

Inside the envelope, have a single page with one actionable idea or concept in the body of the letter. An example might be:

Mr. John Jones

Any Street

Any Town, State, Zip

Dear Mr. Jones:

Last year, congressional action impacted the options available to investors who want to minimize the taxes associated with IRA withdrawals. As a matter of fact, you have the potential for delaying the major impact of taxes on IRA withdrawals for up to 10, 15, or even 20 years. All the time these taxes are avoided, the value of your portfolio has the potential to double every seven years.

This is a complex subject and has to be crafted to individual circumstances. I have reviewed and analyzed the changes and wish to discuss them with you. I'll call Tuesday, Month/Day, to schedule an appointment to show you how to maximize the tax deferral and increase the likelihood of your portfolio doubling in a reasonable period of time.

Sincerely,

Eugene A. Kelly, CFA

What does the letter do? First, it alerts the prospect to the reason for the letter, significant changes in the IRA laws. Second, it points out that the impact of the changes varies with individuals and therefore the prospect can't just read about it in a magazine and apply the principles to their portfolio. Your assistance in applying the rules is required. Finally, the letter alerts the prospect that you will call. If there is an interest, your call will be accepted. Even if the interest is lukewarm, the quality of the presentation will usually get the prospect to accept your phone call.

If you tell the prospect you will call on Tuesday, make sure you call on Tuesday. Start early and stay late if necessary. If you are trying to reach an entrepreneur or a professional, most likely they will be in their office by 8:00 a.m,. or still be there at 6:00 p.m. If there is a call screener, it's important to not try to outfox them. Make the call sound like this:

"Good morning, this is Gene Kelly calling. I'm calling Mr. Jones, please."

If they ask who you are or if Mr. Jones is expecting you, respond: "I'm with _____ firm, and Mr. Jones is aware I am calling." If the call is not taken and it's obvious the prospect knows you are calling, leave your name and number for the prospect to call you back. Don't pester them. This is not a contest of wills here. Remember, a quality client knows what you do <u>and needs your expertise.</u> If the prospect is important, plan on going by their workplace before or after the regular work day hours. Generally, they will be there early or late and their screener will not. Remember, you want to be persistent, but not a pest.

With the quality of the direct mail solicitation message and its presentation you will have the opportunity to speak to the prospect. You have one objective, to get to see them in person, nothing else. You don't want a long conversation and you surely don't want to try to give a long presentation on the phone. Ask for the opportunity to meet the prospect in their office at a time of their choosing within the next week. Let them know you work early and you work late. Ask if before or after hours works best. Pick a day initially when you have a clear schedule so they can choose any time they want. Later, as your schedule begins to be full, give the prospect two or three choices. If none of these choices work, then let the prospect give you two choices. You make it work out. Your goal for the call is over. Hang up as gracefully as you can. Naturally, if the prospect wants to talk about their circumstances, that's fine. Gather the information. Under no circumstances should you give any explanation of the subject in your letter.

A final word about this two-step process. Don't send out more than six letters per day, but don't fail to send out six letters every day until such time as the 300 Club is full. At that point, drop to three letters per day to maintain some prospects in the pipeline.

One of the faults of most stockbrokers is failure to keep in touch with their clientele on a regular basis. Out of sight is out of mind. They are out of your sight and you eventually get out of their mind because someone else is paying attention to them. Transaction-based compensation created this lack of continuity. Fee-based management requires a different approach. Your client expects to hear from you regularly because they expect you to be managing their assets daily. An excellent way to keep in touch is to develop a monthly newsletter that communicates your thoughts to your clients. Some advisors publish a newsletter quarterly, but that is not often enough to serve the purpose of a regular communication. With the desktop publishing software available today, a one or two page newsletter is easy to design and print. A print shop can create a number of copies in a short period of time.

It is crucial to keep to a systematic schedule for mailing the letter. If it is dated the first day of the month, it should be in the mail on that day every month without fail. No excuses, get it done. Keep a copy in your files for referring back to if a client or 300 Club member calls with a question.

Have a place on the newsletter where you indicate the letter is for the private use of your clients and friends (i.e., 300 Club). If any of your clients or friends wish to send a copy to someone, they may call you and you will send a sample copy with their compliments. A neat way to ask for a referral, isn't it?

The newsletter should be newsworthy but not have any specific recommendations. Interest rates, the equity market in general, sector news, index news, market psychology, tax or political news that impacts the markets, interesting background information from published sources (get permission and give credit), and timely subjects that are interesting. It's easy to fill up one or two pages. Do not discuss individual stocks. Talk about investment principles or strategies. For those advisors who are not allowed to write their own newsletter, use information from your firm's analysts. Cut and paste the information so you create a coherent letter while only using the firm's proprietary research. Again, don't use individual stock information. Just general broad information on strategies and various economic sectors. The concept is to impress the reader with your grasp of the market, let them know you are actively managing their portfolio, and give them the feeling of steady and valuable communication.

When you have a particularly good newsletter, you will get referrals to send the letter to someone, an excellent introduction to a potential 300 Club member or client. In your career, you will have the opportunity to give talks to investment clubs or service clubs. Always take a copy of your newsletter with you. At the end of the speech offer a three-month complimentary subscription to anyone in the room. Have a pen and paper for them to write their names and addresses. After they get their first issue, you have the opportunity to call and ask if they have any questions. After their third and last issue, you have another reason to call and ask for a meeting. A monthly newsletter is an excellent way to have a prospect receive something of value from someone of value.

FWIW # 46 .... *Referrals*

Every professional covets referrals and they should because a referral is an endorsement of the quality of the professional's service by a client or acquaintance. A referral is a gift and should be treated as one. Referrals come from four sources: (a) clients, (b) other professionals, (c) 300 Club members, and (d) family and friends. The strongest and most valuable referrals come from clients. When clients speak, it carries weight because they are already partaking of your service and spending good money for it. All of us pay greater attention to someone's opinion who has experienced the situation they are endorsing.

Other professionals, such as lawyers, CPA's, physicians and clergy hold positions of influence and when they choose to give a referral give it with all of the influence they carry. There is another unspoken power behind the referral. These same professionals run the risk of looking bad when the referral turns out tobe less than satisfactory. It is important for you to understand the friendship and esteem represented by this gift so clearly demonstrate your worthiness for the referral by carefully keeping the professional in the loop until the individual becomes a client or you cannot help them. Communicate the end result to the referring professional and if the match does not work articulate why it did not work and what the referred indivdual should do to achieve success with another financial professional.

There will be times a referral will come from a 300 Club member. That might seem strange since the referring 300 Club member has not chosen to become a client. It's not. There could be a number of reasons why the club member has not started to do business with you. Because they recognize your persistence and professionalism, they want to reward you anyway. At times, a member can become your best heerleader and advocate. Acept the gift without calling attention to the incongruity of the situation. Referrals from members instead of their being a client can mean more business.

Friends and family referrals are nice and help validate the closeness of your circle of existence. Treat these referrals with the same degree of care and nurturing you do a stranger's. Keep the referring party in the loop and be just as professional rather than casual.

Why don't people make more referrals? Fear of disaster is the greatest reason, but lack of thought is right up there, too. A close third is not wanting to share you with others, as strange as that seems. You can't deal with the first and third reason, but you can eliminate the lack of thought excuse. Make it easy for referrals by (a) having clients bring friends to seminars, (b) allowing people on mailing lists to have someone receive your monthly client commentary, (c) sending out an annual client feedback sheet where you ask for a referral, and (d) having a sign in your office requesting the opportunity to help someone your client knows.

You never know what client, professional, prospect or friend will make a referral. Most of the time you will be astonished by the source. Consequently, you must treat everyone you come in contact with like they are the ultimate source of all future referrals. In and of itself this attitude is a great way to conduct your business and a sure way to receive as many referrals as possible.

Every professional advisor hs a targeted trading area. It might be one city block or building in New York or it might be the entire United States or even a hemisphere of the world. It also can be a specific group or type of people. Often the trading area is defined in terms of geography. If so, get or make a map of the trading area. Keep it where you can see it, but not where your colleagues or clients can. It's none of their business.

Beginning a career usually means having no clients or strong prospects for clients. It also means having time to see and be seen. As your career prgresses, the time will be a luxury you can't afford giving away by going long distances. Begin your career by prospecting on the outer edges of your sales territory. Go out and see these people. These personal visitscan later be reinforced with telephone contact when the required time in the office means the trps are infrequent.

As the outer edges are thoroughly canvassed, start working back towards the center and your office. one properly, the mix of accounts represents all areas of the territory and any future trips out of the office can be a combination of seeing clients and meeting new prospects.

Only a novice on the way to another career talks about performance to a prospective client. It's a no win situation. Even the best investment managers in the world, now and in the past, have periods when they cannot outperform or math the market indexes. Make no mistake, clients don't hire you because you're funny or cute. They want a professional who can grow their portfolio over time. Performance should not be the focus. Understanding what investment objectives the client has should be the focus. Understanding what investment constraints are unique to the client should be the focus. Being able to craft an investment policy and strategy to meet the objectives within the constraints should be the focus. Being able to communicate all of this to the prospective client should be the focus. Then and only then is it appropriate to show the client that in the past you have been able to take clients with similar situations and assist them in meeting their unique goals.

Above all, during the first meeting with the prospective client, if the prospect mentions performance twice, understand that you will not be able to satisfy them, so find a way to gracefully disengage and spend your time finding clients who realize growing a net worth is not just numbers.

FWIW # 49 .... *Fact Finding*

It never ceases to amaze me when I see financial advisors hand a two, four, or even eight page questionnaire to a prospective client to complete nd return in the mail. Talk about impersonal cookie-cutter, fit-in-the-box, slap-in-the-face. And this is someone who has enough ssets to be considered wealthy!

Not only is it insulting, but you miss the best opportunity to seriously connect with and bond with your potential client. As a financial advisor, you should study the questionnaire your firm uses, and learn all about the questions and WHY they are asked. Work out ways to ask the questions in a dialogue fashion. Use the discourse as an opportunity to share information about yourself with the client to make them understand that you are like they are and are the type of person they want to do business with. The client might say they have three children. Ask if they are all healthy. Perhaps you will find out one is a special child that will need large financial sums at some point. You would not have known that from the questionnaire. Ask their ages and what schools they go to. Parents love to talk about their children. All of this information is also relevant to their financial profile. Seek out tidbits of information that shed light on financial needs or potential investment time horizon goals. Perhaps all the children will be out of college when the prospective client reaches age 54. You should have a plan for an increased investment amount yearly after that time. Above all, take the opportunity to show the client how each of these bits of information fit together to make a whole financial picture that leads to a unique set of goals and strategies. By going through this process with the client, your professionalism is clearly demonstrated and they feel special. You also gather significant information to back up what recommendations or investments you plan for their portfolio.

FWIW # 50 .... *Seeing Is Believing*

There is an interesting aspect to the investment business. Many investors know they should be conservative and balanced in their approach to building wealth, but they are not. If asked, they quickly sing the praises of all of the basic rules of conservative investing.

They talk about buying good quality, they talk about low PE ratios, they talk about high quality bonds, they talk about good cash reserves. When asked by a financial advisor what kind of portfolio is appropriate, their description is safe and sane and fiction. The advisor never manages the portfolio because the client really wants some high risk, very volatile, hope-and-a-prayer stock that has made instant mega millionaires of anyone who bought $10,000 worth five years ago.

Many people say one thing and do another in their portfolio. To avoid wasting time and building frustration, ask the prospective client for a copy of their current statement detailing their real portfolio. See if the portfolio matches what they say they want from an investment advisor. If not, believe the portfolio before you believe the client. See if the current portfolio is appropriate for that client. In many cases, it's not. If it is not appropriate, allow someone else to get in front of the lawsuit that will eventually happen. If the high risk portfolio is acceptable for the client's circumstances and fits your style of investing, put in the effort necessary to become the financial advisor for this client.

FWIW # 51 .... *Silence Is Golden*

The only guarantee in the investment markets is volatility. Volatility means good markets will turn into bad markets. When bad markets arrive, your competitors stop calling their clients. The silence from your competitors is gold for you. Who are your competitors' clients? Your 300 Club. As you have systematically built a relationship with the 300 Club members, you will have learned something about their portfolios. Now is the time to communicate clearly and often with your clients as well as your 300 Club members.

Can you think of a better time to begin a relationship-building call than to offer your 300 Club members information or an opinion about the stocks in their portfolios? Is there a better time to do a review and analysis of prospective clients' portfolios than when the market is down?

Over and over again you will begin to learn that clients want honesty, integrity, and competent leadership from their financial advisor. Make sure you give steady communication to your clients in all markets, not just the good ones, so you will increase your clientele due to your competitor's silence.

FWIW # 52 .... *Cocktail Parties*

The financial advisor at a cocktail party gets picked on, picked at, and picked over almost as much as the hors d'oeuvres. When the stock market is hot, everybody wants to tell how smart they are to own the right stock at the right time. When the market is in the doldrums, they want free advice as to whether or not to keep the stocks in their portfolio. The free advice is the absolute slap in the face. Lawyers and physicians, who will not give any advice for free, are insulted when the financial advisor doesn't make available knowledge for no charge. Besides, a party is not an appropriate place to discuss business. There are ways to handle the situation professionally. First, you have to decide if the person is someone you want as a client or is someone who is currently in your 300 Club. If not, a smile and the following will usually do the trick:

"Well, (name), my clients pay very good money for my opinion on that stock and would be quite upset if I gave my knowledge to you or anyone else for free. I suggest you call your broker tomorrow or go online tonight."

If the person asking is someone you want as a client, or is already in your 300 Club, keep the smile and say the following:

"Well, (name), my opinion is (positive/negative). While I don't recall off-hand the details, I do have an extensive file on that company that I would be willing to share with you. Do you currently own the stock or are you interested in taking a position?"

The purpose of asking the question is to see if they are serious about the company or just making idle chatter. If they say never mind, end the conversation. If they indicate a genuine interest, or disclose the size of their position (1,000 shares, etc.), tell them you will send the information. Don't press the conversation past that point. A cocktail party is no place to carry on a business conversation. You have made all of the progress you can with this individual. Slip out somewhere and make a note of the conversation and then go back to enjoying the party. The next day, prepare a good file on the company and call the person and ask for a time when you can bring it by their office. Don't mail it. Don't discuss it on the phone. The prospective client took your time at the cocktail party. You have a right for five minutes in their office or yours to make this presentation.

FWIW # 53 .... *Friends and Clients*

There is a rule in the financial services business: "Make friends of your clients, not clients of your friends."

When you begin doing business with social friends, there are extra dimensions to both the social and business relationship. First, you know what your client has in the way of finances and assets, and therefore, there can't be any pretense on their part as to how well they're doing or not doing. That openness is challenging since it also keeps them from inflating their financial accomplishments with other mutual friends in your presence. Additional pressure comes from the results of your work when the inevitable mistakes are made or the returns are less than expected. Because of the social relationship, there is a tendency to be less than professional in the contact between you and your friend/client. Unless you clearly set the boundaries from the beginning, there is nothing as uncomfortable as sitting around a party table with other friends and the friend/client brings up an issue that is best discussed in the office, or begins to joke about your prowess as a financial advisor.

None of the foregoing touches on the spousal issues when one spouse is not happy having the other spouse know what is going on in the first one's financial life. Your spouse should not have any idea about your clients' finances or portfolios and that includes the ones who are your social friends. It's hard, however, in reality, to enforce that rule.

From your perspective, you will have a tendency to try too hard or evelop a hesitancy to take risks and your rhythm of investing will be disrupted.

All of these social challenges do not develop in the relationship where the client begins as a stranger and you develop a friendship as a trusted financial advisor over time. Mutual business respect develops usually into a limited social friendship, but always continues first and foremost as a professional relationship.

If you are pressed by a friend to take their portfolio, ask the friend to come to your office to discuss the business relationship. Don't do it casually at your home or theirs. Develop a full list of investment objectives, investment constraints, and an investment strategy to meet those objectives within the known constraints. Be as clear and detailed as appropriate. Send the information in writing to the friend turned client so they can review the material and understand your professionalism. When you contact them to follow up, do so at their office and during business hours. If you are to meet with both the husband and wife, go alone and make the visit strictly business. If you can truthfully not share information with your spouse, at the very first meeting when the husband and wife are together, tell them what they say to you is confidential and that your spouse will not know. Make sure you can truthfully say this. Help them understand that you will not bring up business in the social setting and you expect them to likewise refrain from mixing the two parts of your relationship. Thank them for their confidence and trust and make the best of a difficult situation.

There are two distinct parts to the process of building a successful list of clients. You must be impatient to complete the first part, developing a 300 Club of quality potential clients. There is no excuse for not adding to this elite group of wealthy people every day until it is full. Every day you should also be impatient in trying to take people out of the 300 Club by making them clients. Your nerves should be on edge, your pulse should be racing, and your adrenaline pumping as you search diligently to find the right addition to the club while seeking ways to convert to clients those who have been in the club long enough.

The patience takes place as you build the mosaic of information you need to finally communicate with the 300 Club members the correct information for them to understand you are the right financial advisor for their family. *Prospective clients choose to engage your services on their time table, not yours.* Always remember that fact because it is important that you have a client who will trust you during the challenging markets as well as the good ones. Let them make the decision on their own as to when to engage your services. It will be a stronger commitment to the relationship and to your expertise.

FWIW # 55 .... *Too Many Cooks*

As a successful professional advisor, over time you build up your confidence in your ability to grow clients' portfolios. You know investing and you know that one of the major and sacred investment principles is that there can only be one investment decision maker for every portfolio. Just as in cooking, when too many cooks ruin the meal, too many decision makers ruin the performance of a portfolio. You know these things but you need to always remember that the portfolio is your client's money, not yours. There will be times when you'll be faced with the dilemma of your client wanting you to buy or sell something in the portfolio. Inevitably, what they want to buy is not a good idea or what they want to sell is what you expect to double over the next twelve months. What should you do?

Step one is to gently review with the client the investment objectives of the portfolio, and the strategy designed to meet those objectives. In the process, examine how the stock the client wants fits into that strategy. If it clearly doesn't fit into the strategy, help the client see that fact. Most likely, however, the stock fits but is substantially overvalued because, if it wasn't, the client probably would not have been aware of it in the first place. There are other times the client wants to own a stock that a friend manages or owns. In either case, it's likely it is not appropriate for the portfolio.

Step two, if step one doesn't put the issue to rest, is to remember two things: (a) the portfolio is the client's money and not yours, and (b) the client writes you a check each quarter for your fee. You are the chief operating officer of the portfolio, but the client is the chief executive officer and shareholder of the portfolio. You don't necessarily have to put an entire investment unit in the portfolio, you can buy a smaller amount if that will satisfy the client.

Step three comes into play when client interference becomes excessive. What is excessive? That's up to you, but when you are told what to do twice in a twelve-month period, it's time to have a face to face meeting with the client. In this meeting, again review the performance of the portfolio, review the investment objectives, constraints and strategy. When this is done, look the client squarely in the eyes and ask why they have lost confidence in your ability to manage the portfolio. When they protest that they do have confidence in you, help them understand that every time they tell you to put a stock in the portfolio, not only does it interfere with the performance based upon what that stock does, but it takes assets away from you that you would invest to have the most complete portfolio to meet the agreed upon objectives within the constraints using the strategy that they had approved. Finally, if the rapport with the client has deteriorated and the interference is really becoming burdensome and truly affecting the portfolio performance, you need to terminate the client relationship. A tough decision to make, but one that has to be made to maintain the proper relationship because if the performance does suffer, the client is still going to blame you and eventually leave.

FWIW # 56 .... *Ice Breaker*

There are a lot of financial advisors out there and they all want the same type of people – wealthy investors – as clients. You must have a way of standing out from the crowd as a professional who can know more than the average financial advisor. How to do it? The answer lies in the IRA laws. Sound easy? It's not. IRA rules are constantly changing and there are a number of your competitors, lawyers, and CPA's running around giving bad advice to not only your client, but to people you want to have as clients.

It's safe to say that most people with wealth have IRA's and they have had them for some time. Those investors with defined contribution retirement accounts and 401(k)'s will inevitably roll those assets into an IRA. There are SIMPLE IRA's, SEP-IRA's, Traditional IRA's, and Roth IRA's. When to use each type or move from one type to another is complex and not as clear cut as the math makes it seem. Investors are confused and ignorant about what to do. The financial advisor who can help clients understand how their unique family situation can take advantage of the IRA rules will get to manage all of the assets.

A classic example is if you come across a prospect with a large position in a stock that is significantly depressed in price, but you are confident that the company will rebound in the future. Perhaps now is the time to sell the stock in the Traditional IRA, move the proceeds to a Roth IRA, pay the tax on the move from other funds, and repurchase the stock in the Roth IRA. In effect, moving the stock from a Traditinal IRA to the Roth at a time when the tax will be the least, and reaping the benefits of the appreciation when the stock recovers in a tax-free environment. he only challenge is the assets will have to stay in the Roth IRA for five years.

There are many other aspects of IRA rules and regulations that can be uniquely used for special family situations. Unless you know the rules and regulations completely, you won't know how to apply them and will miss the opportunity to quickly convey to your prospect your professionalism.

Everybody and every firm wants to be a financial advisor since being a transaction-oriented financial services provider has become a commodity available for less than $10 to anyone on the Internet. With more competition comes greater price pressure on fees. There will always be someone who will do the work for less. You have to be prepared for this business dynamic and here's how:

Develop a fee schedule that fully compensates you for the quality of your services. This is the standard fee if anyone inquires what your fees are.

Understand the size and type of business you want to develop. Perhaps you want to concentrate your business on portfolios of $2 million or more. That's fine. You will have plenty of competition and plenty of price pressure. Perhaps you want to do business with institutions. Again, you'll have plenty of competition and price pressure. Quickly learn what kind and size investor you can develop a rapport with and brin your price schedule and cost structure in line to fit that client profile.

Once you know what size and profile of a client you want, be prepared to do what is necessary to win the assignment whenever you have the good fortune to make a presentation to the ideal potential client. It's better to take less for a relationship with the ideal client than to get a full price for dealing with a troublesome client. It goes without saying that troublesome clients don't get a discount.

The discount given, if any, should not be large. Always have your minimum fee for large clients and never go below that amount. If a regular fee is 1%, perhaps .9% is appropriate in competitive situations. Make sure the client knows your professionalism, your focus on their family, and your accessibility and you will not have serious competitive pressures on your fees. Another way to assist a new client in understanding the value you bring to the relationship i to fulfill your fiduciary duty and negotiate a substantial commission discount with the brokerage firm. If you can use the Internet, get a low flat fee for your client and let your client know that you have done this in their best interest. Experience and knowledge will always carry a premium price.

FWIW # 58 .... *No Holy Grail*

If you make above average total returns for clients, they will stay with you forever, true or false? False. It's hard to believe, but there are some people who will find a reason to stop doing business with you in spite of your making them money. The psychological dynamics of people and their money will fill volumes and is not worth your time as it relates to losing clients whom you have handled professionally and correctly. You cannot allow someone else's quirks to cause your focus on what's right to become distracted. Thank them for their past trust and confidence and move on to filling the space with someone who appreciates a quality financial manager.

FWIW # 59 .... *Pruning*

As your business grows, it gets unruly in some ways. You spend too much time with the wrong clients and have stress pressures from others that affect your ability to serve all clients. It's tim to carefully prune accounts so your practice is stronger andcan grow to the next level of business.

Step one is to know your clients and your capacity. First the capacity. Many firms have limits as to the number of client contacts handled by financial advisors. A lot depends on technology. With the right technology, the number of client contacts – the person you communicate with who controls the accounts in a family – can be more than the number at a firm with a low technology workplace. The hours a financial advisor enjoys working will influence the number of clients as well. You know what's right for you by examining the communication impact of each client. Let's examine the issue.

Each client can be catalogued by the amount of time it takes to communicate with them on calls the client initiates. You will have your regular rotation of communicating with your clients by phone, letter, e-mail, or fax. These communications are initiated by you on your schedule for your purpose. What you want to understand is how often the client calls you and initiates interaction. How often will you be asked to interact about issues other than the portfolio? How often are the contacts just nice-to-have conversations rather than need-to-have ones? How many times does the client attempt to influence or interfere with the investment strategy? ***Don't misunderstand. Client reliance on you for a wide variety of issues is job security and should be welcomed.*** You will know when reliance is replaced with unnecessary and burdensome domination of your time.

Begin by categorizing the clients into low, moderate, and high maintenance. Post the following numbers alongside each name: portfolio size, annual fee, and how long they have been a client. Everyone in the high maintenance column should pay you more money in fees and have a bigger portfolio than anyone in the other two columns. Everyone in the moderate column should be larger than anyone in the low column in terms of portfolio and fees paid. If this is not the case, the smaller portfolios in the high maintenance column should be examined. Have they been loyal clients for a long period of your career? Fine. Keep them. If not, put them in the pruning file. Go through each account in each column until finished. Add up the pruning file and see if the total portfolio value and fees are more than 10% of your annual amount. If so, re-examine the group with a less critical eye and bring the total under 10%. In particular, if anyone in the pruning file has been a client for three years or longer ask yourself, have they changed or have you changed? Perhaps you are busier and don't have the time you had to devote to the client in the past. That's not the client's fault. If so, before terminating the relationship, try to reestablish the boundary of how you worked together by having a full client's objectives, constraints, and strategy update and meeting. A three-year client is valuable, so don't throw them away quickly.

Once the pruning is down to the absolute minimum, you will have a sense of whom to terminate and whom to put up with. Pruning is an excellent exercise to reconnect on a focused basis with every one of your clients. It will energize your business.

FWIW # 60 .... *The End*

Clients leave financial advisors. Financial advisors terminate clients. In either case, it is difficult for a financial advisor because it represents failure. Communication was wrong. Attention to detail was wrong. Investment strategy or selection was wrong. Something was wrong. To make it better, make sure the breakup is done right.

It doesn't matter who initiates the separation. There is probably a management agreement that dictates the terms of how the process works. A refund of fees unearned and a thirty-day notice are two standard components of most management agreements. Go beyond the required situation. If the client is terminating the relationship, conduct yourself in such a way that you will win their admiration. Once you have received a notice of termination, make all future contact in writing. If the client calls you, write them a letter summarizing what was said on the call and responding to any inquiry they made. Send out a final report as of the termination date even if it is one week after the last quarterly report. If there is any position in the portfolio that needs immediate attention, point it out. Give an assessment of your opinion of all of the securities. The report should list the cost basis for each stock or bond so that you will not have to deal with this matter next tax season when you'll be busy with your own clients.

When you decide to end a client relationship, try to do so at the end of a quarter. If a thirty-day notice is required, send the notice letter thirty days before the period is over. Let the client know you will not exercise your discretionary authority during the notice period. Send a full final report giving all of the information the client will need to go to another advisor. If appropriate, and it usually is not, assist the client with finding another manager by suggesting they get information from three other financial advisors. If you don't know three names to suggest, don't give any. Always suggest they get information from these firms, not necessarily use the firms.

Be professional and polite no matter what the client is like and you will be proud of yourself and in the right frame of mind to replace the client quickly from the 300 Club.

FWIW # 61 .... *Tough Times*

Good economic times and good markets don't last forever. The longer the good times, the harsher the tough times. The more speculative excesses in the markets, the more the correction will be painful. Tough times are what separates the professionals from those who will not have a long career in the industry. There are a number of actions you can take to turn the tough times into growth times for you and your clients.

First, communicate more with your clients and prepare them for volatility and the changes in fundamentals and psychology taking place. There are two distinct faces to a market correction. First, companies earn less and therefore command a lower valuation based upon these earnings. At times, interest rates go up, thereby causing a lower fundamental valuation of all financial assets. Lower earnings and/or higher interest rates change the absolute valuations. Second, the process of changing fundamental valuations causes a shift in psychology and attitudes about the future, so the pendulum swings from GREED to FEAR causing a relative decline in expectations of the future to correspond with the lowering of present valuations. Let your client know what is happening and what they can expect. Help them focus on the positive events taking place without being Pollyanna or naively minimizing the anxiety your client is feeling about portfolio values.

Throughout your relationship with clients it's important for them to understand the quality of the companies you place in their portfolios. Clients who know the quality of their securities will be more willing to look to the horizon and not focus on the daily down ticks. Train clients from the beginning to realize above average returns are possible when a disciplined investment approach buys good quality companies in a declining market. You should have a short list of companies you want to place in your clients' portfolios as well as the stocks' price targets. Share some generalities about this list with your clients during conversations but not the specific names nor the specific prices for the companies.

When times are tough, leadership is what everyone wants. Leadership and discipline are what professional investment managers are paid to give and have when the market is not rosy. Leadership and discipline are the traits of a good communicator, better known as a successful salesperson. Selling is not a natural skill. You are not born with it. Sales ability is an acquired skill that is developed through hard work, dedication, and practice. The secret of selling is COMMUNICATING.

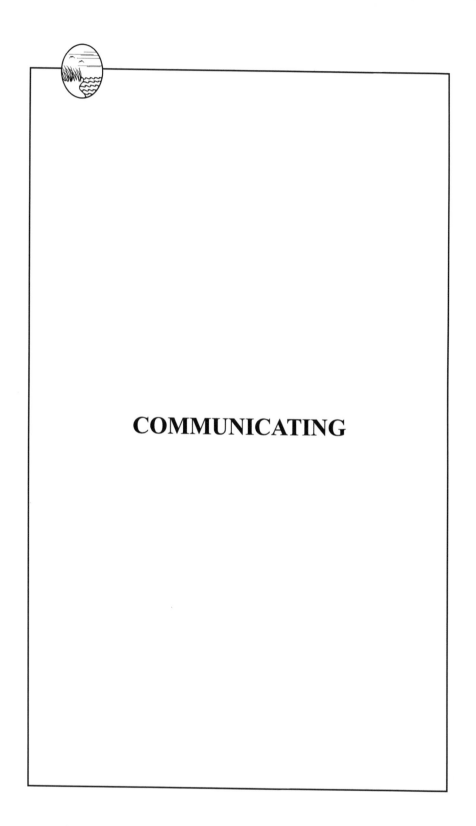

COMMUNICATING

FWIW # 62 .... *Communicating Versus Selling*

Selling is convincing a person to purchse something based upon the features of the product or service. Communicating is understanding what fits the client's needs and using that understanding to ulfill those needs. Since its beginning, the financial services business has been one where securities weresold, not bought. This was true because most investors did not know about securities, their characteristics, and the alternatives for the securities being offered. That's not the case today. Investors believe, and to some extent it's true, that they understand the investment universe and the alternatives to each type of securities being offered.

The Internet is partially responsible for a better educated clientele, but it's not the only aspect. Most clients with assets to invest have studied investing in college and absorbed information from the business media. The focus on wealth creation has spurred many people to try to figure out how to participate in the process. This desire to learn, coupled with the availability of information, is what has changed the landscape of financial services. The challenge for financial advisors is that many investors don't know as much as they think they know.

Investing is a short-term memory activity. Investors' recent experiences and observations are what drive their decision-making process. Couple this with the desire for instant gratification, wanting to be where the action and the money are, and a strong dose of GREED, and the situation is set for mistakes to be made by investors who believe they are smarter than they actually are.

A financial advisor is not going to sell a security today and be compensated adequately unless it is one where the client has an unusual perceived need such as an annuity or insurance policy. Even then, the Internet and competition will continue to reduce the available commission until the advisor will not find acceptable compensation in the transaction.

To achieve above average compensation, a financial advisor has to develop the skill of understanding clients' financial needs and desires, assist clients in realizing those needs and wants, and work with clients to meet the family goals. The majority of clients want to accumulate as much wealth as they can without taking any risks. They know that's not realistic, but they still say and believe that it is possible because they only focus on the winners discussed in the media. They do not focus on risk. A financial advisor has to assist clients in understanding the nature of risk as well as assist them in understanding what type of risk and in what quantity, they, the client, are willing to accept. This educational process is done carefully and in a dialogue with the client. Communicating knowledge and molding the knowledge to fit the unique situation of the individual client is the essenc of financial advising today. The client begins to understand that the financial advisor's expertise is valuable. Couple the knowledge and experience with the access to securities through low cost channels and the client realizes the total cost of using a financial advisor is worth the cost because the knowledge imparted is the true service provided.

Communicating is a language all its own. It must be learned to succeed in the financial services arena of the future. Selling is over. Clients will buy from, not be sold to, the financial advisor who can show them the balance between risk, reward, and personal circumstances moving towards a higher net worth.

In FWIW # 8 and FWIW # 11 the habit of winning and the keys to success, knowledge, and motivation were explored. As you become more successful and mature the motivating forces in your life change. What motivates one person turns off another. Sales-oriented individuals are generally motivated by recognition. The recognition can be from their peers, their firm's management, their social circle, or their community as a whole. Put recognition together with competition and the sales-oriented person is focused on being the best during that particular campaign. You have to understand what motivates you and cultivate the various ways to make sure that you have your focus on your personal motivating factors. For some people it's accumulation of things, for others it's a spirit of adventure through travel. Make sure you understand your own special motivating factors.

Accumulating possessions seems to be deeply rooted in the psyche of achievers. How it exhibits itself is different in all of us. One person wants to live in a big house in the best neighborhood while another wants to have two, three, or even more homes scattered throughout the country or world. One wants to collect antiques while another is an automobile buff. Still, others connect with jewelry. The list of motivating forces is infinite because it is truly personal. The possession you want is external but the determination to achieve the goal is internal.

All successful people are driven from the inside and are emotionally involved with the driving force. Motivation is not rational and logical, it is emotional and illogical to a large extent. Why want a 20,000 square foot home when a 2,000 square foot one is ample? Why want a $200,000 original oil painting when a $200 print is the same image? Don't fret over the senselessness of what motivates you. Nurture it. If antiques are your passion, immerse yourself in them. If travel gets you tingling, plan the trip of a lifetime. Reinforce your motivating element so it grows and becomes the pulsating focus that keeps you going during the tough times. Exercise it so it is lean and potent and almost overwhelming. Couple the motivation and knowledge and end up with success.

FWIW # 64 .... *Different Strokes*

Whenever a financial service or security is sold and a commission is paid upon the sale, it is a transaction. Lip service about a relationship might be in the marketing literature, but there is no relationship unless the transaction is consummated. This transaction-oriented business takes a particular approach to completing the exchange of knowledge which is different than one where the client pays for access to knowledge over a long period even if no transaction is done. The two approaches are different because the two clients are different. Let's examine both.

Penny-wise and pound-foolish is an appropriate description for a large number of investors. They go on-line to Internet brokers to save on the commission and in many cases end up paying more than they need to for the security. Mutual funds are an even better example. Instead of paying an up-front commission for a Class A mutual fund share, investors believe they will save the commission and buy a Class B or C share with a declining sales load over one to seven years. Little thought is given to the fact that the expenses per year of the Class B or C shares are higher than those on a Class A and the loss of portfolio flexibility is substantial since the back-end sales load is a barrier to willingness to sell the security. These investors will not enter into a relationship which is fee-based even with unlimited transactions because they are focused on the fees rather than the performance. It's their nature, and you, as a financial advisor, have to understand that fact and accept it. Very few, if any, of these clients will give you discretionary authority over their account. Too many of these clients will seriously impede the growth of your business. With proper presentation and preparation, they can be acceptable clients in thebeginning of a career and an extra profit center to supplement the main part of a mature business. It needs to be clearly understood that financial advisors without a brokerage connection should just pass these clients by. There is no future for the independent financial advisor with these investors. Advisors at a brokerage firm can have a successful relationship with these clients. Banking-based advisors who have other business such as loans and CD-based investments as well as a cross connection to a brokerage service can effectively and profitably interact with these transaction-oriented non-discretionary investors. Using mutual funds and being passive in terms of initiating security recommendations will be necessary. The most effective way to profitably develop a relationship with these clients begins with the first fact-finding interview.

You have to be in control of the relationship in all areas except the actual order entry. This control is seized and maintained by helping the client clearly understand that while they may decide whether or not to buy an investment, you are accepting responsibility for growth of the portfolio, therefore, if your guidance is not taken enough times, you will not handle the account. The dialogue might go something like this:

> "Mr(s). (name), I understand you want to maintain final authority over the buy and sell decisions. I also understand you prefer to pay for my services on a transaction basis. The agreed upon commission will be ____ ¢ per share. Over time, my firm's expertise in executing orders should enhance the price you pay over what you would pay at other firms, thereby absorbing much of this commission. It is important, however,

for us to agree on some aspects of the portfolio management. First, you and I will agree upon a strategy to grow your portfolio. We will review that strategy every 18 months and make what changes are necessary. Between these regular reviews, I will make buy and sell recommendations to you. While you can veto the recommendation, as long as it is within the strategy, I will urge you not to. If you want to buy and sell securities on your own, that's fine, but let's do it in another account. This portfolio is one you are paying me to manage. The only way to successfully grow the portfolio is to agree to a strategy, stick with it, and measure the results at the end of the period. Don't you agree?"

With this non-discretionary transaction-oriented client, you will have to invest the portfolio rapidly. A patient, opportunistic approach will not work. Every time you call the client with a recommendation, the entire process has to be reinforced. Without this constant renewal of your control, the process will end in failure. A typical call to add or subtract from a portfolio will go something like this:

"Good morning, Mr(s). (<u>name</u>), there is an opportunity in the market that fits your investment strategy. As you remember, we decided there would be four investment units in the Consumer Defensive Staples area. We currently have three. You need to add

500 shares of SLE to the portfolio. It will complement the (name the other stocks in the sector). The funds will come from the cash reserves. I expect it will take one to two years for SLE to hit our objective of 75%. Shall I go ahead and continue implementing the investment strategy?"

This type of reinforcement is needed constantly to keep the client focused on the objective and not on the transaction. Smart investors who understand the process of accumulating wealth respond quickly and appreciate the process. The ones who don't should not be clients for long.

Since you are being paid by the transaction, it should be understood the portfolio has to be large enough to generate the proper revenues for you if managed ethically within the agreed upon investment objectives and constraints. What are proper revenues? At least $1,500 a year for a relatively new advisor with a large amount of excess client capacity. Perhaps $10,000 for a seasoned advisor who has a full complement of clients.

The discretionary fee-based client is ideal for advisors. Care has to be taken to insure that the communication between the client and advisor is clear and complete from the beginning. Written objectives and constraints and the strategy to meet the objectives within those constraints helps. Making sure expectations are reasonable is important. Once the relationship and expectations are in focus, there should be regular but infrequent communication as to the portfolio management progress. In the early months, contact will be more frequent and then begin to taper off as the client becomes more comfortable with the advisor's approach. Eventually, quarterly and then semi-annual meetings to discuss performance and review and update the objectives, constraints, and strategy will be the majority of all contact. Naturally, a monthly newsletter communication as well as short non-specific or question-answering telecommunication fits into the relationship. The goal of interaction is not to reinforce the action plan, but to reaffirm that the process is on track.

Two different kinds of clients and two different ways of dealing with them. Your personality and work habits will dictate which type of client fits best in the business mix. Recognize early what works for you and then stick with that business model.

FWIW # 65 .... *Practice, Practice, Practice*

How often have you heard the comment, "He's a natural salesman?" Well, there's no such thing. Sure, some people can communicate an idea better than others, but anyone can become above average in communicating with practice.

The same person who goes to the tennis court, golf course, or shooting range, and practices over and over again to get good at a sport, will not spend the time to write out a three-minute presentation about their financial advisory services. They pretend they don't want to sound canned. The only way to sound and be natural is to be so familiar with the points you are trying to get across that you will make your points in as few a words as appropriate and in a logical order. To do this requires practice and practice.

There are basic principles in the financial services business. How these principles relate to each type of security are important to understand. Clients don't always understand what impact various factors have on a security. The best way for you to be able to help them is to have prepared in advance an explanation of investment dynamics and have thought out how personal client circumstances can influence and shape choices in a portfolio.

Communicating is selling, but selling is not necessarily communicating. There is a language to communicating that is foreign to everyone but the most astute salesperson. Learning this language is not easy. Being able to shift smoothly from ordinary English or Spanish into the language of communicating is a challenge. Practice might not make perfect, but it does make for successful communicating.

FWIW # 66 .... *The Language of Communicating*

Step one. People do not buy things. It doesn't matter whether the thing is tangible, like a car, or home, or jewelry, or whether it is intangible like a stock, a bond, or an estate plan. People don't buy things, they buy benefits. Therein lies the language of communicating. Things, tangible or intangible, have features. The novice salesperson extols these features and doesn't understand why the customer usually walks away. Step one in becoming an effective communicator is understanding features of what you're selling. When financial services were primarily a transaction business, it was easy to make a list of the features of a particular security. The maturity, the interest rate, or the dividend, or the class of stock, or the size of the company are all features that could be listed and give a description of the nature of the security. In the relationship, fee-based business, it is somewhat harder but still achievable to create a list of features. What are your credentials? What services do you offer? What access do your clients have to you? You can add to the list. These are the features of the services you are selling.

Step two is to understand what advantage each of these features gives the client. Is your monthly newsletter designed to give the client real insight into your investment strategy as opposed to your competitor's newsletter? Are you willing to meet on weekends or evenings with clients unlike your competitor who only meets from nine to five? These are the advantages you have over your competitor in the eyes of your clients or prospective clients. Most people don't see the advantages so you have to help them see them. Advantages are far superior to features for getting a prospective client's attention, but they are not the real communication language. Benefits are the right words.

Benefits sell, nothing else does. In some easy situations, clients instantaneously translate features to advantages to benefits. An example is an aspirin. The feature is the small white pill. The advantage is it's easy to swallow. The benefit is that it works fast and reliably time after time. When a client has a headache, they instantly go from the feature through the advantage to the benefit. They focus on the benefit.

Investments and their benefits are harder to focus on than aspirin. Clients don't even know the features, much less the advantages. In many cases, they do not know what benefit they want from their portfolio and they don't have a clue as to how to achieve the benefit. Your function as a financial advisor is to start with clarifying the benefits the client wants from the portfolio. This is accomplished through goal setting and identifying constraints. Take time with your client to completely identify the goal setting. Don't overestimate your client's ability to know what they want or what constraints they have. Most people have no idea how they can quantify and correlate their assets and liabilities with their wants and needs. For instance, a person with a child who wants that child to go to an expensive college thinks they have to have $200,000 set aside in addition to all of their other assets to pay the cost. That is not necessarily the case. Your function is to identify the goal to understand the magnitude and likelihood of it (is the child capable of going to an Ivy League school?) and to show the client how to reach the goal within the constraints of their family. Perhaps scholarships and student loans enter the picture. Perhaps there is enough time for compounding of asset returns to work. Your activities of identifying goals, identifying constraints, and mapping out a strategy to meet the goals are the first benefits your client recognizes in doing business with you.

With practice you will begin to speak benefits naturally. You will begin to probe your client's thoughts using the language of communication, Features, Advantages, Benefits. One important question in gaining insight into your client's knowledge and desires is to simply ask the question: What do you want your money to do for you? Once you've asked this question, don't say another word until the client speaks. By your silence, your client will be forced to speak. Some clients will be uncomfortable and make a joke. They will tell you they want their money to grow 100% a year which is foolish. Others will answer crisply and clearly, knowing exactly what they want their money to do for them. In some cases, after the client stumbles around and can't give you a good answer, you might have to prompt and lead them by suggesting goals such as education, retirement, or travel. Make them begin to verbalize before you help, however. It is a powerful tool because the client invariably identifies, for you, the benefits they want most. Once they have begun, their thoughts and goals begin gushing out and you can now assist in prioritizing and understanding what you need to do to make them a satisfied client. Your language begins to translate features of various securities into methods of giving the client the benefits they are seeking.

FWIW # 67 .... *Loudest Ears*

The most effective communication is achieved with the ears and not the mouth. It's a fact that short questions elicit long answers and long questions are answered with just one or two words. You want to ask short questions and then listen. Only when the client has told you all you need to know about them should you even begin to share information about how you can achieve their goals.

FWIW # 68 .... *Never Ending*

Every day you are in danger of losing every client. There is always someone else who is smarter than you, hungrier than you, and more charming than you. Every day you have to reinforce and help your clients understand why they chose you as a financial advisor. Every day you have to give to your clients more service and more attention than they believe they are due. Achieving this business goal takes planning and diligence, but it is worth it.

FWIW # 69 .... *Secret Ingredients*

What makes you special enough for someone to entrust their life savings and the future of their family with you? Citigroup, Merrill Lynch, J.P. Morgan, Goldman Sachs, and a host of other financial services firms offer essentially the same service as you. Why will a business, a pension plan, or a family see something in you to the exclusion of all of the other firms? If you are going to be successful, there has to be four ingredients in your business.

First has to be knowledge. Knowledge in at least four areas is necessary. Knowledge of people and the characteristics of people is important to be able to communicate with them. This knowledge is learned through dealing with a variety of clients as well as through reading about people and psychology. Since you are dealing with successful individuals, reading biographies of successful people helps. There are also books and courses that teach you how to identify personality traits and how to communicate with every type of person you will meet.

Investment knowledge is imperative and requires ongoing continuing education. To be a professional investment advisor instead of just a salesperson requires in-depth knowledge. Committing to the Chartered Financial Analyst (CFA) program is important in having a comprehensive understanding of the body of knowledge surrounding investments. Obtaining a Certified Financial Planner (CFP) designation will become a basic requirement for financial advisors in the future. Not all areas of investing will be right for you and your clients, but what is excluded should be a conscious decision, not one made by ignorance.

A thorough understanding of estate planning is necessary in selecting and matching investments with the client circumstances. Unless you have taken the time to know what alternatives individuals have in making estate planning decisions, you will not maximize your client's estate and minimize their estate taxes. For example, do you know about disclaiming? This simple technique can literally save or cost substantial taxes for just about every estate yet the majority of people don't know its possibilities.

Finally, knowledge of all taxes is essential. Taxes on IRA's, capital gains taxes, income taxes, itemized deduction rules, depreciation rules, Schedule 179 deduction rules, and alternative minimum tax rules. The list can go on and on. You need to have enough knowledge to know when to refer a client to an attorney or a CPA and help that client to formulate the questions necessary. You do not need to be the expert, but you need to know enough to be able to raise questions when appropriate.

Experience is the second secret ingredient that will make you a specialist in the eyes of your client. Experience cannot be bought, it cannot be studied, it must be lived. You can shorten the process by paying attention to every detail of your business, thereby receiving more experience per day than the average person who goes through life ignoring the details and difficulties. Decision-making is a way of gaining experience. Making decisions inevitably leads to making mistakes. Mistakes are the seeds of experience and learning. While the financial services business likes to give the appearance of using mathematically certain information, it is actually a place where decisions have to be made with less than complete facts. Mistakes you have made in the past assist in making future decisions better and correctly.

The third ingredient in success as a financial advisor is the personal touch you have with your clients. In the age of e-mail, voice mail, and automated phone switchboards, your caring about your client and their business or family helps build a relationship that is difficult for your competitors to break. A genuine and sincere conversation about their children or parents will mean a great deal to your clients. Don't you know how many times you have wanted someone to care about you and some of the challenges you face? Well, your clients are the same way. Let them know you are interested in them and not just their money. Take a few minutes longer on the phone or in a meeting to ask, "How are you? What is going on in your life?" Stop and make them respond by sitting quietly and looking them in the eye if meeting them in person. By the way, if you smile while talking on the phone, your clients will know it. Remember an event coming up and call them afterwards to see how it went. What's great about personal caring is it costs nothing and is worth more than most of the activities that you can do.

Service is the most important ingredient in developing and maintaining a successful financial advisory practice. The object is to make each of your clients feel they are receiving far more service than they are paying for. Meeting in the evenings or on weekends with busy professional clients helps. Speaking to children or parents and giving advice to guide the family in areas not related to the portfolio helps. Service comes in many ways and at different times.

Find ways to satisfy your client and make them feel special, it works wonders.

FWIW # 70 ....*Positively Positive*

Every recession and depression ever experienced in this country has been and always will be the platform from which positive people become rich. Every top of the market has been a time when buying stocks or bonds worked out in the long term even if there were glitches in between. Clients won't stay with someone who is negative for long. Clients want leadership, and pessimists aren't good leaders. That doesn't mean you have to be a Pollyanna. There are times when caution pays off; however, prudent investing is not being a pessimist. There are rhythms and cycles to all aspects of life including the stock market. You should look at market corrections for what they are: opportunities to buy high quality companies at attractive prices.

When you see a market under pressure, find the best companies and determine at what price they will be good values. When the market is widely exuberant, seek out the companies with the best relative value. Always focus on what you can do that makes the best sense in the present environment. Not only will your clients respond to your positive leadership, but you will be more confident in what you do.

FWIW # 71 .... *Understated Image*

It's human nature to want to be recognized. Why strive for success if you can't enjoy it? Being a financial advisor is a service business, and, therefore, your personal relationship with your clients is an important part of the success of your business. Many clients want and expect their financial advisor to be successful – just not more successful than they are.

Most financial advisors develop a clientele with similar personality characteristics to their own. Some are flashy and some are discreet in handling their personal wealth. Make sure you understand what approach appeals to you and your clients. Once the approach is chosen, make sure you develop your public image in a way your clients are comfortable rather than jealous with your success.

FWIW # 72 .... *Non-Discretionary Client*

FWIW # 64 highlighted the differences between discretionary and non-discretionary clients. A closer look at working with non-discretionary clients is in order. Financial advisors who work for brokerage firms and banks and some insurance firms often have relationships with clients who are not comfortable allowing the financial advisor to make all of the investment decisions without prior consultation. In the universe of investors being assisted by investment managers, there are far more non-discretionary potential clients than there are discretionary ones. Most financial advisors will not work on a non-discretionary basis because of the time it takes as well as the fact that clients are not disciplined in their approach to investments. Clients have a hard time buying securities when they should be bought and an even harder time selling them when they should be sold. One of the basic principles of portfolio management is that there can only be one decision-maker in the successful portfolio. Non-discretionary clients, however, represent a wonderful opportunity for the financial advisor who cannot, nor should not, accept discretion. If the method of compensation is transaction-based, a financial advisor should be very careful in accepting a discretionary role in the portfolio. The potential for conflicts of interest is too great and looks so much clearer in hindsight than it does in the future. The key to successfully managing on a non-discretionary basis is clearly establishing an investment objective and strategy with the client and getting the client's approval of the objectives and strategy before beginning the management process.

Start with the objective for the portfolio. Will there be an income requirement to fund withdrawals? Will there be a focus on doubling the portfolio in a certain period of time? Is the portfolio taxable or tax-deferred? What is the risk tolerance? Which of the major portfolio risks are acceptable to the client and which are not? Is the client trying to pay for something such as retirement, education, or the freedom to work independently? It's important at this stage to take the extra time to build the details of the objective so the client will later connect what you recommend with the stated objective.

Once the objective is reduced to writing in a clear and concise manner using easily understood words, you have to use your skills as an investment professional to develop the strategy you believe is appropriate for meeting the objective. Here, more general information is used since an investment strategy is a dynamic process. You can make general guidelines within which a professional can operate for the long period. Step one in the strategy development is the selection of the type of securities to be used in the portfolio. Cash reserves, fixed income securities, common stocks, and real estate are the primary asset groups. Should futures contracts be a part of the process? How about gold? Should options be used? After making a list of the asset types to be in the portfolio, percentage ranges are necessary. Using the asset type as a heading, identify some general characteristics of the securities to be placed in the portfolio. For instance, under fixed income, decide if U.S. Treasury securities, corporate bonds, corporate preferreds, U.S. government agencies, unit trust, municipal bonds, foreign bonds, or mutual funds will be used. Go through each asset type and develop the characteristics that give your client an understanding of what it takes to flesh out a portfolio into a dynamic group of securities capable of meeting the client's objectives.

Once the strategy is developed, place on a single piece of paper the investment objective and a clear narrative about how the objective will be met through the investment strategy. Allow the client to ask as many questions as necessary for the client to be comfortable and committed to the objective and strategy. Then clearly look the client in the eye and say, "Mr(s). (_name_), this strategy has a high probability of meeting the objective that we have outlined. It can only do so if a disciplined approach is used in selecting the appropriate securities. You can be assured that when I or my assistant calls you to buy a stock or bond for the portfolio or to sell a security, it is what, in my professional opinion, should be done to meet the objective. If you choose not to follow my advice, the portfolio will not perform as you expect. Keep these objectives and strategy handy and you will see how each recommendation adds to the total."

When it comes time to make a recommendation, it's important to begin each conversation clearly showing how the recommendation fits in the overall strategy. The recommendation should go like this: "Mr(s). (_name_), there is an opportunity to fill a gap in your investment strategy for meeting the objective of (_name the objective_). In the strategy, there is a position for a consumer growth company. I recommend you purchase 1,000 shares of XYZ Company to fill this position. Shall I go ahead and add to the strategy?"

Notice, the conversation is short and totally focused on the security fitting the strategy. If you allow yourself to be dragged into defending the specific security, you will either oversell it, which means when it's time to remove the stock from the portfolio the client won't want to do so, or, the client will say no to the purchase. If your recommendation is turned down more than three times, you will not control the performance yet you will be held responsible for it. Usually a portfolio in place for eighteen months will perform up to expectations and it's easier for the client to see the professional way it has been developed. At that point, the calls are relatively easy. However, no financial advisor can do as much business handling non-discretionary portfolios as an advisor handling discretionary funds.

FWIW # 73 .... *Just Say No*

Clients are hard to develop, particularly good ones. Sometimes an advisor comes across a situation where the potential client has the asset base for a significant amount of fees and/or commissions. The problem is the chemistry is wrong, all wrong. When the ability to communicate is challenged and there isn't enough background education or common interest to work together, the financial advisor has to be confident enough to pass up the fees and just say no to taking on the client. In doing so, it should be done as professionally as the account would have been handled. When it's done, both parties will be better for it.

FWIW # 74 .... *Confidentiality*

A successful advisor went to see a prospect and should have gotten the account because the advisor already worked with many of the prospect's peers. In his presentation, he told the potential client about his success with these individuals who are well known to the prospect. The advisor was trying to make the prospect comfortable in the advisor's experience and expertise. The advisor did not get the account. The client went to another advisor, who, when asked by the prospect to name some clients, was told no, it was not appropriate to divulge the names of clients. It does not matter who the client is. They don't want anyone to tell their business to someone else or use them as a non-approved referral source. Use this desire for confidentiality as a way to build your reputation and professionalism by making the following statement if asked about your clients: "Mr(s). (name), at my firm we are conscious about the confidentiality of our clients and do not divulge their names without permission. If, when you see the analysis and recommendations we propose to you, it is important for you to verify our abilities to manage the assets as we outlined in our report, we'll get permission to have you speak with a client who has similar objectives." If the analysis and recommendations are solid and top quality, a referral or reference will not be needed most of the time.

FWIW # 75 ....*Bonding*

No one likes to feel they are being pumped for information like the scenes on television where the police are asking the suspect rapid fire questions and giving nothing in return. The object of the first meeting, from your perspective, is to see if the chemistry between you and the potential client is good and lends itself to a satisfactory working relationship. This is done by sharing information. For you and the potential client, your information gathering becomes a bonding process. Whether you use a loan application, a securities industry account application, or some other form as a starting point, it's important to get complete information for the "WHAT WE KNOW" page of your proposal. Your first step is to learn what you need to know about the prospect. Don't have an application with you, don't just ask questions, have a conversation. Talk about some of the information they give you. For instance, do you have children (grandchildren)? What are their ages? Are they boys or girls? Where do they go to school? Do you participate in the education expense (for grandparents)? Is there a regular gifting program in place? Are you aware of the educational and medical gifting provisions in the tax laws? While going through this process, you can and should mention your children (grandchildren), some appropriate stories similar to their experience, and some way for them to understand that you know what they are going through as either parents or grandparents. Don't allow the conversation, however, to center on you for long, just long enough to establish rapport with the prospects. Conducting an interview correctly takes practice, practice, and more practice. Think about the small areas where you have the opportunity to share with the prospect without shifting the focus from them completely. You'll build a better relationship from the beginning if you do so.

FWIW # 76 .... The Evil I

If you could learn how to make presentations to prospects so they would be more attentive and responsive, you would be interested in learning how to do it, wouldn't you?

Well, you just did. Most people would have posed the same question in this manner: "I can teach you how to make better presentations to prospects so they will be more responsive. I bet you will be interested in learning it, won't you?"

What's the difference? In the second more common way of speaking, "I" comes before "you." The message delivered to the prospect is that I, the financial advisor, come before you, the prospect. You should always make sure that the prospect believes the focus of the relationship is on them and their objectives, not on you, the advisor. There is one point in the relationship, however, where it is important for you to communicate to the client your credentials. During the short period where you are the focus, use a matter-of-fact description which under-embellishes the facts, but clearly shows your accomplishments and abilities to manage the prospect's money.

If the prospect is a non-discretionary account, there is one other place where "I" should be used clearly and that is when asking for the order. Don't make any hesitation in the fact that you recommend the investment. That is the time to let the client know that you are a leader.

FWIW # 77 .... *What's In A Name?*

We all like to hear our name spoken. Have you ever been in a crowded room or airport and heard your name spoken? It sharpens your attention and senses. In making a presentation to a prospective client, you should take advantage of this natural instinct. Once in the introduction, once in the body of the presentation, and once in the close is about right. Too much becomes pandering and sounds like a sales presentation. But never underestimate the power of the prospect's name in talking with them.

FWIW # 78 .... *Presentation Material*

The material used to communicate your professionalism is critical in making the right impression. Tailor the material to the audience. For a group, use PowerPoint or some other digital presentation composed and projected from a computer. This is the latest and slickest way to get your message across. It is also startlingly effective if your competition is using slides or overhead projectors. It takes time and money to perfect, but it's worth it.

When preparing material for one on one or for a couple, don't get too fancy. Make sure your material is in some form of binder, not just a series of pages in a folder. Use good quality 25 lb. cotton content paper. It has a heavier feel and is clearly visually superior to 20 lb. paper. Some people feel charts, graphs, and color are necessary to jazz up a presentation. If the content is weak, perhaps so. But the most effective presentation of quality content is simple format, clear words, and tables.

A proposal to a prospect, when there is more than one document, should definitely be bound so there is no opportunity for one or more of the pages to be mislaid or lost.

Binding machines and binders are not inexpensive, but neither is the effort to find a viable client. Making sure the prospect and later client knows you are a top quality professional in communicating with them is as important as any part of your business other than performance itself.

When you have legal compliance issues to contend with, the best way to streamline the process is to get as much of your presentation pre-approved as you can. Work with your compliance people to get some paragraphs of your material accepted beforehand so the turnaround on any proposal is quick. Being responsive to your client's interest is the key. Keeping the frustration level low is the goal.

FWIW # 79 .... *Extra Mile*

Be willing to work longer, work at night or evenings, travel to the prospect or client, study harder, miss more fun, get up earlier, and be willing to do what it takes to ethically and morally get the business.

FWIW # 80 .... *Specifically Vague*

Many times, when talking with a prospect, an advisor will begin to share their current perspective on the markets. That's only natural and part of the communication process. It's crucial, however, to stick with general aspects of a strategy rather than specific recommendations. If you share with a prospect that you are buying XYZ, ABC, and DEF companies, you open up the possibility that the prospect will not use your services since you have given your best ideas for free or, more likely, the prospect will defer making a decision until the named securities have had time to either perform or not perform. Either way, you have allowed the momentum of the relationship to be put on hold. Structure your presentation to convey your knowledge of how to meet the understood specific and unique goals. By keeping the presentation and prospect focused on the objective, you will keep them interested in you as a person who can achieve that objective for them.

FWIW # 81 .... *What They Want*

Clients sometimes don't know what they want in terms of objectives for their portfolio. They don't know what kind of constraints they impose because they don't think they impose any constraints. ("Don't lose any money" is not considered a constraint.) They do know one fact: they want to be the most important client you have. It's imperative to you and your practice that each and every one of your clients **KNOW** they are the most important clients you have. When you are talking and are engaged with a client, make sure that at that moment and time your focus is totally on them and nothing else.

FWIW # 82 .... *Spouses*

In this age of two income couples, it's rare for one spouse to be the sole decision-maker about family finances. When one spouse seeks you out, it is difficult to ask if the other spouse should be in on the discussion. One effective way to do so and to distinguish yourself from your competition is to ask if the prospect would like to schedule the fact-finding meeting or the discussion of recommendations in the evening or on a weekend to allow both spouses to be part of the process. More times than not, the prospect will welcome the flexibility and opportunity for you to explain the investment strategy to their spouse rather than having to do it themselves.

FWIW # 83 .... *Performance*

Business news is focused on performance, yesterday's performance. It is always focused on what happened in the immediate past. Some investors are the same way. They are always jumping from one mutual fund or advisor to another based upon the newly released quarterly performance numbers. Don't fall into the trap. You cannot build a practice trying to satisfy the impossible. Sure, you can outperform in the long term, perhaps five or six years or more, but you can't do it every quarter or every year. And if you obtain clients based upon promised performance, when you fail to perform they will leave quickly. Always remember, to outperform over a six-year period with the entire portfolio, you are going to have to under perform with some portion of the portfolio for a shorter period of time.

You have to keep the prospect focused on meeting their specific and unique objectives within their specific and unique risk tolerance. If you do, and if you are professional, you will deliver performance and satisfaction and have a long term client.

FWIW # 84 .... *Perfectly Imperfect*

Investment management is based upon making decisions after analyzing and weighing the available information. The problem is there is an abundance of information available on any investment you want. Trying to analyze every piece of information available from the brokerage firms, the news media, the chat rooms, and the Internet will lead to *paralysis by analysis*. The search for the magic piece of information that will keep you from making a mistake is a futile one. Good investment management is a cumulative experience where the decision-making skill is based upon all of the mistakes made in the past. There is a way to sharpen and shorten the process.

When making investment decisions, it helps to keep a page in the security file that lists or discusses the reasons why you bought a particular security. You can make additional notes as time goes by. When the stock either meets expectations or disappoints, you can learn from the experience. Three results will come from the process: (a) you will learn to make better decisions from imperfect information, (b) you will learn from your mistakes and have less likelihood of constantly repeating the same mistake, and (c) you will find it easier to make decisions with confidence.

A final word about all of the data available for investment opportunities. A good analyst seeks out facts from all sources and ignores opinions from all sources. That doesn't mean you can't value another's opinion, it just means you better recognize that someone else's opinion will not help you learn anything from the investment if it goes bad.

FWIW # 85 .... *How Much Is Enough?*

How much prospecting is enough? There is never enough. The fact of life about this business is that client relationships end. Investors in asset accumulation phases of their life grow old and become net users of their portfolios. Clients die. Clients leave for a multitude of reasons. Some because they are quirky and some because you just don't do well for them. Unless you have a steady stream of people you can help, your business will not grow properly.

What needs to happen is an evolution of how you prospect. Referrals become the dominant source of new business. When you are out in the community, people hear about you and your business and they come to you more than you going out and seeking them. Your contact with people in the community gives you the opportunity to speak to them directly when you know they have a need for your service. In other words, prospecting becomes an intricate part of your life, not a specific duty to be performed separate from everything else.

FWIW # 86 .... *Prospect Storage*

Every financial advisor has a list of wealthy people who will do business with them if asked. At least that's what they think. This private reserve of potential clients is called ***prospect storage***, and it's a pipe dream. Why not call them right now? Well, the right investment isn't available, the stock market is still going down, or interest rates haven't peaked yet. The truth is, prospect storage is a lack of self confidence. These wealthy investors aren't going to be called because they will either turn down the advisor or even worse, say yes, and their portfolio will decline. Emptying the prospect storage bin into the 300 Club is a matter of motivation and product knowledge, the two keys to success in communicating properly.

FWIW # 87 .... *Say It Again, Sam*

Even though a financial advisor develops individual portfolios to meet the unique objectives and risk tolerance of specific clients, it is usually done in the context of a developed investment style and within basic investment principles. Just as rehearsals and repetition create the illusion of spontaneous presentations in the theater, the presentation of information to assist the prospect in evaluating the quality of your service has to be smooth. That comfort level and clearness and completeness comes from consistency of saying the same thing over and over.

FWIW # 88 .... *Overwhelming BS*

Financial advisors who operate with discretionary authority have to convince the prospective client to do business. The challenge is significant; however, by focusing on the client's wants and needs, it is accomplished on a regular basis. The non-discretionary advisor has a tougher challenge as a regular part of the advisor/client relationship: making sure the client agrees to the portfolio development and management to overcome the fact it is not easy for the client to buy when a stock should be bought or sell when a stock should be sold. This difficulty leads to the advisor attempting to overwhelm the client with factual information and opinions in the hope the huge pile of information will impress the client and solicit a positive response. This is the wrong approach for two reasons.

First, the phone call clearly puts the client in the driver's seat and that is a disaster to performance. While the non-discretionary advisor has to consult with the client prior to executing an order, the conversation should focus on the overall strategy and how the advisor has selected the particular security to fit within the strategy. The client is being *informed* rather than *asked*.

Second, giving the client too much information can be a problem when the client begins to misunderstand that changes take place over time and, therefore, will not be willing to sell a stock when appropriate. You will have to unsell the same company and look foolish in trying to do so.

The presentation should be carefully constructed (see FWIW # 64) and focused on the strategy, not the individual security. Make your presentation three minutes or less. Let the client then ask questions. Answer the questions completely but concisely. Attempt to limit the conversation to how the security and the underlying company fit into the overall strategy, not the quality or the current price of the stock.

Once a referral or your own prospecting efforts have landed the opportunity to see an investor, a plan for the initial meeting needs to be developed. There should be two objectives in the initial meeting. First, determine if the chemistry between the prospective client and you is a good one. It is critical the two of you will be able to communicate smoothly. Second, enough information should be gathered to be able to analyze the investor's situation, formulate investment goals and constraints, and make recommendations to meet the objectives within the constraints. By doing so, you will be able to determine if this investor will become a client immediately or a new member of the 300 Club.

If at all possible, go to the prospect's home or office to meet. Sure, this travel is inefficient for you, but remember, the key to success at this point is to be able to communicate and find out as much as possible about the prospect. By going to the investor, you can (a) have them as relaxed as possible in their natural surroundings, (b) make the prospect feel important by your going to them, and (c) you can observe their surroundings and get a better insight into their personality. For instance, the approach for someone whose office has a wall of plaques, photos, and degrees is different from someone whose home is tasteful but modest and displays a large collection of photos of their family.

In the initial meeting, you should say as little as possible. Your primary focus is finding out information about the prospect. The secondary focus is building the investor's confidence in your ability to get the job done. When the meeting is over, you want the investor to have the distinct feeling you were interested in their well being and can develop a solution to meet their financial goals.

FWIW # 90 .... *Who's Who?*

Everyone has a personality. You will be able to communicate best with most personalities if you understand the various types and how they respond to various approaches. To begin the process, you have to understand what type of personality you have. Not necessarily the one you want to have, but the one that is you. If necessary, go to a psychologist and have some testing done. The cost is inconsequential if it makes you a better communicator. Buy books on personality traits to get a better understanding of yours and the types out there. The subject is too complex for this book but essentially there are four personality types: A, B, C, and D. We have all heard about the A type personality. Usually the connotation has been negative. That's not the case, however, if you can communicate with this person. You will be able to have a great deal more latitude in managing a type A's portfolio than you will a type B or C person's portfolio.

The B personality is a person who is stable and analytical. A traditional individual who takes pride in doing what is considered the conservative and proven method of investing.

C type personalities are always going to be your best friend and be easy to deal with if you are of the same friendly, open type of personality.

Then there is the D type of egotist who must be the center of attention. If you try to deal as an equal, you won't get the business.

Don't dismiss personality typing. It works and is important in achieving a clientele that maximizes your earnings potential. Study it on a regular basis to improve your ability to connect with prospective clients.

FWIW # 91 .... *Dial-A-Goal*

It doesn't matter if you are a banker, a non-discretionary financial advisor, or a discretionary financial advisor. It doesn't matter if you work for a community bank, an international bank, a wire house, a regional broker, an investment counselor, or own your own firm. Every time you pick up the phone to talk with a client or a prospective client, you should have a minimum and a maximum goal to accomplish with that phone call.

If the call is to find someone for filling a vacancy in the 300 Club, there are certain attributes you need to know about that person. A call to a 300 Club member should have a specific logical reason and should improve your known profile of that individual and move the club member closer to being a client. Client calls should be specifically to reinforce some aspect of your relationship.

There are several good client relationship electronic software systems on the market. Find one you're comfortable with and use it. Develop a list of the information you require for each potential client. Have it in the software so you can prepare for the call before picking up the phone. Business development is challenging, however, with planning the process can become as efficient as possible.

FWIW # 92 .... *Mission Accomplished*

Every phone call or visit with a client or prospect has a goal. When that goal is achieved, hang up or terminate the meeting. You cannot improve the situation if your goal has been met. Thank the client or prospect for their confidence in you, assure them you have their best interest as your objective, and move on to the next item on your agenda.

FWIW # 93 .... *The Right Bait*

Sometimes it is necessary to gently nudge a prospect or client into making a decision to use the advisor's services or make a particular investment. Even though these circumstances are rare, they are real. When the situation does come up, the advisor has to appeal to the client or prospect's emotional side. FEAR, GREED, or some other emotional issue such as a strategy for educating children or taking care of parents becomes the focal point of the discussion. When the situation presents itself, care must be taken by the advisor to be factual and clear in the presentation. Over embellishment is out. It's also unnecessary. Assisting the client to place the investment decision in terms of the long term goal is not only wise but necessary, particularly when dealing with non-discretionary clients. Here is a way to assist a prospect in making a decision to use your firm. "Mr(s). (name), making a decision to accept guidance in developing your portfolio to enable sustainable growth over a six-year market cycle is not easy. You have to decide if a disciplined approach that seeks out under-valued securities and builds them into a coordinated strategy to achieve long term capital gains is better than what you have experienced in the past. What particular part of the strategy I have outlined makes you uncomfortable?" At that point, you should have (a) specific issues you can address, or (b) the client makes a decision to use you or not. Any vagueness or delay is a decision not to use your services. Don't press it, but don't waste your time. Some investors cannot make good business decisions and you will end up with an unhappy client who will disrupt your entire practice if you pressure someone into making a positive decision when they are not ready. There are plenty of investors who need top quality service from an advisor like you, so don't waste your time with someone who is hesitant.

FWIW # 94 .... *Selling The Sizzle*

"Sell the sizzle and not the steak" is an old adage in the selling business. It's another way of saying sell benefits and not features. What is sizzle in the financial advisory business? Is it performance? Is it popularity of the sector or securities in your portfolios? Is it your firm? No to all of these.

Anyone who builds a business based upon performance is building a short term career. Even the best money managers in the world can't sustain performance year in and year out. Someone who outperforms in one type of market rarely outperforms when the market rotates to a different perspective.

There are clear industry segments to the stock market. Pharmaceuticals, consumer non-durables, basic industries, industrial, telecommunications, technology, and utilities are just a few. There are industries within each of these broad macro sectors. If you base your sales presentation on being good at one or a few when that sector rotates out of favor, as they eventually will, your reason for being will cease to exist. You have to be seen as a financial advisor who can participate across the entire market spectrum.

You and your firm and its expertise are important to the client, but the client really makes a decision just based upon you and not who works for your firm, or the company you are recommending. The client wants to know, of course, whether or not you have the demonstrated ability to grow portfolios, but once that is out of the way, what the client really wants to know is if you can assist them in achieving their goals. *Meeting client objectives is the sizzle you want to be selling*. You have to develop in the client's mind a mental picture of the client and you going hand in hand to the promised land – whatever that is for your client.

FWIW # 95 .... *Build On Success*

A great number of advisor/client relationships begin slowly as the client commits an amount of capital that is enough to engage the manager but not too much to the point where the client worries about it. This is natural and not to be thought of as a problem. As a matter of fact, you can turn it into a plus. Here's how.

When a client is pleased with the progress of the portfolio, which usually takes twelve to eighteen months after initially engaging your firm, they will indicate their pleasure. At that point, you can ask for more assets to manage by saying: "Mr(s). (name), thank you for your trust and confidence. My firm and I enjoy having you as a client and believe we can continue the success we have had. If it is a help to you, I would be willing to prepare a written analysis showing how the portfolio we manage complements or supplements your other portfolios. Would you find that helpful?"

The statement is not threatening. It allows the client to make the decision about adding to the portfolio. What it does do is take the good will you have accomplished and use it to get the opportunity for an active review of the client's other assets. If those assets are not as professionally managed, you will be able to point that out. You will then be able to show the client *how much faster they can reach their objective by having those other assets managed by you*. If there are no other assets to manage or the client doesn't want to leave another manager, you can use the opportunity of a pleased client to say: "Mr(s). (name), my business is like all others in that from time to time a client will leave us due to death or a life change that requires steady liquidation of a portfolio rather than the accumulation of assets through portfolio growth. If you know of someone who wants or needs an analysis and review of their portfolio, I'd be pleased to see if our services will help them. Thank you for your trust and confidence. I look forward to our continued successful relationship."

Casually asking for a referral is not threatening to your ego nor to the client.

FWIW # 96 .... *Most Expensive Presentation*

Non-discretionary advisors who, for whatever reason, do not interact with clients in a fee-based manner, have the challenge of selling a client on a particular security. If that relationship is based on transactions rather than fee-based, you have to develop a clear, concise, and upbeat presentation of the benefits of owning the particular security. What better place to start developing a list of features to be turned into benefits than with the front section of most annual reports. Some of the best minds on Madison Avenue have developed the presentation of corporate outlooks even when times are tough for a company. You can read the multi-million dollar presentations in the annual report, determine the important functions of the company now and in the future, and then translate these features into advantages and benefits for your client.

FWIW # 97 .... *Cross Selling*

Banks, insurance companies, mutual fund companies, and brokerage firms are all moving into each others' business. It's highly likely you will eventually find yourself part of a large organization. Being part of a multi-service, multi-investment firm makes sense for you and for your client. However, finding the synergies is not easy. Here are the ways to maximize your revenue by utilizing all parts of your organization.

First, make a list of each section of the overall organization. Does your firm make loans, sell insurance, have CD's, offer brokerage services, offer investment management, and offer checking services? See how the various securities and services fit on a risk spectrum.

Second, obtain from each organization an application form the client will have to complete to utilize their specific services. Review each and select the form that requires the most detailed and complete set of facts. This document becomes the basis of your WHAT WE KNOW interview. Study it and work the information needed into a conversational interview.

Third, look for opportunities to help your client. In your conversations, let them know about special services offered by your firm. While discussing the portfolio management, share with the client your ability to assist them with a business loan. If interest rates appear to be stabilizing at a low rate, check with your clients about refinancing their mortgage. Are you uncomfortable with the concept? You shouldn't be. In regard to mortgage loans, say the following at the end of a conversation that you have had with a client about their portfolio: "Mr(s). (name), before I go, I mentioned that our research indicates interest rates will be stabilizing around current levels. If our research is correct, you should examine your current mortgage to see if it will improve your situation to refinance that mortgage. While I'm not an expert in that area, my friend, John Doe, is. Would it be helpful to you if he were to call to see if he can save you money or shorten your mortgage maturity?"

Perhaps your firm sells insurance. You might tag onto the end of a conversation with a client the following: "Mr(s). (<u>name</u>), by the way, you might not be aware that insurance companies update their mortality tables on a regular basis. What that means to policy holders is that the same amount of insurance currently owned might cost less than what you are paying now. While insurance is not in my area of expertise, making sure my clients have the best total financial and investment profile is. Will it help you if I ask my friend, Jane Doe, who is an insurance expert, to review your insurance policies? Naturally, the review will not be of any cost to you."

See the point? The strategy is this:

(1) Tag onto the end of a portfolio discussion.

(2) Clearly let the client know you are not involved in these related areas, but you have a friend who will assist if you request their assistance.

(3) The logic of the review is to keep the client's financial and investment profile on the cutting edge.

Cross selling is like any other communication. It is smooth and easy when focused on the client's well-being. As with other communication, cross selling takes practice, practice, and more practice.

FWIW # 98 .... *Ask and Ye Shall Receive*

You are not going to get the portfolio management assignment or the order unless you ask the client or the prospect for the right to do business with them. As some point, you have to look them in the eye and ask them to allow you to assist them in growing their portfolio. If you can't do that, you are in the wrong business.

FWIW # 99 .... *Cheap Date*

Want to get rich? Want to have the largest revenue stream at your firm? Want to have everything you ever dreamed of? Here's how:

MAKE SURE ALL OF YOUR CLIENTS BELIEVE THAT THEY GET MORE SERVICE THAN THEY PAY FOR.

What does that mean? Allow your clients to discuss with you financial and investment issues even though the issues are not part of the portfolio you receive a fee for managing. Talk to them about what their other managers are doing. Help them with the assets they manage themselves. Help their children if they have assets. Tell your client you will help the children develop a portfolio without a fee until the portfolio reaches $100,000. Why? Because you want to be indispensable to your clients. A client paying 1% fee with a portfolio of $500,000 that grows at 12.25% a year for ten years will pay you over $88,800 in fees during that period. When your client dies or your client's children become successful on their own, who better to help them with their new wealth than the person who was kind enough to help them develop their first portfolio. Doing more than what the client expects is just good job security.

Now, you would be foolish to allow a wealthy family to take advantage of your top quality service without allowing you to manage sufficient assets. What are sufficient assets? That depends on you and your assessment of the situation. There is no firm rule. Trust your judgement in assessing the potential for helping the family and gaining additional assets in the future.

FWIW # 100 .... *Walking the Talk*

A comfortable and true presentation of your abilities and the proper investment objectives and strategy for a prospective client will get you more clients than you can handle. Once signed up, you have to be able to deliver the proper growth for the acceptable risk. How to perform in all market environments is a matter of having a tested and reliable investment philosophy and strategy. The next section discusses how you can make money for your clients in all market environments. Sometimes the method will outperform the S&P, other times it won't. Given a six-year period where part of the time is a bear market, the strategy will out perform the S&P 500. It seems simple, but it's not. PENDULUM INVESTING™ works.

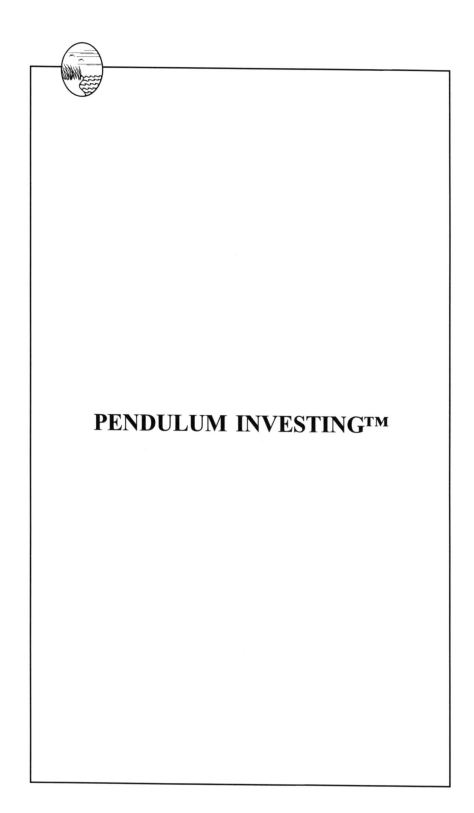

PENDULUM INVESTING™

FWIW # 101 .... *What Road To Travel*

Investing has more than one road to success if you define success as achieving an ever-increasing amount of capital through the years. It's not like a maze where there are dead ends. Each path can achieve success with some ***luck, skill, and discipline***. It's best to think of the process as choices to be made over and over again as the two main roads to success crisscross and intersect. These two roads represent **investing** and **speculating.**

Investing and speculating are both processes and attitudes. If you try to mix investing process with speculative attitude, you will have difficulty and likely not be successful. The same is true for the speculative process and investing attitude. Your clients have no concept of most of these principles. Therefore, it is critical that you, the financial advisor, are able to understand the concepts and are able to recognize the traits exhibited by your clients and therefore can develop an investment philosophy and strategy your clients can embrace. The beginning is understanding the process of investing and speculating.

What are stocks or bonds to you? Are they pieces of paper with lives of their own? Are they pieces of paper that represent an operating business with sales, earnings, and assets? Both? What do you really feel about this concept? Are you more interested in what the ten best gainers were in the market today rather than the earnings reports? Do you look first to see what has been moving in the market to select your potential investments for clients, or do you analyze and understand specific companies that have good businesses before deciding what price to pay for the stock?

Investing is a process of looking for good businesses with the potential to increase sales and earnings in a steady manner over a long time period, perhaps five to ten years. Some investors, successful ones I might add, believe a one hundred-year perspective is appropriate. An investor strives to know all of the pertinent information about the company with specific emphasis on corporate liquidity, management quality, business franchise and barriers to competition, expansion potential, and earnings growth potential. This type of corporate fact gathering is called fundamental analysis and is both time consuming and difficult to do, although the Internet and an emphasis on investor relations by the companies have made more information readily available to analysts and anyone interested in the company. Only when a sound understanding of the business is arrived at, will an investor determine what price should be paid for the company. This price is grounded in the analysis of the company, however, it also takes into consideration the stock's relative value to bonds and other securities in the same industry and the market as a whole. Gauging a stock's relative value to other securities is important to an investor and is an exercise shared with the speculator.

Speculators are interested in price changes, not in fundamentals. They want to know what is moving in the market, both up and down, and what is the potential for capturing the price movement profitably. Speculators don't spend any time with fundamental analysis unless it is a special circumstance where a dramatic change is possible and they speculate that the change will or will not happen. The example is when a company teeters on the verge of bankruptcy or is a potential takeover target. Speculators make extensive use of market analysis better known as technical analysis where the buying and selling of shares and the rhythm of that buying and selling is more important than the operating of the business. Because speculators are only loyal to short term profits, they are quick to abandon a stock that disappoints their expectations or even appears to be diverting from the expected price path.

A good investor understands speculative techniques. A good speculator understands and does some investing techniques. While being true to their own path to success, excellent investors and speculators never mistake their chosen proper attitude for the improper one. Everyone in the investment business is part investor and part speculator. In many cases, the amount of money being managed determines the mix of the two attitudes. Someone with $50,000 might be a speculator, but give them $500,000 and, all of a sudden, investing becomes important. Another person who has accumulated $50,000 over a number of years and understands the difficulty of doing so, might never have a speculative attitude. A crucial function for the financial advisor is to understand the complexity of potential clients' attitudes towards their portfolios. This is done by allowing the clients to express their attitudes and expectations about the portfolio's potential progress. One major indicator of a potential client's attitude is if the client has the portfolio on the Internet and updates it during the day, at night, weekly, or monthly. Someone who updates nightly or more than once a day has a highly speculative attitude no matter what protest they make to the contrary. You have to understand that fact and make sure you design a portfolio that will match their attitude.

It's helpful to you to use the metaphor of two roads crisscrossing and intersecting, but leading to the common destination of success. Time after time, the driver on the investing road must make a decision: "Do I stay on the longer and slower road of investing or do I detour onto the shorter but more perilous road of speculating?" On the investing road it can take a long time to meet your destination of success since the speed limit is slower. It appears the speed limit is 15 miles an hour and you have thousands of miles to go. A little voice keeps saying, "Are we there yet? Are we there yet? Are we there yet?" The temptation builds a little bit at a time to take the more speculative route where the cars are whizzing by at what appears to be 100 miles an hour. At every intersection and crisscross, the speculative road looks to be just as smooth, wide, and straight as the investing road. The problem is it's not. Further down the speculative road, out of sight from the intersection, are potholes, road debris, and hazards that not only block the road, but can cause serious damage to the portfolio. Hit one of these potholes or run into one of these roadblocks and it will take time to repair your portfolio and return to the last intersection to get on the straight, narrow, and safe investing road again. Time and money are lost and will have to made up.

There are other times short stretches on the speculative road can help speed the journey without any problem. These short periods of speculation enhance the overall portfolio's progress because they are successful. They are successful through skill, discipline, and plain ordinary luck. Since luck is uncontrollable, part of your function as a financial advisor involves determining the amount of capital to put on the speculative road and improving the probabilities of winning. If you are primarily an investor, you will not be successful for long dealing with speculators. If you have a speculative attitude, investors will not communicate with you properly. Listen for what the potential client wants from the portfolio. Ask to see the current portfolio so that you can see if what they say is the same as what they do. If the portfolio was constructed by a former investment manager, you have the good opportunity to probe for the client's opinion of what is right about the current portfolio and what is wrong with it. Your prospect's comments will tell you if the attitude they have is for investing or speculating and you will sense if you have the opportunity for a successful relationship.

FWIW # 102 .... *Hurdles To Success*

There are three hurdles to success for any investor or speculator. The first is inflation. Inflation is the loss of purchasing power over a period of time. It is caused by government creating too much paper money for any given economic condition and thereby creating more demand than the current supply of goods and services can meet at stable prices. In the past, inflation has taken the form of a general increase in all prices, primarily tangible assets and goods and services. During the 1970's, not understanding inflation, investors and speculators sold their common stocks and fixed income securities as inflation rose. It wasn't until the early 1980's, with interest rates in the high teens, that some sharp investment people recognized that the value of the underlying assets and the business franchises of companies were not reflected in the then current prices of stocks. The almost assured decline of interest rates was a contributing factor in what became the beginning of the longest and most explosive bull market in history.

At other times, inflation is exhibited in just one or two economic sectors. The price of oil is an example. By the early 1980's, reputable and experienced analysts were espousing clear cases for $100 a barrel oil. Soon thereafter, the price declined to single digits. Real estate skyrocketed during the 1970's and early 1980's as investors and speculators poured money into the asset class because "they weren't making any more land." With the stroke of a pen in 1986, the real estate tax advantages were reduced or eliminated and prices began plummeting. Savings and loans and banks, who for fifteen years made safe real estate loans, went out of existence as over-valued properties were dumped on the market.

Inflation is a hurdle for a well-managed portfolio for three reasons: (a) it erodes the purchasing power of the income from dividends and interest, (b) it erodes the purchasing power of the asset principal in fixed income and cash reserves, and (c) it inflates the price of the security class in demand so much that it becomes inevitable for a sharp price decline.

Inflation is helpful to a portfolio when the businesses represented by the stocks have significant pricing power and the ability to maintain profit margins thereby passing along increased cost through increased sales resulting in increased profits. Usually, the flexibility and operating methods are apparent sooner or later to all investors and the demand for the company or its shares skyrockets as the demand overwhelms the supply in a typical inflationary manner.

Taxes are the second hurdle successful portfolio management has to overcome. There are three kinds of taxes: (a) income taxes, (b) capital gains taxes, and (c) estate taxes. The lowest tax rate is capital gains tax. To achieve this tax rate, the investment has to be in a taxable account and held for a specified period. Any asset sold after being held less than dictated time will have the profit taxed at ordinary tax rates.

Ordinary tax rates range from 15% to over 41% for high income investors. Dividends and interest from investments are subject to ordinary income tax either at the time received, or if the investment is in a tax-deferred account, when income is removed from the account. Whenever the tax is paid, it is a significant hurdle to overcome.

If the income tax and capital gains taxes don't take most of the assets assembled during life, the estate tax will take up to 55% of everything left at death.

There are ways to minimize the effect of taxes on a portfolio, change ordinary income taxes into capital gains taxes, and significantly reduce the estate tax. Pendulum investing and portfolio management use these techniques as part of an overall strategy. Your function as a financial advisor is to understand these tax hurdles so that you can plan for them in the overall strategy.

The final hurdle, probably more significant than the other two, is the fact that investing is fun. Tools and knowledge are at a market participant's fingertips with the click of a mouse. Portfolios can be tracked trade by trade all day long. Market volatility daily brings to mind the question of "What if?" What if I buy it when the stock goes down $3 and sell it when it goes up $3? Analysts are on television daily and in the newspapers daily making a case for their favorite stocks. The stories make logical sense so what if I buy when the analysts first recommend the stock and sell it when it hits the announced target? These analysts are paid a great deal of money to know what they are doing, right? Commissions are cheap, only $9.95, $19.95, or $29.95 per trade. In some cases, only 5¢ per share. There is no real reason not to make a few extra dollars by quickly getting into and out of a stock, particularly in a tax-deferred account where there are no tax consequences until the money is removed from the account.

To the non-professional market participant, being an active investor or speculator means making buy and sell decisions based upon news and share price movement, two primary characteristics of speculating. A stock that does not move fast enough is sold to buy one that is moving. The entire portfolio is changed when it appears to be out of favor. Taking action is a sign of virility and being in control. Buying a stock that subsequently goes up is a tremendous shot of adrenalin to the ego and self-confidence of the decision-maker.

The constant manipulation of the portfolio and its security positions has become a hobby to many people. All of the actions, however, increase the tax hurdles and increase the likelihood of making mistakes in security selection. Mistakes mount as more psychological pressure is felt by the portfolio owner to "make up" for the mistakes of the past by finding a stock that will go up faster than ever before.

As a professional financial advisor, you can seriously minimize the activity hurdle by your disciplined approach to the markets and the portfolio. Through your knowledge of taxes and the client's objectives, you can minimize the income, capital gains, and estate tax hurdles for the portfolio. Through portfolio management, you can develop a portfolio that minimizes the risk of inflation and takes advantage of the benefits of inflation.

FWIW # 103 .... *Reverse Image*

Ever buy a car? Ever buy jewelry? Ever buy artwork? Ever buy real estate? Ever buy these things on a whim? For example, buying the car. When buying, usually people will check the price of what they want with the prices of comparable automobiles and more than one dealership.

Jewelry is the same way. Before buying a ring or a bracelet, usually several different pieces and several different stores are shopped until you are satisfied that the best buy is achieved.

Buying real estate is even more intense with comparisons of values within the neighborhood or location. What is the roof like? How about the room sizes? What about the size of the lot, the square footage of the house? Not until it's clear the best value is obtained is the contract signed. Even then, numerous inspections are done to make sure you are getting what you thought you were buying before putting your money into the investment.

People act differently in the stock market. They hear someone on television talk about a company and they buy it without the least bit of investigation of the company. In some cases, they don't even know what the company does. *Investing without investigating* it's called. In effect, market participants take the stock market's advantage of instant liquidity and turning it into a negative. Why do investors and speculators alike succumb to this fault? GREED primarily. Wanting to make a fast, easy buck by taking advantage of someone else's knowledge for their benefit. A secondary reason is the speculators know the necessary effort to understand the investment will take time and hard work, both of which they aren't inclined to do. It is better to try and hitch a ride on someone else's efforts than expend their own time and energy studying the investment. Most non-professional investors and speculators don't know how to analyze and utilize the information that's available to them.

Can you imagine someone wanting to sell their diamond ring because the store was having a sale on diamonds? How about someone wanting to sell their home because interest rates have risen causing home prices to go down? In both cases, the prices of the ring and real estate have actually declined because of market conditions. But no one panics or wants to quickly sell before prices go down even more. In the stock market, it's different.

Let a share price start to decline and a flood of market players will sell for fear that the price will go down even more. These sellers are not just non-professionals, but also professional money managers who are concerned about short term profits. There are a number of stocks like Hewlett Packard (HWP) in the 1998-2000 period when the stock went from $52 to $118 over the course of twelve months and then fell back to $60 in a thirty-day period only to rise to $140 over the next six months. The price fell because the selling was sustained and determined. Why? What changed in the company or market at the beginning of the thirty-day period, leading to the price decline, that was subsequently reversed in the next six months, leading to more than a doubling of the share price? The 30-year U.S. Treasury Bond interest rate went from 4.75% in the Fall of 1998 to 6.75% in January of 2000, but no one was dumping real estate, nor jewelry, nor art and antiques. What makes the psychology of the stock market so much different than these other asset classes?

Just as the stock market's advantage of liquidity is turned into a negative, the market's transparency of prices and information is turned into a negative by speculators. The psychological impact of daily watching your net worth decline is too much for many people. They think about the stock going to zero or remember stories of the Depression when all was lost. Seeing the price decline is the problem, not so much the decline itself. Being able to do something about the decline, i.e., selling the stock before it declines further, compounds the intense psychological aspect. The rationale in most people's minds is this: "If I don't sell, it (the stock) will continue to fall and my net worth will decline as well. If I do sell, my net worth will stop going down, and I may be able to buy the stock back at a lower price or buy another one that is going up." Makes a goodargument for selling, doesn't it? Can you imagine having the local real estate prices reported daily and beginning to think of real estate in this way? Of course not.

Stock market participants are their own worst enemy when it comes to turning the advantages of stocks, low transaction cost and price and market transparency, into a disadvantage. As a financial advisor, you can use your professionalism to keep your clients from allowing this to happen. Your research and analysis will allow you to understand the intrinsic value of the companies represented by the shares in the portfolio. Helping your clients focus on the long term growth of the portfolio will assist them in understanding that they are participating in the economic growth of your region, the U.S.A., or the global economy. Your use of portfolio management discipline assists your clients in not panicking when one or more securities they hold come under intense and irrational selling pressure. Your use of pendulum investing will enable you to position your clients in the stocks where FEAR is dominant thereby giving them an attractive entry point for potential long term capital gains.

FWIW # 104 .... *A Secret*

Many financial advisors feel they must be active with a client's portfolio to justify their fees or generate commissions. Nothing can be further from the truth. Taking a little money and doing a lot with it is not the road to success as a financial advisor. Taking a lot of money and doing little with it is the secret. Embedded in this secret is the implied fact that a disciplined approach leads to selecting quality companies when they are attractively priced. Once selected, the companies are allowed to operate according to plan and the stock market is allowed to reflect the increased earnings over time.

FWIW # 105 .... *Loose Lips*

It's human nature to want something for nothing. Couple this trait with an intense and often illogical aversion to paying a commission or fee and you have the practice today when supposedly ethical and moral people will seek advice from a financial advisor then turn around and use that advice without paying for it by making a trade with a deep discount broker. They see absolutely nothing wrong with this practice, even if they lead you to believe that you will get their business if only you will share with them your knowledge and expertise.

In other cases, potential clients are sincere in seeking out your services and want to know what securities you are buying. In an effort to be open and honest about your firm, you will give them the one or two names of companies currently being placed in client portfolios. Alas, invariably, these are the one or two companies that will have some negative news and decline shortly after your sharing their names with the potential client. The prospect was confident in your services and postponed making a decision when the shares declined. You lost a potentially good client for no good reason.

The decisions you make are based upon your years of experience and the special knowledge of what is right for each individual client. Never give away for free what makes you unique. Never make a general recommendation that might or might not fit the person you are talking to at the time.

When discussing with a potential client what you do and how you do it, speak in generalities and broad concepts about managing and growing portfolios. If you need to use specific examples, use the ones from three or four years ago that have now met their targets. When pressed for specific current recommendations, say the following:

"Mr(s). (name), my client's pay my firm a significant fee for our best current ideas. It is not fair to them to discuss the investments that we are putting in their portfolio with someone who is not a client."

If they take offense to that response, it's likely they would have not become a client at all.

FWIW # 106 .... *Tax Knowledge*

You have to understand taxes, but don't have to be an expert. You need to know what experts you can call on when you want a clarification of a client's situation. Your firm probably has a tax department able to field questions, or if you work for a small firm, at least a CPA who can be called on to answer questions. If your firm does not have a tax department or access to a CPA, perhaps one of the brokerage firms or banks that you deal with does. Failing that, it is in your best interest to develop a relationship with a CPA where you exchange some advice given to them personally for answers to tax questions.

You do have a need to know the following:

(a) Income tax brackets, personal deduction levels, and what triggers AMT.

(b) How to compute capital gains taxes including the depreciation recapture aspect.

(c) The complete ins and outs of IRA's (this is more complex than first thought).

(d) The rules for 401(k) contributions, withdrawals, and loans.

(e) The estate tax brackets and exemptions.

(f) The step up in basis in various deductions from estate taxes.

(g) Charitable trusts, both lead and remainder and annuity and unit.

(h) Grantor trust and their tax ramifications including the concept of dynasty trust.

The tax knowledge is necessary for you to be able to recognize opportunities to enhance your value to your client. For instance, suppose a couple have separate assets and one spouse has a degenerative illness that will eventually claim their life while the other spouse is in good health and will probably outlive the ill spouse. A review of the family assets to insure taking advantage of the full unified credit deduction from estate taxes is in order. At the same time, assets with very low cost basis and high market value will make sense to be in the estate of the spouse more likely to die first since the step up in basis will benefit the surviving spouse if the assets move laterally to the surviving spouse.

Taxes are complicated and change yearly as Congress tinkers with the tax code. Understanding them is critical in your client relationship building. Your focus, however, is not to give tax advice but to guide the client in structuring the proper questions to ask their tax advisor.

FWIW # 107 .... *Six Principles*

Rules for investing are made every time the market shifts from one cycle to another. A few months or years later, the rules change again. There are, however, a few basic principles that never change. Follow them and you will grow your client assets in a reasonably steady and consistent manner over a three, five, and ten-year period. The following is the bedrock of good portfolio management.

1. A long term approach is necessary. The more decisions that are made, the higher the likelihood of making a mistake. It's nearly impossible to determine what a stock price will do in the next six months, but highly probable good research will be able to determine what a stock price will do three years in the future.

2. An investment portfolio is like a business. It needs good cash flow as well as good assets. It's important to have above average cash flow from dividends and interest in the portfolio even if that portfolio is taxable. It is crucial in taking advantage of the most important aspect of a tax-deferred account, namely the ability to generate income without paying current taxes.

3. Stocks represent real businesses, not just pieces of paper. A portfolio should make sense as a collection of businesses that complement each other and assist the owner in participating in the long term growth of the economy.

4. Successful portfolio management comes when there is only one decision-maker. No one is right all of the time, but with disciplined research and management principles, a manager can be right most of the time. If two different people are making decisions, mistakes will multiply.

5. Income and capital gains taxes have to be minimized. Taxes,

however, cannot be the dominant factor in portfolio decisions, just part of the strategy.

6. Continuity of investment style is crucial. When the inevitable period of time comes where a particular style is not working as well as others, the discipline to keep with the basic principles is necessary.

These six investment principles will work for a disciplined investment manager. Applying the principles is an intricate part of the portfolio management process.

FWIW # 108 .... *Risks Are Real*

There are countless risks associated with each investment decision, but there are fourteen that are more likely to be involved with portfolio management. These fourteen are as follows:

INTEREST RATE RISK - Rising interest rates usually require a higher return potential from the investment, known as the capitalization (cap) rate. The higher the cap rate, the lower the value of the investment for any potential amount of total return.

CREDIT RISK - Other than U.S. Treasury securities, all investments carry some amount of credit risk. Even the strongest of companies runs the risk of credit problems due to mismanagement, fraud, or a difficult operating environment for an extended period of time.

INFLATION RISK - Inflation is a product of the government. In the U.S., the elected government officials change every four years.

The government's response to external and internal forces in the economy can change and is unpredictable.

POLITICAL RISK - Increasingly, the specter of political interference in the economy is exhibiting itself. From anti-trust action to political "tilting" of government spending, economic shaping is evidenced every day.

CATASTROPHIC RISK - A major terrorist attack, earthquakes, hurricanes, flood, or some other natural disaster can and do happen with more regularity than imagined. There is, however, nothing you can do about these events except avoid companies where the geographic risk is high. Generally, it's best to accept the risk and focus on the risks that you can control with more certainty.

RECESSION RISK - The business cycle is real and inevitably leads to a recession. Some stocks are more resistant than others to recession just as high quality bonds are safer than low quality debt in a recession. While a risk to be dealt with when buying stocks during an expansion, a recession is the best time to invest.

MARKET SYSTEMIC RISK - This is the risk of the stock market, real estate market, or bond market falling out of favor with investors in general. A decline due to investors withdrawing money from the asset class affects all of the securities in the class, even the good ones. This is a real risk focused on asset allocation.

SECTOR RISK - On a regular basis, one economic sector or another (see FWIW # 151) has difficult supply and demand problems which lead to under performance in the marketplace. The risk is similar to the market systemic risk in that all securities in a sector decline, including the good ones.

ASSET CONCENTRATION RISK - The truly best way to accumulate serious amounts of wealth is to have all of your assets in one or two securities, assuming those securities are moving higher. When the stock, however, falls out of favor or fails to go up, the damage to the portfolio can be significant.

COMPANY SPECIFIC RISK - This is a similar risk to asset concentration risk, however, it is the result of some event happening in the company that causes the sales and earnings to not grow thereby causing the expectations for the company's future to decline.

VOLATILITY RISK - Stocks and bonds have taken on an increasing amount of volatility risk with wide swings in price being commonplace. The causes of this volatility are many (see FWIW # 114) and will not go away. Short term performance, less than nine months, can seriously be impacted by specific security and market systemic volatility.

LIQUIDITY RISK - Clearly related to volatility risk is liquidity risk in a specific security. If there are no buyers or sellers, massive price changes can take place in a short period of time. Portfolio liquidity risk is potentially even more devastating in times of emergency or market volatility when securities must be sold no matter what the consequences.

TIME HORIZON RISK - Investors seek out companies with the potential to grow. By definition, fundamental sales and earnings growth takes time. Speculators want fast action from their investments. The market, as a whole, demands concrete changes in fundamentals before it will recognize and reward operational improvements. If a market participant wants an investment to meet expectations in one year, but the fundamental changes will take three years, there is a serious time horizon risk. If a portfolio is designed to double in six years, and the investor wants it to double in four years, there is an additional time horizon risk. If the investor is 80 and the portfolio is designed to perform in ten years, statistically there is a potential time horizon problem since the investor will have to live past the average life expectancy. Matching portfolio expectations and realistic portfolio time performance is an important part of an advisor's assignment.

IMPATIENCE RISK - Solid portfolio growth takes time and most investors don't want to wait. They want action now. If the action doesn't materialize, impatient market participants will go elsewhere to find something that will move now.

Fourteen major risks in portfolio management and investing. Which risk is the most costly in terms of money lost and missed opportunities? Without a doubt, *impatience risk* is the greatest risk most investors face. This risk creates unnecessary transaction costs, taxes, and raises the likelihood of making bad decisions because it creates more decisions.

Your client probably won't identify half of these risks. You should identify these risks for your client in the beginning of your relationship. In doing so, you educate the client. Further, you can show the client how each risk impacts their specific situation. You can help them identify which risks they are willing to take and in what degree. Understanding risks is part of setting the overall investment objectives for the client.

FWIW # 109 .... *Investment Objectives*

Most clients do not have a clear objective for their portfolio, therefore you have to understand what a portfolio's objectives are, even if the client doesn't. Usually, the client expresses the objectives in terms of meeting some important event such as retirement, education of children, freedom to start a business, or some other dream-oriented point in their life. Through probing questions, you, the financial advisor, have to be able to quantify the dream. For instance, perhaps your client wants to be a full-time artist in ten years and currently has $250,000 in a portfolio. Through your probing and questioning, you find the client will need $35,000 a year from the portfolio starting in the tenth year. Well, if a withdrawal rate of 5% is considered appropriate (the appropriate rate depends on the client's attitude and economic conditions in general) the portfolio, at the end of the ten years, must have a value of $700,000. To go from $250,000 now to $700,000 in ten years will require an annual compounded rate of return of 10.84%. Understanding the current economic environment and rates of return available will help you identify what emphasis must be placed on each of the risks to be able to achieve the return necessary from the portfolio over the next ten years. Naturally, client circumstances will impact the risk decisions as well.

Many speculators and investors think of investment objectives in terms of how much reward they want. That, however, is only half of the equation because reward and risk are inextricably linked and you can't have high reward without high risk even if the risk is not as readily apparent. Clients don't understand this **unbreakable** connection. You have to help them understand it so that they don't feel misled when risk rears its ugly head and deals the portfolio a blow. When you professionally explain the positives and negatives of the investment objectives, you build a special confidence in your client. It's well worth the effort.

FWIW # 110 .... *Investment Constraints*

"I want to make as much money as possible and as fast as possible" is what most everyone will respond when asked the question: What type of returns do you want on your portfolio?

The problem is the prospective client doesn't want to take any risks! Even if risks were not the issue, you, as the financial advisor, can't allow the client to accept unlimited risks if you want to keep your license. Every client has constraints on the portfolio you manage. Let's examine some of the more common constraints:

<u>Liquidity</u>: Unique client factors impacting the cash flow into or out of a portfolio. Cash disbursement demands not met by dividends

and interest must be met by selling portfolio assets. Ask your client about their expectations and their requirements so you do not have an illiquid portfolio structure and strategy with sudden demands made for money from the portfolio.

Tax Implications: Is the portfolio taxable or tax-deferred? What is the client's tax bracket and will the portfolio income change the tax bracket appreciably? Will capital gains trigger AMT? Will the tax-deferred status allow for a more flexible and speculative investment policy? Will the tax-deferred portfolio be inherited by a beneficiary who has a longer life to draw out the money than the original portfolio owner? As you can see, tax implications impact investment objectives, constraints, and strategies.

Life Expectancy: Client life expectancy impacts the portfolio investment strategy. Life cycle events like children going to college, marriage, or retirement will impact the strategy. Every portfolio should have a specified time period for measuring performance. Perhaps it is five, six, or ten years. Within the portfolio, each security will have its own time to meet objectives. There will be definite maturities on most of the fixed income securities as well as expected times for the common stocks to meet their stated goals.

Legal or Regulatory: Tax-deferred portfolios have rules and regulations dictating the type of assets and procedures for withdrawing cash from the portfolio. Trust accounts have certain requirements and fiduciary obligations that will affect the investment strategy. Custodian accounts have issues that must be disclosed and understood if the investment strategy is to be implemented properly.

Unique: ***Clients are unique and so are their portfolios***™. Perhaps they have grown children or grandchildren they are supporting. Perhaps a spouse has a terminal illness or disability of some kind that makes the investment strategy constrained. It can be as simple as a client not wanting certain stocks to be bought or sold. Whatever unique aspects about the client that you find should be listed in this section if it pertains to the portfolio.

The number of circumstances causing a portfolio management or investment strategy constraint is unlimited. You must discover as many as possible so you have an investment strategy as tailored as appropriate.

Make sure your clients participate in the constraint search so they will understand why you develop the strategy you do. Without their understanding, you will lose the engagement because your proposed strategy will either be too aggressive or not aggressive enough. Explaining the constraints and how they impact the investment strategy will build your professionalism and credibility in your client's eyes.

FWIW # 111 .... *Investment Strategy*

The investment strategy identifies the following:

* Asset classes and types to be used in the portfolio

* Potential asset allocation range

* Characteristics of the securities if necessary

* Investment unit size

* Maximum initial sector allocation

* Target cash flow to portfolio

* Investment style, if any

Your intent in the investment strategy is to develop portfolio security parameters within which you will meet the objectives. This doesn't mean you confine yourself to an inflexible strategy. For instance: identify the type of money market fund that will be used to keep uninvested funds.

You can identify fixed income assets that may be comprised of corporate bonds, corporate preferreds, municipal bonds, U.S. Treasury securities, and REIT's. Listing the type does not bind you to using all of these, but it does give you the flexibility to use them. Client constraints may prevent using one or more and, if so, don't list it. For example: it doesn't make any sense to place municipal tax-free bonds in a tax-deferred portfolio.

Security characteristics are important to identify. Perhaps the portfolio's enabling document requires each security will pay a dividend. You need to identify that characteristic in the investment strategy. Perhaps your client only wants investment grade debt securities or maturities no longer than ten years. These restraining requests should be in the investment strategy as well as the investment constraints.

Naturally, the initial size of each investment unit should be identified (see FWIW # 129) and through the process, the number of investment units will be known. What will be the sector concentration risk? Depending on your client, you will want to limit the amount of assets initially placed in any one macro-economic sector.

Should the portfolio asset allocation be rebalanced when it changes from an initial allocation? If so, at what point? Is this a mechanical requirement? In other words, a risk to you, the manager, if you fail to do so properly?

Target cash flow is critical to be included in the investment strategy because it significantly impacts the overall portfolio risk profile. If you and your client agree to a 4% cash flow at a time when the S&P yields 1.5%, you cannot develop a highly aggressive portfolio of growth stocks. If 1% cash flow is the goal, the portfolio won't have many, if any, utility stocks and bonds. See the importance of identifying the target cash flow?

If specific securities, such as mortgage-backed bonds, are not to be used and the client has specifically raised the issue, note the client's directive in the investment strategy. If the client has not specifically requested a restriction, by leaving the security type out of the strategy, you infer you won't use it.

The investment strategy allows the client to review the portfolio's components without constraining you in how you mix and match the various income and growth securities. You are allowed to meet the objectives within the risk tolerance and constraints without being encumbered. Whenever you feel a shift in strategy is needed, you can address the shift with the client, receive their agreement, and amend the original strategy *in writing.*

To clearly protect yourself from clients misunderstanding the objectives, risks, constraints, and strategy, present these guidelines in writing and have clients sign the document. If your firm will not allow that process, then have a specific meeting with the client where you review in detail the specific features of your assignment seeking questions and comments each step of the way. Make notes of their questions and comments and place your notes in your file. After the meeting, write the client and thank them for their time in going over the objectives, risks, constraints, and strategy.

Clearly explaining the relationship and strategy for meeting client goals is not just to protect you. It's to help them be better clients. Everyone's happy when the market goes up and interest rates go down, but that doesn't happen all of the time. Since the bear market is the most important time for developing future long-term, above average growth, helping your client understand the investment strategy will keep them from panicking at the very time they should be trusting you the most. Educated and committed clients do not panic when the market is under pressure and endorse the concept of finding quality investments at great values during these times.

FWIW # 113 .... *Perspectives*

The stock market has a casino mentality. Short term action is wanted and, to a great degree, needed by a significant portion of market participants. With all of the literature espousing a long-term perspective to stock investing, why the contradiction in viewpoint by so many? There are several reasons.

1. Transaction costs are next to nothing. Large institutions will pay 2 or 3¢ per share or, in some unusual circumstances, nothing for a trade. Even your average retail investor can execute a transaction for a fixed amount ranging from $5 to $29.95. In many cases, the cost is between 3¢ and 8¢ per share. Transaction costs are not much friction to the transaction, particularly with the decimalization of quoting stock prices.

2. The spread between the Bid/Ask prices has narrowed significantly on most stocks. Where 3/8 and 1/2 used to be the norm, 5¢ to 10¢ is more common, thereby allowing an investor to exit a position, study the market situation or news, and reenter if appropriate.

3. Computers have enabled many trading floors to improve their knowledge of a security's volatility. Volatility has increased and, with the narrowing of the spread and lower transaction costs, the profit potential for quick in and out trading has multiplied. Many of these trades do not even have human origin. The trades are generated by computer programs based upon and involving volatility information flow.

4. Many more portfolios are in tax-deferred accounts than ever

before. With the tax-deferred status, potential loss of profit to the tax collector is no longer an impediment to a transaction. Brokerage trading floors pay taxes on their net profitable trading, but that is considered a cost of doing business just like generating commissions.

5. Most stock mutual funds are not interested in being tax efficient. They consider themselves speculative vehicles designed to seek out profit wherever it can be found. They understand many shareholders use tax-deferred accounts and taxable shareholders are forgiving of the tax consequences if enough money is being made. Outperforming the S&P 500 or some other index is the objective and it is best done by moving in and out of sectors or securities with greater or less momentum than the index itself. In addition to beating the index, mutual fund managers must compete with their peers in their own fund category on a 90-day basis. Poor relative performance will cause investors to pull money out of their fund and give it to their competition or another fund category.

6. The entire market has become performance oriented. Even long term investors watch the business news looking for the daily performance of one or more of their stocks. Investing is the hobby of choice for millions who know they want to be invested for the long-term but are always looking for the special of the day. Playing the game is exhilarating and fun – at least in a bull market.

Should you cater to this casino mentality? Not if you want to have a long-term career as a financial advisor. If you get a chance, go into any of the major trading firms and survey the average age of the traders.

Very few wear bifocals. It is difficult to succeed managing assets on a short term perspective due to the taxes, your fee, and the fact that not every trade will be successful. Besides, who wants to trade for 10%, 20%, or even 40% gains? As a financial advisor, you want the opportunity to see some of your transactions return 300%, 500%, or even 1,000% over a five or ten-year period. This is really making serious money for your clients! Don't fool yourself, it can be done, but not often. It doesn't take many of these trades to overcome some mistakes.

Your clients want discipline and intelligence applied to their portfolio. What they don't want is to lose money. Trading is a fast way to lose money. Long-term investing is a steady way to grow a portfolio.

Market volatility is an attribute, neither good nor bad. You can either allow it to be negative or positive for your clients. Portfolio management will align the impact of market volatility with your client's unique objectives and constraints. In developing objectives and constraints, you determine the size of the client's portfolio investment units. Those not suited for high amounts of asset concentration risk will have more investment units than those able to accept large amounts of this risk.

Knowing what price you want to pay for the securities you want to own allows you to pounce when volatility gives you the opportunity. In a similar fashion, studying the normal daily volatility of a stock will assist in reducing transaction costs to zero or even a negative number.

Inevitably, a stock you own in your client's portfolios will be hit by a downdraft in the market. If your initial premise for owning the stock was and still is correct, you will add to a successful position at a favorable price. Volatility increases the requirement that you hone your management skills to a razor sharp edge. If you do, it can incrementally add to your performance over time.

FWIW # 115 .... *Time Lines*

One investment management aspect not often discussed is the **time line**. With market volatility and a casino mentality, numerous unusual opportunities are offered by the market on a regular basis, but not all at once. As a financial advisor, your function is to grow your clients' portfolios. In the past, a new assignment would include a massive liquidation and reinvestment in a short period. The infusion of capital at one time made sense because the price volatility in the stock market was not significant and it was appropriate to get into the market to capture all of the returns available. Today's high octane market is different. Blue chip stocks can move 5% to10% per day while smaller more speculative stocks in the spotlight can move 10% to 20% per day. There is no reason for massive capital infusions if the portfolio management requires investments over several macro-economic sectors.

Any security you place in a portfolio has a time horizon for meeting your objectives. You should consciously seek out some companies that will meet their price objectives in 1.5, 2, or 3 years (see FWIW # 130). One effective use of the time line is to plan to be fully invested in six to nine months unless unusual circumstances and market or sector volatility dictate a faster allocation of capital. Adhering to this plan will result in the last investment units being invested when a few initial positions with 1.5 year time horizons are starting the momentum towards their price objective. Your clients will then be able to see the portfolio management process in action and be more confident in what you are doing. The all-at-one-time approach erodes confidence in your abilities if the stock market has a sharp sell off within a few weeks of the commitment of capital.

While you might plan a six-month or even nine-month time horizon for committing capital, significant downward price action of some or all of your potential investments will hasten the process. After all, the objective is to buy low. If the stocks you want to place in the portfolio decline significantly in a short period, there is no reason you shouldn't seize the moment and invest in the companies.

Individual stocks experiencing sharp share price downdrafts are a regular occurrence today. It is dangerous buying a company with an extended price pattern. A mutual fund or pension fund wanting to take a profit can drive a share price back down to the year's low.

Prior to 1987, orderly markets were important; today they're not. Even shares considered to be market leaders experience selling pressure dips from time to time. There is an old saying in Iowa that if you don't like the weather wait fifteen minutes and it will change. The stock market is much like Iowa weather; so are stock prices. Understand what you want to buy, what price you want to pay, and then be patient. Over a six-month to nine-month period, you will usually invest at your price.

FWIW # 116 .... *Bear Times*

A bull or a sideway moving stock market can be difficult for sticking with the discipline of a time line. A bear market is just the opposite. You and your clients use short term memory in setting a stock's target price. There is a flaw in this process. When a bull market gives way to a bear market, it rarely does so with prior notice to investors, it just happens gradually. The bull market thinking does not change. So, when a market leading stock experiences a decline of 15%, most investors, still on bull market time, sense an opportunity and seize the former high flyer before it resumes the climb to great wealth for its shareholders. The problem is, however, the former market leader does not go to new highs. The shares might rally some and then fall to a new low for the period. The results are a portfolio entering a bear market with the fallen angels of the prior bull market bought at high prices.

Using a time line helps minimize the assets bought with a bull market perspective in a bear market environment. Using a time line helps you recognize a shift in the market's overall direction. Waiting for opportunities and realizing they are becoming more plentiful is a good indication of a change in market direction.

FWIW # 117 .... *Cash Flow*

Cash is not a dirty four-letter word. Dividends and interest in a portfolio are important components to successful long- term investing even though their presence reduces the short-term growth rate. Let's examine the issue of portfolio cash flow.

A portfolio is a business. Just like any other business, unless there is cash flow from some source, the portfolio will be forced to sell one asset for another as opportunities or withdrawal demands emerge. The decision to switch from a current portfolio holding to a new opportunity doubles the potential for making a bad decision (one sell and one buy instead of just one buy decision) and will usually come at a time when the current holdings have not met their investment objectives or tax consequences of selling are not attractive. On the other hand, a steady stream of cash flow, as well as stable-asset-value securities used to generate the cash, will allow you to not disturb the portfolio's growth component until it is appropriate.

Assets that generate high cash flow usually have stable asset values. Bonds, preferred stocks, REIT's, and utility stocks are examples of the securities providing investors above average cash flow on a regular basis. These securities can move in price, particularly the REIT's, when interest rates change, however, the change in share price is not significant and will reverse as interest rates move back to the level they were when you invested in the income security. There won't be any serious declines (unless credit quality changes) and there won't be any giant gains because these securities usually have a maturity date or call provision anchoring the price close to par value or intrinsic value. Sharp swings in market levels do not impact these securities thereby lending more stability to portfolio values during bear markets or just normal market corrections. Your clients will like this feature of stability when market indexes are declining. What they don't like is the slower growth when the indexes are moving sharply higher. Portfolios with mostly growth securities and astute stock selection is important. Portfolio under performance is usually experienced in the short term since utilizing the cash flow correctly overcomes stable-value assets in the longer measured periods.

Think in terms of the time line. The market gives opportunities regularly. Most portfolios can't take advantage of many opportunities because there are not sufficient funds. Your clients with good portfolio cash flow can use that cash flow to seize the opportunities when available. Perhaps a full investment unit will not be possible, but some positions in the special situations can be taken. Depending on where the growth securities are in their development, it's possible it will be appropriate to switch one of the fixed income, stable-value assets for the growth opportunity presented by the market. Selling stable-value assets for growth assets should only be done if all growth securities in the portfolio have not met their objectives, or a short wait will change the tax year thereby allowing a shifting of capital gains into a new tax year. Allowing securities to meet their full potential and minimizing taxes help the portfolios compounded returns over a five-year period in the same way cash flow generates steady and reliable returns each and every year.

If a portfolio generates 4% a year in cash from dividends and interest over a five-year period, a minimum 20% growth is achieved if security prices don't change at all. To double the portfolio in five years, the growth securities will have to appreciate 80% if the 20% gain from cash is achieved. Without the dividends and interest, the security selection will have to average 100% growth, a significantly harder achievement since not every decision works out as expected. There is another more important factor for you to understand. If a portfolio declines by 10%, for instance, from $500,000 to $450,000, it must go up 11.1% to get back to the starting point. If a compounded 14.86% is the objective, recovering from a decline of 10% and achieving the current annual rate of return objective, 14.86%, on the initial $500,000, will require 27.62% to meet the growth required. The cash flow, being steady and consistent, will reduce a portfolio decline of 10% by the amount of the cash flow. Recovery, when it does come, begins at a point closer to the initial value and, therefore, does not take as much to recover. Adding to the recovery speed are all of the new opportunities placed in the portfolio with the cash flow during the market decline.

Special situations are an overlooked advantage of high portfolio cash flow. Most portfolios have investment units ranging between 1% and 4% of the asset value (see FWIW # 129). A portfolio with 2% investment unit size and 4% cash flow can add two new investment units per year. The *company specific risk* for these new investment units can be different and higher from the initial portfolio profile since you are risking an amount of assets capable of being replaced by current cash from dividends and interest within a six or twelve-month period. The overall portfolio growth profile will improve by using the majority of dividends and interest for the growth component with only a minority of the cash flow for adding to the income component itself. Assuming your growth securities do grow, the cash percentage return on the portfolio's market value will decline, so it's important to calculate your cash flow returns using historical cost basis rather than market prices. There still will be a shrinking of the percentage cash return, so every two years, adjustments should be made by using proceeds from securities meeting their growth objectives to invest in securities with above average cash flow.

What is above average cash flow? It depends on the level of interest rates as well as the equity risk premium. The equity risk premium indicates the overall investors' attitude about stocks in relation to bonds. Using the S&P 500 Index dividend return, it's easy to see that if the S&P return is less than the 10-year U.S. Treasury return, the expectation for capital gains is significant and, therefore, investors are not focused on risk, but are focused on potential gains in the future. Conversely, dividend yields greater than the 10-year Treasury yield will imply a significant negative attitude towards future stock appreciation.

When the S&P 500 Index dividend return is less than the 10-year Treasury, and you want to fully utilize the advantages of cash flow and still have the potential for appreciation, set your target cash flow at double the S&P 500 Index yield up to, but not more than, the 10-year U.S. Treasury yield. For instance, if the S&P 500 dividend yield is 1.75% and the 10-year Treasury is 5.5%, set your portfolio cash yield at 3.5% (1.75% x 2 = 3.5%). In a circumstance where the S&P 500 dividend rate is 3% and the 10-year U.S. Treasury rate is 5.5%, you would set your portfolio return at 5.5%, the same level as the 10-year Treasury. When the S&P dividend return is greater than the U.S. Treasury return, use the same rate as the Index and focus on the quality and sustainability of the dividends for the companies you select.

Cash flow is important, even if it is taxable, in keeping a portfolio moving forward in all market environments. Learn the ins and outs of using cash correctly and watch your clients increase their respect and admiration for your expertise.

FWIW # 118 .... *Portfolio Management*
Portfolio management is a dynamic process. It is alive and changes

constantly based upon changes in the client's circumstances and the market's response to business, social, and governmental interaction. The process starts with the client's objectives, constraints, and a strategy to meet those objectives within the constraints, but it doesn't end there. Using the client profile, an idea of what macro-economic groups to include in the portfolio, as well as security quality, emerges. A physician beginning a career with $100,000 has a portfolio much different than a person over age 50 with $100,000 to invest.

Even though you want to use a time line and cash flow to seize special opportunities when they are presented, you want the securities bought to fit with the current assets in the portfolio. To insure all parts of the portfolio complement and supplement each other, you have to plan how the portfolio will eventually look when fully invested. Will it be appropriate for the portfolio to be all technology, telecommunication, and biotechnology stocks? In other words, a higher risk growth portfolio? Should the portfolio mix basic industry stocks with technology and in what quantities for each? Until you know the ultimate goal for the portfolio profile, you can't prioritize the importance of the special opportunities presented by the market. Any group of stocks may do an adequate job over the *very* long term, a carefully and thoughtfully assembled group of companies representing the appropriate sectors of the economy designed to meet the client's objectives, will give your client the opportunity for above average returns.

There is more than one way to make money in the stock market.

Growth portfolio management seeks to maximize the capital appreciation through assembling a collection of growth stocks. The macro-economic sectors represented are few and asset concentration high. This is a high-powered approach with a significant degree of volatility. By definition, the securities are not from dividend-paying companies, but companies that choose to plow available cash flow back into the operations to sustain the high sales and earnings growth rates.

Value investing places in the portfolio common stocks that represent special value in relation to the assets, sales, earnings, and business franchise of the company issuing the securities. There are many yardsticks used by value investors, some of which are rigid and not focused on the business as a going concern.

Contrarian portfolio management seeks to find those companies that are completely out of favor with investors using the premise investors' opinion changes over time. There is a great deal of validity to this concept of changing opinions, however, most contrarian investing does not take into consideration the intrinsic value of the underlying company, just the fact it is out of favor in the marketplace.

Balanced investing uses one or more of the equity portfolio management styles for some of the assets and fixed income investing for the remainder of the portfolio assets. A balance between these two opposite asset classes is matched with the investor's objectives and constraints for growing the portfolio.

Fixed income portfolio management concentrates only on securities designed to generate cash flow with only secondary regard for capital gains. This management style is characterized by steady cash flow and relatively stable asset values.

Pendulum Investing™ is a portfolio management strategy developed by Marshwinds Advisory Company. It has characteristics and principles which allow a portfolio to participate in all market environments, no matter which traditional portfolio management technique is in vogue. It seeks to identify the factors influencing current share price in relation to a company's intrinsic value.

Portfolio management is necessary to bring some semblance of steadiness to a portfolio's growth. Without it, the possibilities and probabilities of losses increase and the risk of major losses increases significantly. As a professional financial advisor, it's important for your career and your clients' portfolios that you determine the portfolio management style you are intuitively comfortable with and learn how to apply it to your business.

FWIW # 119 .... *Pendulum Investing™*

Pendulum Investing™ integrates fundamental analysis of economic, political, and business conditions with the investment markets' perception of these areas of endeavors. Analysts understand fundamental analysis of these areas because the research work deals with statistics. GDP growth, money supply growth, taxation, electoral districts, registered voters, political parties, corporate sales, corporate profits, inventory levels, and interest rates are easily calculable by any analyst with pencil and paper, much less a high-speed computer or access to the Internet.

In some cases, such as economic data, the analyst is looking for stability and direction of the particular statistics. For instance, is GDP growing and at what rate? Is that rate accelerating or slowing? How about the money supply and its velocity? There are a number of economic factors and measurements important to the direction and health of the investment markets, the litany of them can be found every day on broadcast business shows. Whether the indicator has any real meaning or not is important to you in regards to how the investment markets act or react at the time the information is released. Many of the touted measurements of economic data are not as important as the market believes they are when taken in context of a three to five-year period.

Political factors are important when time series for the data is longer term. There are cycles to politics and much overlapping of the cycles as the generations of the population age and power is shifted from one group to another. Human beings' tendency to use recent memory for decision-making makes it important to try to gauge the actual position in the political cycle from the perceived position. The human trait of trying to typecast or label political parties and politicians leads to differences between the actual situation and the perceived situation. Look at the 1992 victory of the liberal Democrat Bill Clinton over the conservative Republican George Bush. Economically, Bill Clinton turned out to be more conservative than George Bush; yet, many investors using their label mentality exited the investment markets at just the time the markets were beginning a record bull rune. Politics have always mattered in dealing with investment markets and today it is more critical than ever.

Specific business fundamental analysis is the measurement of activity, profitability of activity, change in direction of activity, and potential for activity to become more or less vulnerable due to outside macro-economic factors or micro-economic company specific events. There are a number of different ratios and analytical tools available to investors that will slice and dice a company and its performance into separate analytical functions.

Pendulum Investing™ has its base in fundamental analysis where a subjective determination is made of *intrinsic value.* Intrinsic value is subjective because a certain amount of interpretation is necessary to make the past and present statistical data meaningful for a projection of the future. It's clear a company growing at 40% a year will not be able to sustain that growth rate, otherwise, they will take over the world. Decisions have to be made to arrive at a sustainable growth rate. Nevertheless, an intrinsic value is determined. In effect, this value becomes the center pole and mid-point on a pendulum's arc. It represents what the company is believed to be worth.

The investment markets are not unemotional. Anyone who says they make investment decisions unemotionally is either not telling the truth, doesn't have any assets in the markets, or doesn't know their own self. Every human emotion can be found in the investment markets every day. Love, hate, and desire are all there in some amount. As a whole, these emotions tend to cancel each other out leaving just two: FEAR and GREED. These two emotions form the crossbar of the pendulum with FEAR on the left and GREED on the right.

The pendulum itself, in constant motion and moving from left to right or right to left, is the collective markets' attitude about the fundamental data that is available at any given moment. At all times, the pendulum is influenced by investors exhibiting FEAR and GREED characteristics. Since individual investors have different tolerances for these emotions and are influenced by them in different degrees and at different times, the level of FEAR and GREED is always shifting. Even at extremes, there is a certain measurement of each emotion to be found in every security.

The function of Pendulum Investing™ is to measure the FEAR and GREED to see where the pendulum is in relation to the intrinsic value of the particular security. Only by understanding the difference between market perception and reality can a financial advisor find the investments that give clients the ability to have above average portfolio growth in the long term. A patient investor can wait for just the right investment to come along before committing capital. Pendulum Investing™ gives the disciplined investor the tools to find the right investment.

The investment markets have a short term perspective and Pendulum Investing™ uses a three to five-year perspective thereby giving adherents an opportunity for above average long term returns. There are increasing numbers of investors with a speculative perspective looking at stocks as simply pieces of paper fluctuating at the whims of the market. Speculators do not focus on intrinsic value thus giving Pendulum Investing™ an opportunity for profit.

Where Pendulum Investing™ differs from growth investing is in the basic attitude about the company. Growth investing looks for a company that is already growing and recognized in the marketplace. There is very little FEAR in the share price as just about everybody knows the company is doing well or the Fed is lowering interest rates or a sector of the economy is improving. Pendulum Investing™ is excellent for finding the right point to enter a portfolio position for a growth stock. Every stock, even the best performers, has a period when there is doubt about the future. The doubt can be about the company, the market as a whole, the economic sector, interest rates, or some other situation that increases the FEAR component in a share price of even the best company. It's during these periods Pendulum Investing™ signals an entry point.

Pendulum Investing™ differs from value investing in that Pendulum Investing™ does not determine intrinsic value based solely upon the easily measured statistical data of a company. There are no cut and dried yardsticks to measure against. The management quality and business franchise are just as important as the current ROE or price to book value. A particular situation might be a good value investment, but not right for Pendulum Investing™ because the relationship between GREED and FEAR is in balance even though the price is a good value.

Even though Pendulum Investing™ seeks out those situations where FEAR is dominant in a share price, it differs from contrarian investing in a major way: Pendulum Investing™ can identify an attractive situation in a growth stock as easily as it can in a contrarian investment or even a value investment. Contrarian investing only pays attention to the market's attitude about the company. Pendulum Investing™ adds subjective fundamental factors that can make a difference in FEAR and GREED over a three to five-year period of time.

As with any investment philosophy, Pendulum Investing™ is not perfect. It does not work in every situation. It also has a significant short term time horizon risk. When FEAR is dominant, it's important to attempt to understand how long it has been dominant and at what place FEAR is in the journey to capitulation by investors. Emotional extremes can be significant even if they only last for a short period.

Pendulum Investing™ works and it focuses on what is important in this era of instant information: the interpretation of statistics in regards to the market's perception of those statistics and their meaning. It is an investment philosophy allowing investors the capability of operating in all market environments. Pendulum Investing™, however, is not simple.

FWIW # 120 .... *Pendulums*

The following are some of the pendulums an investor wants to understand as to how FEAR and GREED control the position and direction of the pendulum:

Global Politics	Global Currency
Global Money Supply	Global Interest Rates
Global Taxation	Global Equities
Global Bond Markets	Geo. Regional Politics
Geo. Regional Currency	Geo. Regional Money Supply
Geo. Regional Interest Rates	Geo. Regional Taxation
Geo. Regional Equities	Geo. Regional Bond Markets
U.S. Politics	U.S. Currency
U.S. Money Supply	U.S. Interest Rates
U.S. Taxation	U.S. Bond Markets
U.S. Equity Markets	Macro-Economic Sector
Industry Sector	Value Stocks
Growth Stocks	Large Capitalization Stocks
Mid Capitalization Stocks	Small Capitalization Stocks
Dividends and Interest	Individual Company Pendulums

Thirty different pendulums that influence the movement of each and every security no matter what market or where it is. Powerful moves come when several pendulums align themselves and move from one extreme to another. The weighting of each pendulum is more important the closer the pendulum is to the actual security.

236

However, there are times when any one or two broad pendulums can significantly impact the most obscure stock or bond.

FWIW # 121 .... *Scientific Art*

Have you ever wondered why a stock will drop 20% because its earnings are 2¢ less than the expected amount, or why a stock jumps up 15% when earnings exceed expectations? The answer is market participants are seeking some way to reduce the uncertainty in selecting investments by attempting to reduce the process to a science. It all began with the academic community back in the 1950's.

In an attempt to compare investment returns of various money managers, formal analytical analysis was applied to identifying risks in portfolio management and matching the risks with a client's objectives. Dr. Harry M. Markowitz was the first to put forward the concept of **modern portfolio theory (MPT)** in the 1950's. Markowitz turned the concept of portfolio management from the idea of stock picking to the idea of assembling a portfolio of stocks that accepted the maximum risk profile of the client and gave, in return, the most certain expected returns for the level of risk accepted. A full understanding about Markowitz's work can only come from a textbook. What is important to understand here is the idea effective diversification only comes from a portfolio composed of stocks that fluctuate in response to different factors in different ways. For example, financial stocks might decline due to a threat of inflation, while oil and gas stocks will rise in anticipation of inflation. In other words, Markowitz indicated a portfolio manager can create a portfolio that cancels out the individual security risk while accepting only the minimal market systemic risk for the client's objectives.

Here's the point you have to understand: to operate under MPT, the portfolio manager has to make estimations of the following:

1. Projected expected rates of return including dividends and interest and potential capital gains or losses to be earned in a given period.

2. Estimates of the potential range of returns for each security assuming the first estimate might be wrong (better known as standard deviation).

3. What the effects of each outside influence impacting the portfolio will have on every security in the portfolio.

4. Any constraints placed upon the portfolio manager by the client.

The essence of MPT are judgements made by the analysts and portfolio managers. In most cases, these estimates are based upon past historical data because there is nothing else to use in such computations as standard deviation and the impact of some influencing factor on a particular security. While not impossible because of the high-speed computers available, the profession simplified step three by relating every security to an index, thus developing what is termed *beta* today. The beta is a measurement of the implied volatility relationship of a stock to the S&P 500 Index or some other index. A beta of one implies the same volatility as the market index. A beta less than one implies less volatility than the market, and more than one implies greater volatility.

As a financial advisor, you can grasp the significance of all of these estimates. The majority of factors are based upon the past, looking into the rearview mirror, so to speak. To improve the results, analysts plug into their models their expectations for the future earnings. Trying to use the past to predict the future. Not a bad idea, but one that raises the potential for error even higher because it is predicting events rather than extending a trend line into the future. That is why analysts like to be in the same grouping with other analysts covering the industry. It's why analysts have gone to seeking "guidance" from company management. If analysts are uncomfortable with doing the analysis, why not ask the management for the answers to the test?

How difficult is it to truly forecast earnings? Very, to say the least. Take the average company in any industry. Each company is subjected to three types of factors influencing revenues, cost, and, therefore, profits: (a) industry factors such as competition, suppliers, customers, and economic conditions influencing the industry; (b) external factors such as the general economy, weather, politics and governmental issues, technology changes, Federal Reserve policies and currency exchange rates, particularly in the area of the global economy, and Internet advances; (c) company specific factors such as management continuity, plant and equipment operating efficiencies, union relationships, personnel availability and competitive wage pressures.

These factors listed don't even scratch the surface of the information necessary to make earnings estimates, yet the analysts and portfolio managers using MPT believe the earnings estimate must be to the exact penny they forecast or the entire model is wrong. Does anyone in June of any given year know how severe the winter weather will be thereby causing logistical disruptions to many companies' revenue and cost structure? Earnings estimates are educated guesses and not mathematical certainties making the MPT computations scientific.

William F. Sharpe took Markowitz's work further and developed *capital asset pricing theory (CAPT)* detailing the nature of the market's pricing function when investors are guided by two principals: (1) risk aversion and (2) desire for an optimum portfolio through diversification. Sharp makes six assumptions in setting up his theory (obtain the full theory and assumptions from a textbook) that are not wholly realistic in the investment markets. For this discussion, CAPT is like MPT, it requires assumptions and estimates that are not hard facts, but educated guesses susceptible to all the risks of being wrong. For example, CAPT assumes investors are risk adverse, but substantial money in the markets is operated by professional investors seeking out and creating risk. Think of the hedge fund community and mutual funds that only invest in one or two industries, or major investors accepting significant leverage risk, asset concentration risk, or company specific risk. There would never have been the technology mania of the 1998-2000 period if the basic CAPT assumptions were correct, nor would there have been any mania if it were true. If all investors are not risk adverse, then what does that do to the functioning of the investment markets and how it relates to the CAPT?

Should MPT and CAPT be ignored? No. As a financial advisor, you have to understand the way these theories operate in the real market because so many participants use them. They are part of the market dynamics. You can actually use the market's reliance on these theories to your advantage.

As a portfolio manager or financial advisor, it's important for you to understand MPT and CAPT reliance on diversification and the true definition of diversification. Having assets in six different industries that are all in one macro-economic sector is not diversification. Neither is owning ten global stocks if they are all in the telecommunications and technology area. Having true diversification is not easy in a market lead by just one or two industries or sectors. Therein lies the art of the process. You have to take the scientific tools realizing they are not as scientific as touted and use them to create a portfolio designed to give as steady and consistent growth as possible, meaning relatively diversified, within the tolerance of your client's willingness to accept stable growth over volatile growth. Now that takes an artist!

In this age of instant information about economic and company statistics, share prices adjust within minutes of company announcements. If the market expects good news and gets bad news, 10-20% can be taken off the price of a stock within minutes. Whenever you are determining the levels of FEAR and GREED influencing the current share prices, there are three primary questions you must ask in the analysis:

1. *What can change?* Make a list of the factors in the analysis that could be different within a probability range. How old are the CEO and other key managers? How susceptible is the company to competitors or customers using the Internet to change the competitive dynamics of the industry? How susceptible is the company to logistical issues in both supplies and selling products to customers if there is a major weather change? Remember the Taiwan earthquake and what it did to semiconductor supplies? You can't plan for a catastrophe but you can gauge its impact on a company or industry.

2. *What are catalysts for the change?* Will currency factors cause a competitive advantage or disadvantage for a company? How about retirement age of a dynamic CEO as faced by GE in 2001? By thinking about the potential catalysts, you can do a much better job of applying probability weighting to each scenario.

3. *When will the change occur if the catalyst happens?* Some events happen quickly. A CEO retires and the new CEO wants to make a mark as soon as possible. Often, major write-offs take place within months. Some major industry and company structure shifts happen gradually. The consolidation in the paper industry started in 1998 and is slowly concentrating the industry in fewer and fewer

companies spread around the world. Eventually, the paper industry will achieve significant pricing power although it could take years.

Answering these three questions correctly will lead to above average returns in a three to five-year period of time. Understanding that every stock will not present a chance for change is part of the process. The stock market gives investors who ask these questions plenty of time to act or react since the pendulum for extreme cases of FEAR and GREED do not shift quickly. There are many times it's clear a change is coming, but the market's attitude about a company or industry does not adjust quickly. These are situations where serious, long term, above average returns are likely.

Answering these three questions correctly leads to above average returns using MPT and CAPT as well. Here's why. Remember beta? Beta is the measurement of a stock's volatility in relation to the market's volatility as measured by some index, generally the S&P 500 Index. The concept is to have a portfolio beta less than 1, the market's volatility profile, and returns better than the market's returns. Beta measures the past. You're interested in the future. A low beta stock with evolving fundamental changes that will increase earnings has a high probability of outperforming the market. So you see, using Pendulum Investing™ can work in a market dominated by both short term speculation and MPT/CAPT.

FWIW # 123 .... *Seeing Double*

Your clients don't understand the ramification of what it takes to accomplish certain portfolio growth objectives. For instance, by late 1999, if you inquired about a new client's rate of return expectations after five years of 20%+ growth in the market, they would say 20% is a minimum expectation. Your client had forgotten about the first half of the decade, 1990 through 1994, when the stock market had one good year and four mediocre or poor years.

To assist them in coming to terms with what they want and to assist you in interpreting their desires, it's advantageous to help them picture the length of time it will take to double their money. For instance, the following is a way to begin moving the client into a thought process for understanding portfolio growth:

"Mr(s). (name), you currently have $_____ in your portfolio. You have indicated you want the portfolio to grow. If in six years, the portfolio value is $_____ (double the current value), will you find that an acceptable goal?"

Most investors have not thought about the amount of money associated with achieving a double of the portfolio. They are usually taken aback by this concept and are amazed by the potential to double their money. You, on the other hand, have assisted the client to focus on a rate of return close to, but above, the long term stock market trend of 11% compounded. A double in six years has a compounded 12.25% rate of return.

An aggressive client may want to double the portfolio in three, four, or five years. Well, that's their choice. What you can now do is to assist them in understanding what they think they want. Doubling the portfolio in these time periods requires the following rates of return:

Three Years 25.99%

Four Years 18.92%

Five Years 14.86%

If the stock market averages over the long term, fifty years, an 11% compounded return, the implied risk for achieving 14.86%, 18.92%, or 25.99% is substantial. You can discuss with your client the major risks (FWIW # 108) and which ones their portfolio will accept. Will it be leverage? Will it be credit risk? How about very high asset concentration risk? Usually, walking through the risks it takes to achieve the target return will help the client understand that prudent investment management uses compounding of reasonable rates of return instead of high risk to speed up the returns. How many clients do you know who will be unhappy with having four times their current portfolio value in twelve years? That's right, four times. Well, a compounded 12.25% annually for twelve years takes a portfolio of $100,000 to $400,162.32. You can achieve that kind of return using portfolio management techniques discussed in this book and using good quality companies' shares. You need both portfolio management and good quality securities because there will definitely be periods of time in the ten years when stocks are in a bear market. Above average, long term portfolio growth is enhanced considerably by using portfolio management techniques during these difficult periods.

Substituting the effects of compounding for speculative risk not only makes some sense from a fiduciary viewpoint, it also improves the probability of success. Take a calculator and play with the numbers. It will amaze you and raise your awareness of the value of compounding.

FWIW # 124 .... *Single Focus*

As a financial advisor, your ***single focus is to grow your client's portfolios within their risk tolerance and constraints.*** Notice, your focus is not just to grow their portfolios. Your focus is to grow the portfolios within their risk tolerance and constraints. There is a world of importance and meaning in adding the risk tolerance and constraints to the above sentence.

FWIW # 125 .... *Consistency*

Understanding who you are (FWIW # 10) is critical in building a financial advisory business. It is just as important in being successful at managing portfolios. There are several different investment philosophies such as growth investing, value investing, small cap investing, and Pendulum Investing™, and infinite variations of each. You have to choose the one that works for you and you are intellectually comfortable with. Learn it. Read about it. Understand how the style works with technical analysis. Understand how to use the style in conjunction with portfolio management techniques. In other words, immerse yourself in the nooks and crannies of the investment style. Then, don't be surprised when it doesn't seem to work. There are times when every investment management style does not work. The financial advisor cannot do anything right. This situation is the normal pendulum of the market moving from one investment style to another as the first becomes so popular most investors rush in to use it and the guiding principles responsible for the investment style's above average returns no longer work.

What appear to be long periods when growth investing, or value investing, or contrarian investing are out of favor generally will cause an advocate of the style to doubt the wisdom of staying with the same philosophy. The temptation is to abandon the known for the new. It is a mistake. Properly used portfolio management techniques will keep the portfolio growing at some pace during out of favor periods in the markets. Using the experience and skills developed and honed over time will help you find the absolute best companies at terrific prices because the market is focused elsewhere. Eventually, the market's momentum will shift and your investment style will come back into favor. The excellent investments you found when they were out of favor will be the engines of above average growth going forward.

FWIW # 126 .... *Taxable Versus Tax-Deferred*

Your bull's-eye is to grow your client's portfolio within their risk tolerance and constraints. Where they have their assets in regard to taxable or tax-deferred accounts makes a difference and can add an incremental return to your performance numbers.

When all of the assets are in taxable accounts, there is the penalty of paying taxes yearly on the current income from dividends and interest as well as the capital gains resulting from any sell transactions. These taxes reduce the returns even if the taxes are paid from other monies. Municipal bonds may be used for fixed income assets and cash reserves, however, if you target a significant cash flow from equities, the tax will cut the return. The compounding effect in the portfolio is reduced by these taxes.

Portfolios that are tax-deferred do not have the problem of yearly taxation. In exchange, when the assets are withdrawn, ordinary income taxes are paid on everything withdrawn, even gains from selling assets. No wonder the government lets the profits accumulate. They take up to 39.6% of the total. If you die before withdrawal, the tax gets even more complex.

The ideal situation is when a client has assets in both taxable and tax-deferred accounts. You manage two portfolios as one and place the assets in the appropriate account to minimize both current and long term taxes. This is the opposite of what many advisors do. For example, suppose you buy a stock for $30 that over the long term will probably rise to $300. Where do you put it? In the taxable account or the tax deferred? What about a cyclical stock that pays a reasonable dividend and has the potential of doubling in the next two years? Where do you put that? What about a 20-year bond at an above average yield that is non-callable? The bond is a corporate bond, but has an equivalent municipal bond with an after tax yield that is almost as much, but has a maturity date half as long. Where would you put the two bonds? Which fixed income security would you select?

First, the stocks. The growth stock goes in the taxable account. It doesn't pay a dividend so current taxes are not increased. The potential payoff is huge so you want to make sure the gains are taxed as low as possible at the capital gains rate. You might not sell that stock until after you have died and have a step up in basis. For sure, it is unlikely you will sell that stock anytime in the foreseeable future. The cyclical stock pays a good dividend and will likely be sold in two to three years. Consequently, you want to place that stock in the tax-deferred portfolio. Current taxes are not paid on the current dividend and taxes on the gains are deferred for years even though they will be higher when finally paid.

The same holds true for the fixed income security. Other than client liquidity requirements, all fixed income investments should go into the tax-deferred account. In the example above, the corporate bond without a call feature and a long term maturity will not just give the overall portfolio good cash flow to assist the compounding effect, but, since it cannot be called, will have good volatility when interest rates decline. With a bond of that nature, there is the potential for

15% to 30% capital appreciation sometime in the twenty-year period. Avoiding a tax and swapping the bond gives additional flexibility to the portfolio so it fits in the tax-deferred account. The shorter municipal bond will not give the additional potential capital appreciation because the maturity is shorter. The muni interest is tax-free so it makes sense to have the bond in a taxable account.

Allocating the assets between the taxable and tax-deferred portfolios is best accomplished by listing all of the securities you want in the overall portfolio in order of the income component for each security with consideration for the client's need for available liquidity. Start with the highest current income security on the list and allocate it to the tax-deferred account. Go down the list until all of the tax-deferred assets are utilized. The remaining securities with the least current income and highest capital appreciation potential will end up in the taxable account. You have effectively limited the current and long term taxes to their lowest amount.

You will also notice the tax-deferred account will be generating the bulk of the annual dividend and interest income for the portfolio. Therefore, the compounding effect will be enhanced in the tax-deferred account. Unless the client adds to the taxable portion from other funds, most future new positions will be added in the tax-deferred portfolio. That's ok. You have to continue to look at the overall portfolio allocation to make sure the proper balance between growth and income assets is maintained. If a growth asset is applicable and monies are not available in the taxable portfolio, put it in the tax-deferred account.

Since the tax profile of each client is unique to them, you will still have the lowest tax profile if you adhere to the principles discussed in this book.

There are literally tens of thousands of stocks in the global marketplace and even more bonds and preferred stocks. All of these securities are in over two hundred different industries in twelve or more different macro-economic groups. You can't follow or understand them all nor do you want to. If your firm has a research department, the selection of securities you use in your clients' portfolios is made for you. Some trust departments and investment counseling firms seek out expert advice from one research firm or another to develop the universe of securities they use.

Limiting the number of securities followed by you or your firm makes good sense. It gives you the opportunity to understand the companies better by being able to dig deeper into the fundamental aspects of the operating business as well as all of the technical analysis factors of the stock. The question is this: How do you create a universe so you will participate in all market environments? The key concept is that you must be able to have some stocks performing all of the time. If you work for a firm with a research department, they will have selected the universe of companies and should have analysts following a diverse group of industries. That makes your job a lot easier because you only have to learn how to use the research generated (FWIW # 141).

If you don't have access to a research department at your firm, you have to develop your own universe. Start by deciding how many companies you feel is appropriate for you to follow based upon the clientele you have. If your clients are aggressive, high income professionals, you might only have fifty companies in your universe. If you have a number of clients where diversification is an important portfolio management technique, you may have one hundred stocks. The concept is to have an adequate number for your clients' portfolio size and temperament.

Start your search by looking at the macro-economic sectors of the global economy. Depending on who is drawing up the list, there are approximately twelve macro-economic sectors for investors (FWIW # 151). Some sectors will not be right for your investment style. Value investors do not have an easy time investing in pure technology or small non-profitable companies. Growth investors don't have much use for most Basic Industry companies. Narrow the list of sectors if you feel it is appropriate but always have at least seven in your universe. Look next at how you view the world's economy from the standpoint of growth and importance. For instance, the global economy will continue to grow and, therefore, various forms of transportation are important to the smooth flow of commerce even though these companies are cyclical in nature. Their heavy dependence on capital, labor and energy stymie earnings growth. In the same fashion, technology and telecommunication are rapidly expanding industries in the Capital Goods-Tech sector that must be represented in your universe of companies. Review the sectors you want represented and allocate the number of securities in your universe to each sector. If you have one hundred companies, perhaps your allocation will be five to Basic Industries, three to Transportation, ten to Consumer Growth Staples, and on down the line. This is not rocket science and there is no clear right or wrong way to allocate other than the discipline of having at least seven sectors represented in your universe. Remember, the universe is for your use and not for others. Think of your clients and think of your own temperament as to what you are comfortable owning in your client's portfolios.

Now analyze the industries within the sectors and select the ones with the best consistent economic performance over the long term. Pay attention to any recent meaning two or three years, events that may alter the longer trend, but go with the leaders in each industry within a macro-economic sector. For instance, is there better steady but cyclical growth in the use of paper than there is in the use of precious metals? How about chemicals rather than metals in general?

The process ends as you select the companies within each industry represented in your universe. The overriding feeling you will have as you go through this process is of having to leave some good companies out of the top one hundred names. That's a good feeling because it will focus your efforts on comparing and finding the very best companies represented in the world economy.

A final word about your universe. It is not static. At any given moment you might find a company that needs to be in the universe. That's fine. Put it in while taking out one firm from the same industry grouping and sector. Don't remove a Basic Industries stock to add a Financial company. Remove a financial company to add a better one. The discipline of this approach will assist in assuring your universe of companies is the best that you can find.

FWIW # 128 .... *Merchandising*

Whether you realize it or not, you are an entrepreneur, a retailer and, like all successful retailers, it is important for you to have an attractive mix of business from three perspectives.

You should deliberately develop a clientele with different objectives. Different investment objectives and constraints leading to different investment policies and strategies which, in turn, lead to different portfolio composition. Sector rotation or market shifts will impact some of your clients while helping others when you have a diverse clientele.

Diverse client requirements are important, but a diverse mix of investments is critical for the success of your business. Rotation is the nature of the investment business and most participants only focus on what is working now. Inevitably, the market leaders become overbought, stop going up, and begin to decline. Market participants fail to realize this price action is a topping process and continue to buy last year's leaders as next year's leaders quietly begin their movement from oblivion to stardom. The shift is disguised by several rallies and back and forth trading so it is easier to discuss the evolution than it is to recognize it while it's happening.

Your first indication of market rotations can be seen by your constant review and observation of your own universe of companies. If your universe is constructed to reflect a diverse marketplace, you will recognize the rotation beginning. One way to dramatically enhance this awareness is to have software or an Internet site that allows up to one hundred security symbols to be displayed on one screen and indicates up or down price movement either by color or with + and - signs. Take time to group your universe by economic sectors with one extreme on one side of the screen and its opposite on the other side. During the day, you will begin to see shifts in the market flow of funds from one sector or industry to another. Over time, you will see if the shift is long term or temporary.

Merchandising your portfolios is the most important function you do and is the process of matching the quality and characteristics of the companies in the universe with your clients' profiles. Just as important is to deliberately have companies that are out of favor and of various market capitalization size in the portfolio. Companies with high and low betas can be mixed to match the market volatility factor that is appropriate. Fixed income and growth assets combined will give the client a target income stream without hurting the flexibility, liquidity, or long term growth of the portfolio.

Thinking about portfolio construction as a merchandising activity helps in having discipline to place a measured amount of out of favor investments in the portfolio. It only takes one rotation and watching the portfolio respond with spurts of growth for you and your clients to understand the unique value of merchandising properly.

FWIW # 129 .... *Investment Units*

Ever see a situation where a new client has had dismal performance yet has owned some fine stocks? In all likelihood it's because the performing stocks were smaller portions of the portfolio than the non-performers. For instance, a portfolio might have $10,000 in a performing growth stock and $50,000 in a utility stock. The growth stock doubles and the utility stock goes nowhere and the client is frustrated.

Good portfolio development comes in selecting the amount of assets to be placed in each security selection. The amount is totally a function of the client and the client's objectives and constraints. The focus is on how many securities are to be in a portfolio. Perhaps the client is a high-income professional between the ages of 30 and 40 with a temperament that requires aggressive growth. Only five to eight stocks may be appropriate. If so, take the portfolio size and divide by the number of positions. A million-dollar portfolio with five securities will initially have $200,000 in each security.

At the other end of the spectrum may be a tax-deferred client who wants to minimize company specific risk and asset concentration risk, so the portfolio will have forty investment units. In this case, a million-dollar portfolio will have $25,000 in each unit.

By giving equal weight to each of the securities, you are allowing the dynamics of the portfolio selections to contribute to the growth. Over time, the stocks currently moving will change the relationship of each investment unit to the others since the growing stocks have become larger by market action. You then have a decision about re-balancing the portfolio.

There are only two times you should consider diverting from the strict construction of investment units. First, there are some small capitalization, highly volatile and emerging companies in industries where more than one stock is appropriate, yet two or more investment units in the industry is not prudent for the client. In this case, it is acceptable to use half unit sizes for each company thereby allowing the proper dollar allocation to the industry but using two companies instead of one. This recognition of the heightened company specific risk allows the portfolio to participate in a high risk sector without undue exposure.

The second exception to a strict investment unit construction comes in the depth of a bear market where there are unusually large numbers of obvious values. Overdiversification is not an issue because when the time comes all stocks will move higher by a significant amount. In other words, diversification is not a penalty against performance, it is neutral. In these cases, determine the appropriate number of investment units and then double the number so each position is a half unit size. Don't increase the macro-economic sectors, just the opportunity for individual security selection within the appropriate industries.

FWIW # 130 .... *Time Horizon*

Everyone wants their stocks to go up the day after they buy the shares. We all know that, but reality dictates differently. Stocks move up and down for essentially four reasons. Let's examine them.

First, there are times when the overall economy changes and the general investing public's attitude changes from FEAR to GREED or the opposite. This scenario sets up major adjustments in the overall marketplace commonly referred to as the rising of tide or falling tide when all stocks go up or down. By its nature, this phenomenon doesn't happen often.

The second influence on stock prices is the special event or unusual arbitrage activity that is usually driven by speculators who are jumping in and out based upon short-lived information or events. A merger rumor, a dividend arbitrage, or expiring options may cause the price change. By its nature, the event is short term and random. This type of volatility has increased with the advent of Internet chat rooms and no control over who says what about a company.

Fundamental change in the company's operations is the third influence on share prices. It is also the longest lasting and most powerful. As the changes evolve and market participants factor the changes into their valuation models, the share prices begin to move and momentum builds over a long time.

A combination of each of these three factors is the fourth influence on share prices and gives the strongest share price movement over a three to five year period of time. It's safe to say that only the fundamental changes in company operations will lead to sustained share price movement with the potential for five to ten times the original stock price. Fundamental operating changes don't happen overnight. It takes time to make the management changes and implement them. How much time depends on the industry and complexity of the business. Some technology companies can shift the focus in eighteen months. Some capital and labor intensive businesses can't do it in less than three years. Understanding where a company is in the process is important for portfolio management. As part of your portfolio merchandising, you should deliberately seek out companies that you expect will complete their fundamental operation shifts in eighteen months, twenty-four months, or thirty-six months. Naturally, some will surprise you and take longer or shorter time periods. Usually, the market anticipates the change so the stock price will begin to respond in less time than it takes to actually put the steps in place.

No one knows what the stock market or an individual stock will do in six months. There are too many random factors that can influence the short term. Over a 1.5 to 3-year period, the fundamental factors of sales and earnings growth will dominate share prices. That's why it is easier to identify a company likely to have a strong share price change over three years than it is to identify one likely to experience a fundamental business change in eighteen months. The longer the time horizon the easier it is to have the company shares meet your expectations.

A new time horizon is being introduced into the picture. Unless repealed, special capital gains tax considerations will be given to investments held for five years or longer if they were bought after January 1, 2001. While this incentive for long term investing has nothing to do with the operations of a company, it will influence the allocation of speculative capital between growth and value companies. Value investing has always been less risky than growth investing with growth having a greater after-tax payoff. If the tax rate is reduced, those speculators who can obtain control of a company and turn it around and reap the benefits with lower risk will move into these major restructuring situations.

FWIW # 131 ....*Bucket Brigade*

Ever wonder how the Rothschilds, the Duponts, the Rockefellers, and other legendary wealthy families keep having more money generation after generation? It's partly by being smart investors. It's also by being careful investors who understand that a major part of long term wealth accumulation is having liquidity when no one else does. Long term success comes from understanding that every asset class cycles in and out of favor over time. In other words, wealthy families make sure they keep the four asset class buckets full at all times.

As a financial advisor, you have to assist your client in understanding the importance of having some assets in (a) cash reserves, (b) fixed income securities, (c) equities, and (d) real estate. Think of each one of these categories as a bucket that can't ever overflow but can hold more than the other buckets at any given time. In theory, a family, or a client in your case, places a measured amount of resources in each of the four buckets. Perhaps 10% in cash reserves, 15% in fixed income, 40% in equities, and 35% in real estate. A year later, the four buckets have generated 5% in cash income from dividends and interest plus the equities and real estate have appreciated. The cash income is reallocated to the bucket needing more resources depending upon the family's current financial circumstances. The balance between the equities and real estate is examined and adjusted according to the relative risk and reward between the two classes. No matter what asset class is strongest and returning the most profit, all four buckets are kept full to the appropriate level.

Immediately, a novice investor never having spent time through a serious investment bear market believes it is unnecessary to keep cash reserves or fixed income investments. Plow it all into equities or real estate is the attitude. When the inevitable downturn comes or, even more common, when an outside emergency requires quick funds, these investors are left illiquid and in danger of having serious capital erosion. More importantly, these investors don't have the ability to follow the most important investment rule: buy when there is blood in the streets. Above average unusual long term family wealth creation takes place during recessions or periods of social upheaval. The real estate and equities owned by the family during these periods will not be immune to the forces on the market and consequently will not be sources of liquidity to take advantage of bargain prices in other equities or real estate. Only cash reserve or fixed income assets and the portfolio cash flow will insure the client or family adds to wealth at times of bargain prices.

Let's examine each of the buckets:

CASH RESERVES - These assets are money market funds, bonds, CD's, and fixed income securities with maturities or call dates of twelve months or less.

FIXED INCOME SECURITIES - These are bonds and preferred stocks with maturities or call dates of thirteen months or longer. Credit quality can be a mix of ratings, but 90% or more should be investment grade. An emphasis should be on having the highest coupon for the selected credit quality at the time the investment is made. A deliberate effort should be made to have a range of maturities or call dates so some securities move into the cash reserve bucket on a regular basis.

EQUITIES - These are ownership assets of all securities other than real estate. It may include public and private stock, partnerships, and commodities.

REAL ESTATE - All forms of real estate including REITs.

FWIW # 132 .... *Relatively Speaking*

Understand first that *risk and reward are linked and cannot be separated*. The degree of potential reward in an asset corresponds with the degree of risk in the same asset. High reward does not come from a low risk asset.

The next point is to understand that all assets have a relatively stable risk relationship between them. In other words, cash assets have the lowest risk potential and therefore the lowest return potential. Fixed income assets have a higher degree of risk than cash assets if for no other reason than the time horizon and inflation risk, so they have a higher return than the cash assets. Equity investments have a less certain reward potential and therefore a higher risk profile than fixed income assets so the potential reward must be greater than the fixed income assets to attract capital. Finally, real estate is less liquid than equity assets and requires leverage to make a good return so the risk potential is higher and the potential reward must compensate successful investors for that greater risk. This relationship between the asset classes is intuitive and can readily be understood. It's important for you as a financial advisor to constantly check these risk/reward relationships so you can be aware of any change in the relationship which indicates an abnormality in the marketplace.

When there is an out-of-kilter, apparent risk/reward shift, be careful. The asset class relationships can be stretched like a rubber band but they can't be broken and will eventually snap back into place rewarding prudent investors and causing pain to imprudent ones. Just as an inverted yield curve (see FWIW # 135) signals an imbalance in the supply and demand for credit over time, when real estate offers a lower visible potential return than equities, it behooves the financial advisor to find out why. The reasons for a relationship imbalance are many so they can't be easily quantified. It's important to just know the relationship is fixed and when not normal the situation is forecasting a major shift in money flows.

FWIW # 133 .... *T+1=Gold*

Trade date + 1 (T+1) is the settlement time for all security trades after mid-2002. T+1 will speed up the process of having all securities held by brokerage custodians. It will help you in assisting your clients to think in terms of portfolio management rather than individual transactions. By understanding the nature and complexity of asset allocation and communicating the knowledge to your prospective clients when examining their brokerage statement, you will enhance your professionalism.

Bonds have been the stepchild of business for most financial advisors. Traditionally, they are bought and held to maturity. A series of maturities makes sense for a number of investors so the buy and hold strategy fits with a growth component in equities. Times, however, have changed and so has the attractiveness of bond portfolio management.

Volatile interest rates make for volatile bond prices. Volatile bond prices create opportunities for swapping bonds. Bond transactions are usually handled on a net basis meaning there is no visible commission and the yield quoted to the client is competitive in the marketplace. Financial advisors working for brokerage firms have found that bond business has turned out to be more lucrative than stock business. A client buying $50,000 of a stock might pay $8 to $30 in commission. The same size trade in the bond market can put between $500 and $1,000 or more in the financial advisor's revenue account.

Fee based financial advisors usually have a lower percentage fee for bond portfolio management than they do for equity portfolio management. At the same time, bond portfolios are generally larger than equity portfolios, and the clientele more stable and likely to be clients for a long period. The diversity of fixed income clients is extensive. Some clients will be right for the municipal bond market, others are appropriate for U.S. Treasuries or agencies. By far, the majority are corporate bond buyers. Each of these markets have their own quirks and unique trading patterns.

Call provisions have become quite sophisticated and impact the way a bond trades. Knowing how to mix call provisions, maturities, coupon levels, and credit quality allow the professional financial advisor to bring real value to a bond portfolio.

Traditionally, income has been the bond investor's goal. With the current volatility and a professional financial advisor, a bond investor can seek out income and some small measure of capital gains. Aggressive bond management exhibited by moving up and down the maturity spectrum, switching coupons, and seeking marginal gains between credit quality or type of bonds, as well as using options and futures, allows financial advisors to guide clients toward liquidity and flexibility as well as steady and above average levels of growth through interest and some capital gains.

Marketing to bond investors is similar to the process of seeking equity investors. More emphasis, however, is placed upon liquidity, flexibility, and incremental returns from the portfolio. Fixed income portfolio management is a sound way for financial advisors, either fee based or commission based, to bring real value to their clients.

FWIW # 135 .... *Fixed Income Investing*

Understanding fixed income investing requires many hours of study as well as years of experience working in and observing the markets. While the scope of the subject is broad, there are characteristics of bonds, and to some degree preferred stocks, that give the market its ability to be managed for specific results. Let's examine some of these characteristics:

1. <u>Bond Type</u> - There are a number of different bond markets including but not limited to: (a) U.S. Treasury securities, (b) government agency securities, (c) investment grade corporate bonds, (d) municipal bonds, (e) non-investment grade corporate bonds, (f) non-U.S. bonds, (g) zero coupon bonds, both treasuries and corporates, (h) equipment trust certificates, and (i) trust preferred shares based upon debt instruments. All of these securities trade amongst their peers and have an established relationship with the other fixed income type markets.

2. <u>Trading Desk Market</u> - Some bonds are traded on the New York Stock Exchange (NYSE) or American Stock Exchange (ASE), but the vast majority are handled by a trading desk where each trader is a profit center. That means the trader is more interested in profit per trade than finding and passing on a good deal to your client even if you work for the same firm as the trader. Markups on bonds can be high and the best way to avoid them is to only buy bonds when the bonds are part of an initial public offering. As you can imagine, that's not always easy or appropriate when your client has a desire for bonds and there's no IPO available. The next best time to buy bonds is on a Friday when interest rates are rising. Trading desks do not like to hold bonds over a weekend during a period of rising rates. The one time you need to be cautious is when your trading desk, or the broker

you are dealing with, offers you what appears to be an unusual opportunity both in yield and commission credit. *The bond market does not give any extra return for free.* If you cannot find out why this particular bond has an unusual return, you should be cautious.

3. <u>Shifts in the Yield Curve</u> - The yield curve is a plotted line connecting the maturities of the U.S. Treasury securities, or, if appropriate, the maturities of a particular type of bond. While the usual yield curve starts with the lowest interest rate for the shortest maturity and rises in interest rates the longer the maturity, there are influences on the marketplace, notably Federal Reserve monetary policy, that will cause short term interest rates to move above long term interest rates. This condition is called an inverted yield curve. It is an opportunity to take advantage of anticipated future interest rate movement or shorten maturities and bring additional liquidity to a portfolio. More than anything, it means that interest rates are on the move.

4. <u>Debt Issue Size</u> - Some specific bond issues are large and liquid while others are small and hard to trade. Depending on the issuer, the available bonds in the marketplace might cause the price to be more than or less than comparable quality bonds. Slight differences can be taken advantage of depending on the client's special circumstances. For example, a client with a portfolio where buying and holding to maturity is appropriate, will be willing to snap up a bond that trades at a discount because of the issue size.

5. <u>Maturity</u> - For any given interest rate paid by a bond, issues

with a longer maturity will be more volatile than a shorter maturity of the same interest payment. Since interest rates are more volatile today, bond investors have found it attractive to move from one maturity to another in response to changes in prices brought about by shifts of interest rates.

6. <u>Credit Quality</u> - Bond prices and yields are generally quoted relative to the yield on a comparable U.S. Treasury security with the Treasury having the highest quality and therefore lowest yield and the next lower credit quality paying progressively more interest. Bonds can be upgraded and downgraded depending on the fundamental operating environment of the issuing company. Ratings change when mergers take place. It's possible to buy a non-investment grade bond and find the company becomes part of another investment grade company thereby giving your client a good quality bond at an unusually high interest rate. Circumstances can also go the other way when an investment grade company buys another company using debt and the resulting balance sheet and income statement will not support an investment grade rating on the debt. The spread between the various credit qualities is not static. In good economic times, the difference narrows as bond buyers do not fear defaults and seek out the highest cash flow available. When a recession looms, buyers flee low quality debt in favor of top quality bonds to protect against possible defaults. Working the spread is smart and can add a small incremental return when done successfully.

7. <u>Coupon Size</u> - For any given change in interest rates, bonds that

pay a higher fixed amount of interest, called the coupon, will be less volatile than a bond of the same maturity and call feature with a lower amount of fixed interest payments. If interest rates are high and are expected to go lower, a bond with low fixed interest rate payments will move up in price more than the one with high fixed interest payments. If rates are moderate to low and are expected to move higher, a bond with a high fixed interest payment will be more stable in price than a low coupon bond with the same maturity and call provision. It's clear to see that changing coupon levels in a portfolio in response to the interest rate level and its anticipated direction change can add incrementally to the total returns of the portfolio.

8. <u>Call Provision</u> - The predominant call provision is one that allows the issuer to redeem the bond prior to maturity at a set price. The issuer's ability to extinguish the debt before maturity will influence how the bond trades in the marketplace. No one will be interested in paying more than the call price if it is possible they will have to take a loss prior to maturity. Even if all other bonds with similar features are moving up in price, an active call provision will keep a bond close to the call price. There are some bonds that give the bond holder the right to "put" the bond back to the issuer if interest rates rise much above the level when the bond was first sold to investors. While this flexibility for the bond holder is nice, as with all special provisions in favor of the bond holder, it comes at a cost through lower interest payments.

9. <u>Special Provisions</u> - Sometimes bonds have special provisions

such as (a) a sinking fund, (b) special collateral, (c) special financial requirements, or (d) prohibited financing transactions. These are usually obscure and embedded in the debt instrument but cause the bond price to deviate from similar bonds that look the same but don't have the special provisions. It's important to check on these features. For instance, a bond may have a regular call price of 102 but an annual 1% sinking fund provision at par (100). The bond price may be trading in the market at 101.75 which is below the regular call provision but above the special sinking fund redemption price. The risk, however, is that 1% of the bonds will be retired or called at par each year and your client's bonds may be part of the 1%. It's hard to explain how you missed the special sinking fund feature when your client takes the loss.

10. <u>Yield Calculation</u> - There are many ways to calculate a yield. The **yield-to-maturity** was the industry standard for decades until interest rate volatility became so great. It's still used regularly, but is not really meaningful since the calculation assumes all of the interest payments received over the years will be reinvested at an interest rate equal to the initial rate at the time the bonds were bought. With 1.5% and 2% swings in rates annually, this is an incorrect assumption. The **current yield** just takes the annual interest payment and divides it by the price paid for the bond and does not allow any consideration for how the payments are used over the years. When a bond is part of a managed portfolio, the current yield is more appropriate since all of the income from the portfolio is gathered and reinvested in the best

potential investment at the time.

11. <u>Level of Interest Rates</u> - As interest rates move around, bond prices change. There comes a point, however, when the change in bond prices is not as great as the amount of interest to be received. Generally, this level is 12%. At that interest rate, it is clear the bond buyer should seek out the longest maturity with the lowest appropriate credit quality and the lowest fixed interest rate coupon. When interest rates reach 12% or higher in an economy like the U.S., the credit markets will eventually push out marginal borrowers setting up a recession and the eventual decline of interest rates.

There are other factors and dynamics of the fixed income market that you as a financial advisor can use to help your clients extract additional incremental returns from their portfolio. Always remember, however, that unless an unusual change of interest rates is expected, capital gains are greater in the equity markets and the first two functions of fixed income investing are to supply cash flow and give some portfolio price stability. Take the information provided here and use it as a starting point to learn the intricacies of the fixed income markets.

FWIW # 136 .... *Growth Versus Cyclical*

There are only two types of stocks in the stock market. Growth stocks are shares in companies where business generally will produce more sales and earnings each year. This constant growth is attractive to investors because over time they have ownership in a larger and larger economic entity. It's nice to buy a company doing $1 billion in sales and ten years later have a company doing $6 billion in sales and a proportionately higher amount of earnings. Usually the share price will anticipate future growth and assign a higher valuation to growth stocks than to cyclical companies of the same size.

A cyclical company is one where the sales do not grow every year. Industry or general economic dynamics causes customers of the firms to stop or reduce their orders on a regular basis. The only growth experiences for these companies from one cycle trough to another are (a) inflationary pricing, (b) taking market share from competitors, or (c) incremental growth for their products. The stock prices of these companies reflect this inability to grow. Share prices sink as the economy begins to falter and investors anticipate a slowdown in business. Unusual capacity expansions associated with peaks in the business cycle put additional pressure on share prices of every company in the industry. When capacity is at its lowest utilization and there appears to be no hope for profits, share prices begin to creep higher in anticipation of better days to come. The debate about whether or not growth stocks are better than value stocks will never have a clear winner. The fact is most companies are a good investment if the price is right. The challenge is understanding what is the right price. Growth stock higher valuations anticipate continued growth. If the company's operations falter, the share price adjustment can be brutal. Cyclical stock investing is a matter of waiting patiently for the market to anticipate the worst possible time for the company's operations and then buying the stock. When profits are gushing in the door, it is the point to sell the shares no matter how much the analysts say it's different this time.

All growth stocks falter eventually. All cyclical stocks appear to be growth stocks eventually. Having a long enough perspective to see the true character of the industry or the company is crucial to not making a mistake and buying a cyclical stock when it is expensive and missing a golden opportunity to buy a growth stock when it is inexpensive.

FWIW # 137 .... *Fundamental Analysis*

Fundamental analysis is the search for a fairly valued company. Notice the word undervalued was not used. Why? Because most, if not all stocks, are not undervalued in the sense that short term operating problems or industry issues make them worth what the market says they are at that point and time. The difference is in the time perspective. The market has a short term perspective and you, as a financial advisor, might have a longer term perspective. Both the market and you can be right. What you truly want to do is to buy a stream of earnings at a fair price. Quality assets and earnings potential will grow and eventually be recognized. When this happens, the share price goes up because the increased earnings and anticipation of future higher earnings increase the price/earnings ratio. Understanding the operating profile of the company gives you the ability to judge the fairness of the share price.

There are two perspectives from analysts' viewpoints. First is the analysis of the absolute numbers. Is the company a viable business at the moment the financial numbers were compiled? Yes or no, fairly simple. It gets more complex from there. The moment in time could be the precise point just before the company started deteriorating into bankruptcy. It's important to understand the direction of the business. This is accomplished by looking at a series of fundamental data covering at least five years and preferably ten years. You are still looking at just the one company and looking for the pulse of the company to see if it is strong and healthy or beginning to falter.

Understanding the past operatin of a company is only part of the process. The next step is to compare the company to its peers. The company under review may have grown at a 15% rate, but its competitors in the industry might have grown at 20%. The relative position of the company you are analyzing in its industry is important but only if the relative position is not reflected in the share price. Usually, any advantage or disadvantage one company has over its competitors is quickly reflected in the share price through higher or lower price/earnings ratios. By comparing the various financial ratios of the leading companies in an industry, you can begin to understand which ones are favored by the market and which ones are neglected. You can then make a judgment as to which company might be the best investment for your clients.

Investing in the industry leader is usually the best strategy but not always. For example, an industry that has been under severe economic pressure from externl sources will have all companies in deteriorated financial condition. As pricing pressure abates and new revenue flows come into the industry, all of the companies will initially benefit. The industry leader will show earnings improvements, but the weaker, more heavily leveraged survivors will show going from a loss or break-even to substantial earnings improvement. A comparable large movement in share price as the company rises from the nearly dead will follow. The important principle, when faced with this opportunity, is to find the nearly dead, not the dead. Looking at the situation during the past several years of difficulty will show you which firm's management is creative and flexible in meeting the problems of a challenging situation.

You are a financial advisor, not a statistician. There are numerous sources you can go to for obtaining number crunching. The first place to start is with the annual report or 10k document. Companies are required to have at least five years worth of statistics in the document and most companies have ten years. Further analysis of ratios is available through subscription services or online. Supplementing the annual report is best done by seeing if your brokerage firm covers the stock and, if so, asking for the detailed research on the company. You have to be careful with any subscription service, brokerage firm, or online research. Usually, it is a mix of facts and opinion. You want to form your own opinion so extract the facts, analyze them from your perspective, and decide if the company has a fair valuation. Only when the process is finished should you review the other analysts' opinions to see what perspective they have. If there is substantial fear in the share price, you can bet they will differ from your perspectives so you have to be confident in what you see and understand before looking at others' conclusions.

Fundamental analysis includes analyzing the industry dynamics and where the industry development is in relation to the overall economy in the business cycle. From there you progress by examining the business franchise and the management profile of the company. Tenure, age, depth of experience and overall quality of the management is a key component in understanding if the officers are operating with enthusiasm and energy or just taking care of the business until they retire. Observations and non-statistical judgements are backed up with statistical information.

Statistics fall into three broad categories:

1. **Liquidity** - These are the numbers related to current assets, current liabilities, and the flow of working capital. Historically, looking at the current ratio was thoughtto be the only exam necessary, but that is not the case. A company with low inventory turnover can have a huge current ratio and be headed for trouble if inventory is backed up and management is hiding the fact by borrowing intermediate term to pay the accounts payable. The cash and marketable securities component of the current assets ratio is important. Perhaps management is operating with too much working capital. Maybe a

1.5 to 1 current ratio makes more sense in this day of just-in-time inventory management for the industry than a 2.5 to 1. There is no set of ratios as important as the liquidity ratios so work with them and learn to understand what they truly do mean.

2. **Management Quality** - These statistics give the analysts insight into how management takes the revenues available to them and adds to shareholder value.The decomposition of return on equity is important. The gross margin, operating margin, and after-tax margin give a glimpse into management's perspective. The cash flow statement is probably the most telling document because it separates into what the business gives management in the form of operating cash flow, how management spends or invests the operating cash flow, and how management decides to finance the ongoing operations.

3. **Capital Structure** - Decisions about the capital structure and how it influences the building of shareholder equity are reflected in these statistics. Debt as a percentage of total capital, the nature of the debt maturity, off balance sheet financing, and various classes of stock all say something about the way to build shareholder value. Companies in highly cyclical industries have to use debt carefully. An industry mired in a recession and a leading company beginning to borrow money to add capacity can be a clue to a coming boom or a risk to the company's position. You need to know.

Even if you have excellent sources of data for developing your ratios and analytical comparisons, it's critical for you to read the MANAGEMENT DISCUSSION OF OPERATIONS and the footnotes to the financial statements. While mandated changes have made the financial numbers more transparent, there are still insights that can be obtained by these nuggets of information. Lease obligations are clearly defined in the statements but the structure of the lease expiration is detailed in the footnotes. For retail businesses, the information is critical. Pension plan and post retirement benefit plans all have assumptions that indicate a problem or a potential source of future earnings. Footnotes are fun reading for an inquisitive mind.

Your function as a financial advisor is to make judgements about the quality of the business and its valuation in the marketplace. You cannot get bogged down in recreating the wheel when the statistics necessary to make the decisions are already available. You must learn to tailor the statistics and change some of the calculations to suit what you feel is important. Perhaps you have found it insightful to monitor the relationship between annual depreciation and the commitment to new plant and equipment. Adding a few new ratios unique to an industry or to you and your research makes sense. Particularly when you create an electronic spreadsheet and have few pieces of raw data input and automatically have the calculations at your fingertips.

Fundamental data is important to give you a sense of intrinsic value. Statistics are hard numbers and judgements about management, the industry, and the business franchise value are soft numbers. Intrinsic value changes all of the time in response to operating conditions and the ebb and flow of the economy, but it is critical in all types of investing including Pendulum Investing™.

FWIW # 138 .... *Technical Analysis*

Technical analysis is reading the forces of supply and demand for a stock in the marketplace. Some people say it is like voodoo. Voodoo requires participants believe with all of their heart that what is happening is true and real. Technical analysis is similar in that the participants using it must believe in the concepts. The concepts are interesting. First, prices will continue to move in one direction until some unusual event will cause prices to reverse. This is called a trend. Second, looking at past prices and the amount of volume will indicate whether a stock will go up or down. Third, there are mathematical and statistical concepts that support or suppress share prices when prices rise or fall to a designated level. What's interesting about technical analysts is how they believe if a particular share price trading pattern doesn't work out as expected, it's not an error in the analytical theory, but an interpretive mistake.

There are thick books written about technical analysis and its many variations. Point and figure charts, candlestick charts, close only charts, open high low and close charts, stochastics, Fibonacci numbers, money flows, moving averages, and volume are just a few of the many technical tools for projecting stock prices. It's important you understand technical analysis even if you do not totally agree with it because many market participants do.

Pendulum Investing™ defines a relationship between the intrinsic value of a stock and the levels of FEAR and GREED influencing the share prices at any given time. Many of the technical analysis principles and concepts are nt used in Pendulum Investing™ except as a means of testing the FEAR or GREED momentum. For instance, inflection points are sought to find an extreme of FEAR or GREED. If a share price reaches what technicians feel is a support poin, a measurement of FEAR is taken by examining the daily news and the market's reaction to the news as well as the aggressiveness of the analysts covering the company. What happens to volume when the technical support or resistance point is reached? Are market participants focusing on the stock or are the shares totally ignored? Is the evidence that FEAR or GREED is being exhausted in the share price pattern and volume information?

As with any subject or body of knowledge, just taking the time to understand and work with technical analysis will help your skills and your understanding of the ebbs and flows of FEAR and GREED in a stock price. Couple this understanding with the information about the company you develop through fundamental anlysis and your ability to select stocks at a profitable point will increase.

FWIW # 139 .... *Business Broadcast Shows*

The world has found out that investing is interesting and challenging and responded with massive media coverage. From CNBC to NBR to CNN/FN and Wall Street Week, the media attempts to bring the general public sliced and diced daily information spiced with humor and a touch of sex appeal. The problem arises in the fact that 90% of the information is nice to know and useless while 10% need to know information is not enough to make up for the wasted time. It's not all themedia's fault. Investors relish in hearing about today's winners and rumors. It's human nature.

As a financial advisor, the business broadcast channel CNBC is the least expensive way of keeping in touch with breaking news. Covering breaking news is the best feature of the CNBC service. Manufacturing reasons for market movements is not. There are times when movement happens in a stock price, a sector, or the market as a whole when there is no meaning to the volatility. It would be a better public service to admit that fact rather than try to find some manufactured reason that might be misleading in the long run. Interviewing CEO's and companies having some special event on the exchange is a service to those companies but not helpful to investors since the information solicited and available is alredy public information. It appears to be clear that for the access to the exchange the media has to give editorial time to the exchange.

The best information from these services, both radio and television, usualy comes as a casual comment about investing or analytical techniques that adds to the body of knowledge a listener might have. Programs that don't always give answers, but just raise issues, are not seen because they do not give viewers what most of them want: a hot tip. There is no question that listening to business broadcast shows every day will make it easier to converse with your clients who are watching the same shows. The cost, however, in not using the time productively can be high.

It seems everyone has an opinion about investing and specific stocks or styles. As a financial advisor, you better have one too. As a matter of fact, your clients depend on you having an opinion and a correct one most of the time. Your first task in the role of analyst is to learn to separate facts from opinion in the research you read and review. You should try to avoid ever reading others' opinions until you have formed one of your own so you will not be influenced by what they say. This separation of fact from opinion is not hard to do since most research reports show the facts in table form or as statistics. The opinion comes in the essay part of the report. Statistical services only present you with sterile numbers. To shape your intuitive judgement after reviewing the statistics, you should write out why you think a stock should be bought or sold and keep the reasons for later review after the stock meets its objectives or fails. Analyzing companies and the potential gains in their share prices is a cumulative exercise where experience builds upon experience. Success builds upon the deeper layers of making good and bad decisions over time. Consciously being aware of the process improves and speeds success.

FWIW # 141 .... *Using In-House Research*

If your firm has a research department, you have an excellent tool at your disposal. Effectively using the in-house research starts with your realizing that the analysts have multiple roles to play. First and foremost, where possible, they are investment bankers who have the function of saying nice things about your firm's investment banking clients. Accept that fact and you can learn to understand when this role is being played. Second to being an investment banker is generating institutional business for the firm. This task usually requires the analyst to have regular contact with institutions and results in your firm's large clients having professional insight into what the analyst thinks and sees. The third role is grinding out research for your firm's retail clients, trying to have your firm's large base of business assist in supplying liquidity to a particular stock. There is a clear potential conflict of interest when the analyst pushes the research with the retail clients while sending coded signals to institutional clients inferring a different perspective. It appears to have happened and will probably continue to happen. You have to understand it and adjust for the potential issue in your business.

Even with the pitfalls of ethical challenges, you can make your research department work for you. Step one is to review the coverage your firm has of the markets. Discard the analyst's information for sectors and companies you do not have in your universe. Second, set up a file for each company you are going to follow and ask your research department for sector, industry, and company in-depth reports as well as current opinion reports. Study the background material so you will have the facts about the company and its competitors. Keep the opinion pieces for a long period of time along with your opinion of the company and its peers. Every twelve months, go back and read what your firms' analysts have said. Using this rearview mirror approach gives you a unique perspective of judging how effective your analysts are. You should be able to see subtle changes in their words that give you insights into their conviction for what they are saying. This backward reading will tell you which analysts are in sync with the markets and which are not. If you have the open dialogue approach at your firm, e-mail an analyst you respect with well thought out and succinct questions when you have them. Let the analysts know when they have helped you in your business and when you are building a position in one of their stocks. In-house research can be effective in building your business if you put out the effort to use it properly. Remember, these analysts have taken the time to build specialized knowledge of a narrow sector of the market so take advantage of the work they have done and use it for your clients.

FWIW # 142 .... *Instant Info*

There has always been a debate as to whether or not the investment markets are efficient or inefficient in handling information. Actually, the markets are both. Let's examine the issue. When earnings are reported, there are a number of analysts who follow the company and are ready to check certain key points in the numbers such as gross margin, operating cash flow, sales increases or decreases, and return on equity decomposition. Other special and unique figures and ratios unique to a particular company are focused on as well. As quickly as possible, a snap decision is made to recommend holding, buying, or selling the shares. These decisions are made in minutes, not hours. This is an efficient market that analyzes all known statistical data. Hours or ays later, further information can change the opinion and, if so, the market will adjust the share price again. The question, therefore, becomes this: Is instantly adjusted information really useful or valuable?

The answer is yes if you use it properly. As a financial advisor, you will seldom be able to analyze a company as deeply as a dedicated research analyst only following one industry or a handful of companies. What you can do is understand the premise research analysts are using to form their opinions. Since you have your independent opinion, which may agree with or dispute the analysts' opinion, you can give weight to each of the factors the analysts believe is important to the future of the company. After weighing the factors, you will be able to make a judgement about the importance of the information in the short term and long term. You can determine if the issues are company specific or industry wide. By having your own opinion and then dissecting the research analysts' opinion, when the statistical news is released and is instantly adjusted by the market, you will be able to determine if the influence will be long-term or short-term. For instance, if an earnings report is one cent below estimates and the stock drops by 25%, is the problem with the company or the aggressiveness of the earnings estimate? If it is a company problem, was the shortfall due to margin issues, temporary supply chain disruptions, or industry factors. You cannot react fast in the market but you can be ready for the news and tailor the market's reaction to your benefit.

Non-statistical information is not as efficiently processed as statistics. As with most information today, the market's perspective is short term and concrete. If a company is doing well today, the market believes it will do well in the future. Poor industry economics or challenges in operating the company are expected to stay that way forever. These are incorrect assumptions and lead to above average gains for patient investors. These are real opportunities but have to be managed so that too much time isn't spent with the share price languishing on the bottom causing your clients to become disenchanted with your performance.

Instant information processing is a fact of life for the markets and so is the volatility it brings. You have to be paying enough attention to your universe of companies to be able to digest the news releases and the market's reaction to the news.

FWIW # 143 .... *Expensive Free Research*

There is no free research shortage in the market today. The Internet is full of self-styled analysts willing to give you an opinion on a company. Probably the worst can be found in chat rooms about specific stocks. Brokerage companies will supply their clients with free research on the stocks they follow and even give clients access to research from third parties. If all of this material is available for free, what is it worth? The certainty most research conveys can be expensive if taken as the truth. The fact that the information is already known tells you it is built into the share price. What is interesting is how some services will take two companies competing against each other when one company is having difficulty and the other is not and uses the current operating numbers to prove the case that you should put your clients in the better operating firm. Never mind the fact that the company with challenges is selling for a 40x PE ratio and the company clicking on all cylinders is selling for a 120x PE ratio. The market has already adjusted for the known problems. The real questions for you as a financial advisor remain: What can change? What will make it change? When will it change? The only value that you can receive from the mounds of free research available is the time saved from having to crunch the numbers. Find a source that has good statistics and stick with it.

FWIW # 144 .... *The Internet*

The Internet is a great tool but it's not safe to use indiscriminately. The best place to start in researching a company is at the company's web site. This is the place for statistics and company produced propaganda. Serious money is spent on putting the company's best foot forward at all times. What you will see is what management believes is the company's future. Statistics are available as well as the required MANAGEMENT'S DISCUSSION OF OPERATIONS. A time line of information about the company is available for the last three years so you can see the trends in operations. Your initial questions will be formulated by going through these pages carefully.

The second site might be an industry trade organization web page where you can begin to get a sense about the industry and its position in the overall economy. Industry niches and company rankings will become better understood through reviewing these pages. Questions related to the industry and competitors can be formulated here.

You should be developing a sense of where the company fits into its marketplace by now. Is it number one or number two in revenue? How about operating efficiency? Is the management aggressive or passive? Take time to thoroughly understand what info you have received. Go to some of the web sites that supply ratios and number crunching, not opinions. It's very important you form your own opinion before reading others'. Write down your conclusions and thoughts so you will always know what impression you had after going through the raw numbers. Now you are ready for web surfing.

Go everywhere you can find information about the company, its industry, and its major competitors. Go to the competitor's web site to see what their management feels is important in the future. Make notes when you see a difference between what your primary company's management said and what the competitors said. More questions should be generated from this search. The next step is to go to credible investment research sites and to get brokerage research if it is available on the web. Now you are into opinion land. You will begin to see where the various analysts disagree with you. You can begin to see what they think is important. Discipline and patience in picking out the statistics these analysts use to support their opinions will help you in formulating a full range of statistics that you need to use in your research.

Finally, you need to work through the gutter of the Internet chat rooms. Always remember those chat room users are anonymous and trying to pump up or deflate a company's stock. You will be mining the garbage for that one nugget of fact that could be important. Obviously, this is the last stop and not a lot of time should be spent here.

When you are finished surfing the web, you should have a handful of questions to put to the company's investor relations department.

The real beauty of the web is the time and travel it will have saved you in gathering this information.

FWIW # 145 ....*Earnings Yield*

Everyone talks about the price earnings ratio (P/E) in discussing a stock. What is the P/E ratio really? It is the inverse of the earnings yield. The earnings yield is calculated by dividing the earnings of a company by its market capitalization. This can be done in the aggregate or more handily in terms of per share numbers. A company with a $1.20 in earnings selling for $24 has an earnings yield of 5% or a P/E of 20.

If investors are trying to compare all investments to each other, what is more meaningful, the P/E or the earnings yield? If interest rates for 10-year U.S. Treasuries are 6%, and 10-year BAA corporate bonds are 7.5%, doesn't it make sense to talk in terms of a 1% or 5% earnings yield on an investment when looking at a stock? Certainly, earnings are subject to change and fixed income investments are not. However, the reality of accepting a 1% earnings yield hits home when it becomes clear it might take seven or eight years for the earnings yield to improve to 5% and then only if the earnings are going up. The implied hope for a 1% earnings yield company is that the yield will always stay at 1% even if the earnings are going up. Earnings yield causes an investor to think about the return on the investment the same way a business owner thinks about it.

FWIW # 146 .... *Excuses*

Analysts and corporate management look for any excuse to find a way to make the earnings of a company seem better and higher. One way is to promote the use of earnings before interest, taxes, depreciation, and amortization (EBITDA). This is a number that is usually bandied about by management in businesses that have a great deal of interest, taxes, depreciation, and amortization. EBITDA might be helpful if the ITDA were optional or not real costs. The trouble is that they are real costs. Management chooses to use debt in the company's capitalization so there are interest expenses. This is a conscious decision on the part of management. If one company decides not to use debt and another competitor does, it doesn't help to ignore the debt-ridden company's interest expense.

The only way taxes can be optional is to not have earnings. Some companies are bought with debt and interest expense wipes out the earnings and, therefore, the taxes. Use of EBITDA came into vogue in the early 1980's as the decade of 1970's inflation and high interest rates had driven common stock valuations to incredibly low levels. With the prospect of falling interest rates and rising valuations, the LBO craze created massive wealth through financial engineering. When valuations are high and interest rates are moderate to low, the use of excessive debt carries undo risks.

Depreciation is the systematic write-off of long life assets. For a while in the 1980's, the write-off period for these assets was artificially short thereby suppressing earnings more than necessary. Even at today's lengthier schedules, a case can sometimes be made that some assets do not depreciate, but actually rise in value over time. One example used is a commercial building where rental income rises regularly. With routine maintenance, the building becomes worth more, not less, over the years, yet depreciation reduces earnings by a certain amount each year as the cost of the building is recovered over time. The challenge is that some assets do depreciate and wear out with use and to ignore all depreciation is to overstate the earnings and give a false value to the company.

Amortization comes from writing off intangible assets such as capitalized expenses and acquisition costs called goodwill. With purchase accounting methods for mergers and acquisitions and the willingness of corporate management to buy market share rather than to earn it, amortization of these acquisition costs has started to materially affect net profits in many industries. Analysts and corporate management are hand in hand trying to get investors to ignore the goodwill write-offs using a similar rationale as that used for depreciation. Why would a business' value over and above the tangible asset value be considered a cost when the business should increase in value as it grows? In some respects, this is a compelling argument. Managed properly, a going concern will increase in value as earnings increase. The issue, however, is that if management is allowed to ignore the price they pay for a business over and above the tangible assets of the business, there is no discipline to say the price being paid is too high. After all, the purchase transaction is a real one. There was actual shareholder value given for the new enterprise. It is management's responsibility to take the new enterprise and manage it and grow the earnings at such a pace as to justify the price paid. The amortization chart is a way to measure if management has accomplished their goal.

As a financial advisor, you have to operate in the present environment. The Financial Accounting Standards Board (FASB) is changing purchase accounting to remove the amortization of good will. What is important for you is the value received through cash flow in exchange for the price paid as a stock buyer.

FWIW # 147 .... *Fresh Ideas*

The object of the investing world is to buy low and sell high. Don't we wish it was as simple to do as to say? Now, it goes without saying that if a stock is making lows there is something wrong with it, otherwise it would not be going down. Conversely, everything is usually going right for stocks that are moving higher. How can an advisor have an opportunity to find the nuggets of gold amongst the trash? Use the New High and New Low list published each day. There is a method to the process that helps the gold glitter.

Momentum speculators will tell you to only look at the New High list. You should look at this list, but for a different perspective. First of all, discard all of the stocks that are preferreds or in sectors you do not follow in your universe. This will cut the list to a more manageable level. Next, take the time to look at where the remaining companies are in their trading pattern over the last twelve months. What you are looking for is not the company that has been going up for several weeks, but the company that is making a new high because the trading range over the last twelve months has been narrow and flat. Therein lies the goal in the New High list. The longer the trading range and the more narrow the trading range the better. Add these stocks to your universe and place them in the appropriate accounts.

The New Low list contains gold as well as trash, it's just harder to find. Stocks stop going down in three ways. First is what is called a V bottom. These stocks are usually growth stocks that have stumbled. As soon as it appears they have stopped going down, aggressive buying comes in and the stocks rebound 30% to 50% of the decline that took place. The rebound is quick and sharp the same way the decline was. A second bottoming pattern is a derivation of the V bottom where a stock quickly rebounds 20% to 30% and then starts drifting back to the prior low over an extended period of time. The third and most powerful bottoming method is a lengthy basing pattern that seems to go nowhere, not up or down, and can literally take years to develop.

As with the New High list, discard any names of companies outside of your universe or preferred stocks. Take the rest and see what type of price pattern the last six months has experienced. It is difficult to do anything but throw a dart at a company prone to make a V bottom. The other two patterns, however, are an investor's dream. The quick turnaround and slow drift back to the low is excellent for being able to gauge the amount of risk in a stock at any given moment. It will not, however, give you the assurances of when a stock will go up. You can be reasonably sure that if the prior low price gives way to a new low, you don't want to be in the stock in the immediate future. The long extended sideways price pattern is very powerful, particularly if there is evidence the volume is picking up and the fundamental operations of the company are improving. Sideways price action with increased volume is a clear indication that FEAR is giving way ever so slowly to GREED. In this pattern, you not only have a defined risk, the prior low, but you can usually define the catalyst that is effecting the change in the company's fundamental operations.

Obtaining fresh ideas from the New High/New Low list takes a commitment to look at each company that passes the first cut and has to be done daily. This exercise is part of your commitment to excellence and well worth the efforts.

FWIW # 148 .... *Too High/Too Low*

Everyone is looking for a universal answer to the question: When is a stock too high? When is a stock too low? The problem is there isn't a universal answer. It depends on the individual investor or speculator. Here are the rules:

A stock is too high when an investor can't sleep at night or function properly during the day for worrying the price will fall before the shares can be sold.

A stock is too low when an investor can't sleep at night or function properly during the day for worrying the price will rise before the shares are bought.

FWIW # 149 .... *Taxes and Liquidity*

In the 1970's and the 1980's, investors were obsessed with avoiding taxes and owning tangible assets. It was a perfect time for tax shelters in the form of limited partnerships. While the total amount of money that was lost in tax shelters and limited partnerships is not known, the industry's practices were probably the biggest legal fleecing of investors in history. Promoters, investment bankers, and many in the securities industry created securities to allow the "man on the street" to invest like the rich. Windmills, oil and gas drilling, real estate, and merchant banking partnerships to do leveraged buy outs (LBOs) were all packaged with high commission rates and very little, if any, liquidity. Long term investing was the theme so who needs liquidity? Not only were the commissions high, but the partnership structures were challenging. The promoter, who usually had some controlled organization acting as general partner, put up very little money but got 20% or more of the profits. If there weren't any profits, that's ok because the investor got 100% of the loss. In many cases, particularly oil and gas and real estate, the partnerships bought assets from other subsidiaries of the promoter or general partner (GP) paying a "fair" but full price for the assets. Not to worry, there was always an investment banker willing to render a fairness opinion for a fee which may or may not be wrapped up in the organizational cost reimbursed by the investors.

Many financial advisors today can't even comprehend putting their clients in the investments described in this FWIW. That's because a generation of investors was burned to the extent the partnership structure is out of favor. These debacles were twenty to thirty years ago. An entirely new generation of investors will eventually be in an environment where taxes and tangible assets or, for that matter, intangible intellectual property requiring large sums to develop will become enticing again. Remember, investing runs in cycles. Even today, the promoters who prey upon gullible, wealthy investors use private placement or qualified investor offerings to separate those looking for a lightning strike of riches from their money. Your clients are going to see these investments. You can strengthen your relationship with your clients by letting them know you are willing to review the documents and give them guidance. This is no small service.

The documents accompanying a private placement qualified investor offering or limited partnership investment are usually several inches thick and written to say what the law requires, but in a way the reader can't understand the entire ramifications. There are key sections in each document that will tell an observant reader what the facts are. Most every document starts with a summary section and that's where you want to start. Read it through making notes on the important points. Start with the sales charge paid by the investor. What is the percentage of invested money paid by either the investor or the promoter for the sales people to sell the investment? It's possible there is no sales charge if the promoter is doing the marketing in-house.

Second, for a limited partnership, what is the split of profits between the GP and limited partner (LP)? What is the split of losses? How much cash is the GP or promoter putting into the deal? If the investment is a corporation, what price did the promoter and original investors pay for their shares and what price will your investors be paying? How much money will eventually be needed to get the enterprise operating and profitable and how does that compare with the money being raised? What is the projected cash flow analysis? How much of the cash is being spent on salaries and promotional activities?

All of these investments have operating projections. The costs are usually hard numbers, but the revenue projections are pie-in-the-sky numbers pulled together to make the investment look viable. How do I know this? Because if the deal was a sure thing, your client would not get a chance to invest. Take time to think about what the revenue numbers mean in terms of units sold and the capacity to scale up to the projected level. Every operating projection has a starting point. Usually, you or your clients are not the first to see the deal so it's likely the operations are underway when you are reviewing the material. Ask the promoter to give you actual operating numbers for the time the enterprise has been in business so you can compare that to the projected numbers. This request usually gets some back pedaling started. Along the same lines, if the operations are not underway, find out when they will begin and stall until they do start, then ask for updated numbers. If the organizers require a decision before business commences, decline the investment. Why? Because if they were really confident and ready and had the right product or service, the organizers or promoters would be using their credit cards, family money, friend's money, and anything else they could to get going. You, then, would be taking an ongoing business further down the road.

Read the risk section carefully. The lawyers spend a lot of time on this section because it is where the lawsuits arise. Every conceivable risk is discussed in these pages. If the organizers or promoters are getting a special deal in some way, it will be discussed here. If the management doesn't have experience, it will be discussed here. Read these stated risks carefully, hear what they say.

When you are through dissecting the document, write your client a one paragraph letter. Either recommend the investment or don't recommend it. Address your recommendation to the merits of the investment and how it fits into their investment objectives, constraints, and strategy. Don't be ambiguous. State your opinion clearly and forcefully.

FWIW # 150 .... *Packaged Dynamite*

Within all of us is a little bit of Rambo, or Tarzan, or James Bond. A super hero who likes to live in the fast lane. Daily we see the major indexes moving up and down sometimes as much as 3% in a trading day. When this happens, our fantasies and dreams turn towards options, leaps, futures, and derivatives such as exchange traded securities designed to replicate one of the major indexes around the world. Isn't it easy to jump on board when the index starts up and get out when it stops going up? Yes and no. Yes, you can buy it at any time, but it seems to be harder to sell before the index starts to go down again since you don't know when it is going to stop going up until it already has and has started down. Even then, the tendency is to wait for the index to go back up before you sell it.

Exchange traded derivatives, options, leaps, and futures are speculative vehicles designed to reflect and enhance, usually through leverage, the actions of an index, a stock, a bond, or a currency. They are speculative securities with price action as the only purpose. They should never be called investments because they are not investments. They are tools. Tools to try to make quick money for the speculator and tools to assist with portfolio management for professional investors.

Speculators have to not only guess the price direction of the underlying security, but they also have to guess the time frame of the move when using options and futures. This seemingly minor point greatly shifts the odds against the speculator. Why? Because the speculator has to pay a premium for the option or futures contract. The amount of the premium is set by the marketplace and the marketplace is dominated by professional traders who use sophisticated computer programs to calculate the implied price volatility of the underlying security. The premium to buy or sell is a reflection of these calculations and just about removes the opportunity to make money unless some special event takes place in the markets or the company.

There are ways for you, as a financial advisor, to use exchange traded securities that serve as proxies for market indexes and options. Depending on your client's risk profile, you may set up an option writing program. This program is designed to generate income to the portfolio in exchange for giving the other side of the trade the right to sell you stock at a certain price (your client writes a naked PUT) or the privilege to buy your stock at a certain price (your client writes a covered CALL or naked CALL). Market volatility raises the risk and rewards of this type of program. Careful study of the many books covering the subject should be undertaken before adding the speculative strategy to your firm's client services.

At times when you have a new client and want to use a time line to invest in specific companies, it may be appropriate to place some of the assets in exchange traded securities designed to replicate the action of the specific benchmark you have for performance measurement. As the individual securities move into a buy range, you can shift assets from the market related security to the company specific security.

All of these options, leaps, futures, and exchange traded index securities are called derivatives because they derive their value from other investment vehicles. They are tools in some cases, tools that can hurt your client's portfolio unexpectedly. They, in effect, have embedded leverage and that increases both the risk and reward. Are they really necessary for you to have a full and competitive business?

FWIW # 151 .... *Real Diversification*

Many investors today misunderstand the meaning of diversification. They will buy a growth mutual fund, a growth and income mutual fund, a stock market fund, and a global mutual fund and believe they are diversified. The problem is, if you look at the portfolios within these fund categories, the individual securities have significant overlap and the investor is not truly diversified because the fund managers are all chasing performance and that comes from a handful of industries and stocks.

Some investors and advisors feel diversification takes place when a portfolio has thirty or more stocks all in the same industry or economic sector! There might be diversification of company specific risks, but there is substantial and untenable sector risk. What about geographic or country diversification? Portfolio managers and clients will decide to place some assets in Asia, Japan, Latin America, and

European markets and feel they are diversified. Look in the portfolio and you will find mostly tech stocks, telecom stocks, and pharmaceutical stocks for every market or country. With the tendency of the global markets to move in tandem, a dip in one of the sectors or industries will be felt in just about every geographic location.

To achieve real diversification, your clients' portfolios require you specifically place some assets in a number of different macro-economic sectors. A macro-economic sector is a segment of the global economy that is influenced by specific factors and forces different from other areas of the economy. Since the economy is not neatly in separate compartments, there is, of course, substantial overlapping. The key is to focus on the major influences of a sector. To complicate matters somewhat, different investment firms will have fifteen sectors listed while others will have twelve. You don't have to be that precise. Here is a suggested list of macro-economic sectors for you to consider in segmenting your universe of companies:

1. **Basic Industries** - Companies in steel, paper, metal, glass, container, agriculture, and chemical industries.

2. **Transportation** - Airlines, equipment and leasing, rail, shipping, trucking, and air freight.

3. **Credit Cyclical** - Building industries and related materials.

4. **Financial** - Banks, insurance, leasing companies, and all areas of financial services.

5. **Utilities** - Electric, gas, water, and basic telephone.

6. **Consumer Growth Staples** - Advertising, beverages, medical

and pharmaceutical, broadcasting, publishing, jewelry, and schools.

7. **Consumer Defensive Staples** - Food, cleaning supplies, tobacco, funeral services, and food retailers.

8. **Consumer Cyclicals** - Automotive, appliances, audio/visual home products, engines, hotel/motel, leisure products and services, most retail, shoes, and textiles of all kinds.

9. **Energy** - Coal, all aspects of oil and gas, and alternative energy sources.

10. **Capital Goods-Technology** - All technology and electronics, fiber optics, instruments, and telecommunications.

11. **Capital Goods-Industrial** - Aerospace and aircraft, construction, industrial robotics, all types of machinery, pollution control, commercial printing, rubber and plastics, tire, and wire and cable.

12. **Real Estate** - All types.

With the advent of global markets, having a separate category for companies based outside the U.S. does not make sense. Royal Dutch/ Shell and British Petroleum have substantial assets in this country. If a stock based in another country is willing to meet the reporting requirements to be listed on a U.S. exchange, they may be considered in the appropriate macro-economic sector.

Real diversification starts with the macro-economic sectors, moves through the industries within the sectors and ends with companies selected within the industries. When setting investment objectives, investment constraints, and investment policy and strategy for your clients, you will decide the size of each investment unit and how many investment units in the portfolio will be invested in any one macro-economic sector.

Real diversification reduces performance in the short term. There are usually only one, two, or three sectors of the economy leading the market at one time. If you truly diversify your clients' portfolios, you will have seven to twelve sectors represented. Some of these assets will be marking time or be under pressure. The urge to pile all of the money into the winning stocks and sectors is strong particularly when clients call and ask why their performance is not as good as the leading mutual funds that are focused on only one or two sectors. Client pressure is the primary reason why many money managers do not practice real diversification. Clients only realize the value of real diversification in a bear market. Over a full market cycle of five to six years, a portfolio that does have real diversification will grow at an above average rate if the stock selection is focused and disciplined. Pendulum Investing™ allows investors and advisors to be in the right stocks for the long term. FEAR always gives way to GREED and GREED always gives way to FEAR. Diversification enhances the opportunities to be on the right side of these shifts.

FWIW # 152 .... *Tax Swapping*

President Clinton's administration tried to get rid of tax swapping and Wall Street revolted. Tax swapping is a major source of revenue for investment houses and an important tool for financial advisors.

Every financial advisor makes timing mistakes. Each year there are gains that have to be realized for one reason or another. Instead of paying taxes on the realized gains and holding a great stock until it recovers, there is the potential for a tax swap. You can tax swap both stocks and bonds. Bonds are easier to swap than stocks. Preferred stocks are similar to bonds and should be swapped in the same way.

Bonds have six characteristics that can change and therefore make one bond different from another. If you have different securities, even though they are similar, you can sell one and buy the other immediately taking the loss on the first security to offset your other gains while holding the new security until maturity. The six characteristics are as follows:

1. **Maturity** - The bond your client owns has a certain maturity. You can change the maturity and thereby change the characteristic of the security even if you don't change any of the other features of the bond.

2. **Quantity** - Changing the quantity of bonds may assist in adjusting the credit quality, maturity, or coupon amount.

3. **Credit Quality** - Bonds are priced in a pecking order with the lowest yield given to the highest credit quality. Changing the credit quality changes the yield and therefore the price for any given maturity and coupon level.

4. **Coupon Amount** - The stated interest rate on a bond is a major factor in a bond's price. Change the coupon and you change the price

and character of the holding.

5. **Type of Bond** - Moving from U.S. treasuries to U.S. agencies to corporate bonds to municipal bonds to non-U.S. debt is another alternative to factor into a tax swap.

6. **Issue** - Many companies have more than one issue of outstanding bonds. Moving from one bond to another is changing the security and generally qualifies for a tax swap. The same can be said for U.S. Treasury debt and other large prolific issuers of bonds.

Six characteristics that can be adjusted to take the bond your client is holding at an unrealized loss and give the client comparable income and maturity but turn the loss into a realized one which will shelter any realized gains from other transactions. At the very least, a small amount of ordinary income may be sheltered by the tax loss realized in the swap.

Swapping isn't a free lunch. You have to take into consideration the cost of the swap and when the new bond matures or is sold at a price higher than the purchase price, capital gains taxes will have to be paid. These two events happen in the future and, as the old saying goes, "The next best thing to no taxes is a tax-deferred."

Stock swapping is different from bond swapping. Bonds are securities placed in a portfolio to generate cash flow from interest. You generally don't care if you own one bond or another as long as the one in the portfolio has the desired credit quality, income level, and maturity. It's not that way with stocks. Your clients don't want to sell HWP and buy CPQ or else they would have bought CPQ in the beginning. Ownership of a company is specific to the outlook for that company. With tax swapping you cannot buy and sell the same security within thirty days and realize a tax loss. There has to be a thirty-one-day period between the two transactions. The law, however, does not say which transaction has to occur first. There are two ways to turn an unrealized loss into a realized loss to shelter other realized gains and maintain a position in a company that you feel will be appropriate for the long term.

(A) Sell the stock being held. Do it now if the outlook for the next thirty days is bleak and it is unlikely the stock will gain appreciably during that time. It might be that you find a better investment during the thirty-day period. If you still want to own the stock for the long term after thirty-one days, buy the shares back.

(B) For volatile stocks and companies you don't want to risk not having in the portfolio, buy the new shares, hold a double position for thirty-one days, and sell the original shares at the end of the holding period. Make sure you do a "versus purchase on (date) transaction." This is accomplished by having the broker enter the specific date of purchase for the original shares on the order ticket when selling. The original purchase date will show up in the description field on the sales confirmation.

Tax swaps are a regular tool you should use on a routine basis in your business even when there are no realized gains already taken. By collecting realized losses without disturbing the portfolio strategy, you build flexibility and liquidity in the portfolio, having some realized losses for unexpected gains that may not be long term but are attractive to take at that moment.

FWIW # 153 ....*Buy/Sell Psychology*

Don't kid yourself. Buying stocks when the share price is controlled by FEAR is not easy. Selling stocks that are gripped by GREED is not any easier. Keeping a portfolio with real diversification is just as challenging. The most difficult aspect of the job is buying what you know needs to be bought when your client is giving hints they want the latest high-flying stock talked about on every business news show during the day.

You have to have confidence in your analysis and confidence in your strategy. Make the decisions when the markets are closed so you aren't influenced by one day's price action. Remember the times you made decisions in the past and they were the right ones. Remember the length of time it takes for truly great investments to develop. See how the new addition to the portfolio fits with the other companies. Frankly, realize that it is better for you to do what is right and risk losing a client because they want faster growth than to allow the psychology of the market or some other influences to cause you to go along with a strategy not proper for the client. Think of all of the factors and then just do what is right. By the way, doing what's right gets easier the longer you are in the business.

FWIW # 154 .... *What To Sell and When*

The great mystery to almost every investor is when to sell a stock. How do you tell the moment before it starts to go down? Selling is a much tougher call than buying. Part of Pendulum Investing™ is the art of focusing on GREED in relation to a company's intrinsic value. With today's volatile markets, the company may continue to progress and grow, but the shares stall out and decline due to sector rotation, rumors, or just selling by one or more major holders. When the market dynamics shift again, the stock will resume its rise. You don't want to be out of that kind of situation. Actually, there are five situations when you might want to sell a stock:

1. The client needs money or becomes excessively involved with holding the position. If the client is always interfering with your management and wants the position sold, either get rid of the client or the stock. In the majority of cases, it's easier to sell the stock.

2. The company's fundamentals change. Something happens that indicates a change in the operating rhythm such as the resignation of a senior manager, labor problems, supply disruptions, a major product recall, or unexpected jumps in raw material prices.

3. The share prices begin to ignore good news after a long rise in price. Stocks that won't go up when all systems are working will start going down under their own weight. Be sensitive to this issue because it is the surest sign of a top in the price of a stock. Look at the stock's money flows if you think this event is happening. If you don't have access to money flows, look at volume to detect increases in

volume without a confirming price rise.

4. Stock price hits your target. This is particularly important for cyclical stock. When you buy a cyclical stock, you should pick the price at which you will sell it even to the point of entering the order to sell on a good-to-cancel basis. When the stock reaches the sell point, the news will be favorable and the euphoria great so it will be hard to let the stock go if you have not already developed a discipline for selling at a specific price. If you don't, then eventually you will watch the stock go all the way back to where the move began. Growth stocks are more difficult to sell because it is more difficult to pick a target. You can determine if a growth stock is excessively priced by looking at the P/E expansion over a multiple year period. If earnings are going up and so is the price, that's fine. If earnings are going up and the P/E is expanding significantly faster, you have to begin to be concerned. You should begin to watch for the signs in number 3 above.

5. There is a substantially better opportunity in the marketplace. Not just a slightly better value, but one that takes your breath away. Clearly a stock that you know, without a doubt, will double or triple in the next two to three years. When this opportunity arises, go through your clients' portfolios and select the least desirable stock and sell it to buy the new opportunity.

This sell discipline works and keeps the portfolio turnover reasonable and prudent. Notice all of the reasons not listed above for selling a stock. There are plenty of excuses investors use to hide their impatience, but none of them are truly professional reasons to sell a stock.

FWIW # 155 .... *Rumors/News*

Ever watch a stock go up on expectations of good news and when the news comes out, the price declines? The phenomenon happens all of the time. The reverse is true for bad news. Always remember the stock market is an anticipatory market – it anticipates the future, not reacts to the past. Keep that in mind and you won't find yourself caught in one of these news announcement traps.

FWIW # 156 .... *Above Average Growth*

If all your clients wanted was to do as well as some benchmark, they'd buy the benchmark. They want above benchmark growth. The challenge arises when they want it each and every quarter. Let's examine how you can give your clients above benchmark growth over a three to six-year period of time. Most of the major indexes today are market capitalization weighted. The bigger stocks in the index are going to be more important than the smaller ones. As a matter of fact, there have been some years when only a handful of stocks have out performed the averages they were part of. The overwhelming majority of companies making up the index declined.

Here are the ways you can outperform the benchmark you are measured against:

1. Give up diversification. Real diversification diminishes performance in the short term because you do not have just a handful of stocks going up. While the technique of concentrated positions will work part of the time, when it goes against you, the consequences can be serious losses to your clients' portfolios.

2. Buy the stocks going up the fastest. This requires giving up diversification and just putting your money on the hottest stocks in the market. This is just crap shooting and what is called the "Greater Fool Theory." In other words, you expect a greater fool to come along and buy the overpriced stock from you at an even higher overvalued price.

3. Participate in a red-hot IPO market. Easier said than done unless you have billions of dollars and are willing to take the bad with the good from your brokerage connections.

4. Buy stocks with significant FEAR in the price. Pendulum Investing™ is based on the principle that human emotions cannot sustain themselves at an extreme for long. Shares with high degrees of FEAR controlling the price are by definition lower in price than they usually are with the normal balance between FEAR and GREED. A stock at the low end of the normal range and recovering back to middle ground will usually return a greater percentage gain than the market as a whole.

5. Seek out a low Beta stock with significant share price FEAR

for the client accustomed to risk adjusting portfolios and their returns. The stock with a low Beta that is about to have major industry or company specific changes will enable you to get high Beta returns from a low Beta security.

True fundamental company operating changes do not happen overnight. They happen over a 1.5 to 3-year period of time. You can estimate how long the change will take and realize the market as a whole will not generally respond until the last six months of the change. As you build your diversified portfolio, look for companies where there are various time periods until the evolution is complete. Companies that are 1.5, 2, or 3-years away from strong fundamental operating earnings fit together so by the time the 1.5-year workout is meeting expectations, the 2-year is close behind and the 3-year has begun its road to recovery. This cumulative rolling progress will lead to above average returns in three to six-year performance because it is not dependent upon the market averages but upon the corporate management and earnings growth. When the market is reacting negatively to various dynamics, your companies will be resisting the decline. As market pressure lets up, your stocks will likely surge ahead because of their improving fundamentals.

By keeping real diversification and selecting companies with FEAR controlling the share price, you will under perform on some of your investment units in the short term, but be able to outperform on the whole portfolio in the long term.

FWIW # 157 .... *Obvious*

The best investments do not take deep analysis. Quality management selling quality needed goods or services to many people with numerous barriers to competition and a stock selling at a fair price is what all investors are looking for. The problem arises when it takes a lot of analysis and rationalization to be able to develop the perspective necessary to justify the price or the fundamentals.

FWIW # 158 .... *Performance Pendulum*

So you have had above average performance for one or two years and you think you want to run a hedge fund because it's an easy business. Well, don't go to the do-or-die leagues yet. Above benchmark investment performance actually breeds under performance for a period of time in the process. Here's why. Whatever index you are using is probably market capitalization weighted. That means the big capitalization stocks dominate the performance. To outperform, you have to own the top performers in the index and only the top performers and/or you have taken asset concentration risk in a few companies not in your benchmark but moving faster than the benchmark. Either way, you are in the most volatile stocks. The benchmark, however, has the massive bulk coming up behind the leaders that is holding the index back somewhat while the leading stocks are pulling the index higher.

At the point where the benchmark leading stocks stop going up and proceed to go down, the rest of the index may continue higher or hold steady, thereby diluting the decline of the leaders somewhat just as it diluted the rise of the leading stocks. Your clients, on the other hand, have been in the volatile shares without the stability of the less volatile shares in the benchmark. When the shares your clients own start lower, there is nothing there to dampen the movement lower, just as there was nothing there to hold it back on the upside.

You might believe you will sell the stocks before they go lower, but that thought raises a host of issues such as (a) is it in the client's best interest to sell and create a taxable event just so performance won't suffer, (b) is the decline just a normal correction that will be followed by renewed growth to new heights, and (c) where do you place the assets to continue to outperform for the next six months or more?

Outperformance over a six-year period is very achievable if you maintain a long term perspective. Trying to outperform quarterly usually degenerates into a highly speculative chasing of momentum for the sake of momentum alone.

FWIW # 159 .... *Patience*

If you are in a stock too early, the experience looks and feels the same as buying a stock that goes down. The timing has to be reasonably targeted for each company represented in your clients' portfolios. Some of the companies should be at the stage of fundamental development that the earnings growth will be apparent in eighteen months, others at the point the market realizes the change within twenty-four months, while the last group targeted for new above average earnings growth in thirty-six months.

Assuming you are reasonably accurate in your analysis, serious time horizon risk for under performance is in the first twelve months of a client's engagement. It is during this period, when the companies you have selected are developing the operational efficiencies for growth, that you must show leadership to your clients through your patience. You must keep your clients focused on what is happening with each company and approximately when the markets should start realizing the changes and begin to adjust the share price upward.

Unfortunately, eighteen months is a long time in many investors' eyes. While most won't admit it, eighteen weeks is an excruciating time to wait for performance. Your professionalism will be the key to getting the client to have patience and confidence in you. Once the companies begin to respond, no matter how slightly it happens, you and your clients will begin to relax and patiently watch the portfolio grow.

FWIW # 160 .... *Manias*

Pendulum Investing™ focuses on understanding the relationship between a stock's price and the underlying company's intrinsic value. There are situations when there is no logical relationship. In other words, the pendulum is so far to an extreme that no correlation can be found. The investment community calls these situations bubbles. These special crowd psychology frenzies happen on a regular basis. If you invest your clients in stocks that later come into this special zone of euphoria, your clients will reap extraordinary reward. Manias, however, always end the same way: a gut wrenching crash that wipes out most, if not all, of the startling rise. The change happens suddenly. Almost like someone turning off the mania switch.

Many times there is no special warning that the end is close. The more spectacular the rise, the less likely there will be signs of pending disaster. Remember, a mania is not a growth stock that goes up each year because its earnings are going up. A mania is a collective belief that one country, one sector, one industry, or one company has found a new way of doing business that will give it a dominant role to the detriment of all others. This belief is so profound and so clearly based upon some factual evidence that everyone feels they must participate or forever lose out. So you can see, there are keys to a mania:

(1) A large number of investors or speculators know, without a doubt, that the road to untold wealth is found in owning shares in a country, sector, industry, or a company.

(2) There is an element of truth to the fact that the subject of the mania is all that the share buyers say it is.

(3) A concern on the part of speculators that if they don't participate in the mania shares, they, the speculators, will not be able to maintain their relative financial position amongst their peers.

There are other characteristics of a mania that can be found in many books. It is wise for you, as a financial advisor, to study the great manias of history so that it will be easier to spot the next one.

Little known is the flip side of a mania bubble in what Pendulum Investing™ calls potholes. By definition, if a large number of speculators and investors believe one area is the chosen place to be in the market, they withdraw funds from other areas driving down the share prices in these industries and sectors as the heavy liquidation meets the lack of buyers. As the opposite of a mania bubble, pothole pendulums reach an extreme on the FEAR side. Now the real investing begins. In Pendulum Investing™, these are called ***generational opportunities*** where the share prices relative to the intrinsic value are so low the company is a serious candidate to be taken private or bought by another company. These opportunities fit the definition in FWIW # 148 where it's hard to sleep or function worrying that the share price will rise before you can invest.

It's important to remember, a pothole can only go so deep. No one will pay you to invest in a company. Like bubbles, there is usually some truth to the issues that cause investors to flee an industry. As a long term investor, you have some comfort in understanding that you are buying assets and a business franchise for substantially less than it is worth. On the other hand, bubbles have no limits. They usually last longer and go farther than you will ever believe. You cannot apply logic to the situation. The old saying is that trees don't grow to the sky. That's true, but a mania is in fantasy land and everyone knows

Jack's beanstalk did grow to the sky. There is one way to realize the top may be close: when YOU begin to really believe this mania is the only way to make money, it's time to get out.

OPM rhymes with opium and they both have an intoxicating effect on their users and are deceptively dangerous to use. OPM = Other People's Money. Throughout financial history, OPM has been the way for someone with good ideas and little or no money to make a fortune by partnering up with someone who has money. In most cases, OPM comes in the form of borrowed money. In the securities business, it's borrowed money called margin. Using margin is using leverage. Using leverage magnifies the gains and losses in your clients' accounts. Leverage is powerful. An example shows just how powerful. A $20 stock goes to $30. The investor, paying fully for the 1,000 shares at $20, sells at $30 and has a 50% return on the investment. If the stock went down to $10 instead of going up, the investor loses 50% of the investment. A serious loss, but one where capital is left to try again.

If the same investor bought the $20,000 of stock on margin, putting up $10,000 and borrowing $10,000, a subsequent move to $30 or $30,000 will yield a 100% return less the cost of interest for the loan. Double the return of the conservative investor who did not use margin. A drop of $10 or $10,000, however, will completely wipe out the investor's equity. Federal Reserve margin requirements are 50% initial margin. In the 1920's, it was only 10%, and that fact was a major cause in the stock market collapse of 1929.

There are some investors who will not use margin under any circumstances and that is appropriate for them. There are others who should not use margin because they are not psychologically or financially suited to take the risk associated with margin.

The biggest risk of margin is the fact that people don't know when they have used too much until they have. Then it is too late and the investment program falls apart. The Federal Reserve margin requirement dictates that only 50% of a stock's market value may be borrowed from a brokerage firm. This is a major factor in helping minimize this risk in securities. As a financial advisor, you should have conversations with your client about the amount of leverage they have elsewhere in their financial affairs. A client with extensive leveraged real estate holdings is at risk of needing funds from your managed portfolio if a real estate crunch comes. Your investment strategy should make allowances for the possibility of needing emergency funds.

The second major danger of using OPM is using it to buy the wrong stocks. What are the wrong stocks? Precisely the ones your clients want to buy: the fast moving, high valuation, aggressive growth companies. What better way to pile up gains in a hurry with little equity? The challenge comes when these stocks have a price adjustment. The move downwards is even sharper than the upside volatility. Margin calls, requirements to put up more equity, are created and are required to be met in a short time span. Forced liquidation results in many cases and the account is severely impaired or wiped out. Naturally, just after this debacle happens, the stock turns around and goes back up adding insult to injury. This is not a joke, it happens when excessive margin is used during periods of euphoria.

Margin interest is simple interest meaning interest that is charged based upon the amount of money borrowed. Simple interest is far superior for the borrower than compound interest where interest is charged on the interest due. The problem arises when your client does not pay the interest due each month and the next interest charged is made on the money borrowed and all of the past interest not paid. In other words, simple interest is turned into compound interest. Let this non-payment and compounding go on for too long, and the borrowed money becomes substantially more than the equity (assuming the equity is not growing) and the likelihood of a margin call increases. Even if the stocks are going up, it's good business sense to pay the monthly interest expense so the money due on liquidation reflects the money borrowed.

OPM used to buy a specific stock should be earmarked just for that stock. Unfortunately, many clients don't manage their portfolios that way and you should be careful to let them know when a stock they bought on margin is not performing and should be sold. Let me explain the serious danger. Perhaps a client has a $500,000 portfolio fully paid for and wants to buy $50,000 of another stock. Using the portfolio's value as collateral, the stock is bought by borrowing the money. If the new stock was in an account by itself and declined to the point of a margin call, the client would be forced to put up more money or liquidate the position. In the large account, the stock can go to zero and there still won't be a margin call. Investors tend to ignore losing positions when there is enough margin until the stock is a major loss. In a margin account, every stock should be required to perform or be sold. You, as a financial advisor, should know where every stock would generate a margin call if in an account by itself. Since the large account is compiled for margin purposes on a macro basis, you need to make sure a stock performing well doesn't mask a position that should be sold.

Margin interest expense is considered investment interest expense and is only tax deductible to the extent that the taxpayer has investment income. Investment income can be from any source including interest, dividends, and rents, not income from just the assets in the portfolio. As a financial advisor, you should understand the total investment income for your clients who want to use margin. An aggressive investor, not afraid of debt, can develop a portfolio with a total investment income as closely matched by investment interest expense. The net effect is neutralizing current income taxes while using OPM to leverage the potential capital gains, a powerful strategy for the right client.

A second, more conservative strategy is to pay the interest expense from ordinary income the same way your client does when borrowing money to own a home or automobile. They use the investment income, both from the portfolio and other sources, to pay down the debt each year. Paying down the debt regularly is important. Perhaps when a particular security is sold, the debt is reduced by an amount predetermined before a new stock is bought. For example, your client might sell a $50,000 stock position and repurchase a $40,000 stock position thereby reducing the debit balance by $10,000. It may be appropriate to later increase the money owed, but right now your client uses part of the profit to pay off some of the loan and save some interest expense as well.

Margin interest is floating rate interest. That is a major danger in a rising interest rate environment. The interest expense goes up monthly while the collateral is under valuation pressure as the higher interest rates cause the stock market to adjust downward. Having margin debt in a rising interest rate environment is not good. If your client wants it, you have to make sure the portfolio has real diversification.

All of these dangers are real and explode without warning at just the wrong time. There is one self inflicted danger that is guaranteed to take you, the advisor, into a black hole with your client: compounding leverage in a concentrated form. As a financial advisor, there is nothing you can say or do after the fact to defend your allowing your client to do this. Let's examine this situation. A client has $200,000 in an account and borrows $200,000 to buy a $50 stock thereby owning 8,000 shares. The stock goes to $70. Now the account value is $560,000 (8,000 x $70) with a debt of $200,000 and an average cost of $50. Since the equity has increased $160,000, the client can buy an additional 4,571 shares for the $320,000 which includes the equity and a new loan for $160,000. The stock moves to $100. With 12,571 shares in the portfolio, the value leaps to $1,257,100. Subtract the debt of $360,000 and the equity is now $897,100. Not bad for a $200,000 beginning. Well, there is now $567,100 in excess equity, so your client, believing retirement is only right around the corner, buys an additional $567,100 in shares at $100 a piece. The average share price is now $70. The company issues an earnings warning and the shares collapse to $80. While still above the average cost, the equity falls to 37.5%, barely above the level where the brokerage firm will ask for additional cash (17,942 x $80 = $1,435,360 - $897,100 loan = $538,260 equity ÷ $1,435,360 = 37.5% equity). If the stock were to drop back to $50, the equity in the account would be completely gone.

This is an extreme example to make a point: using OPM can be hazardous to your firm, your clients, and your career. Using OPM correctly is fine for some clients and you need to understand a few safeguards to manage leverage so it works for you and your clients. First, always know where the use of OPM will trigger a margin call if there were no other stocks in the portfolio. This way you don't use good money to keep a bad decision. Second, only use margin to own high quality companies where the share price pendulum is controlled by FEAR and the share price has started moving sideways. This basing period of prices not going up or down much is an indication the share price is under accumulation. It's an excellent time to use some OPM to build a position in a company. It might take two years for the stock to respond to fundamental operating changes, but you will have bought the shares at an attractive price. Third, seek out a company with a reasonably safe dividend. If margin interest is 9% and the shares pay 3%, the loan is only half the value of the shares so the net effect is an interest cost of 3% on the loan ($10,000 x 3% = $300 dividend; $5,000 x 9% = $450 interest expense; $450 - $300 = $150 net interest call on $5,000 loan = 3%). Fourth, use OPM for those clearly extreme FEAR situations where the upside potential is substantially greater than the downside risk. Finally, pay the interest monthly.

Follow these simple rules and watch your clients boost their returns on equity in their portfolio.

FWIW # 162 .... *Paying The Piper*

For many clients, there will come a time when they want to systematically withdraw from the portfolio. How do you handle the situation? There are several methods of setting up a program, each with its own special risk and reward. The first issue to confront is the level of withdrawals. For an IRA mandatory withdrawal, the rate can range from 8% to 4%. Most non-IRA clients look for the same range of income. A portfolio can generate 4% to 5% annually in most cases without causing a problem in the investment strategy. Go above 5% and the retained portfolio growth will begin to suffer, particularly if the cash flow into the portfolio is smaller than the withdrawals. Sure, there will be years when a bull market is raging and growth before withdrawals is in the high teens or even the 20% range. There are also years when the portfolio will decline or return less than the 5%. If several of the low-return or no-return years happen in a row, the decline in the portfolio value will be hard to make up. Let your client tell you what withdrawal target to use, then suggest these three alternatives:

(A) Match the withdrawal with cash flow completely. This strategy will usually lead to a portfolio balance between fixed income and growth assets. The higher the withdrawal requirement, the more the fixed income component. There is a flip side to this strategy in that the more the fixed income component, the higher the risk profile can be for the growth assets. Eventually, the growth component will increase to the extent that the portfolio will pay the proper cash and still be able to accelerate the overall portfolio value.

(B) For clients who still want to be primarily in equities, structure a cash flow for the portfolio that is 60% to 70% of the withdrawal rate. If the client wants to take out 6% from the portfolio, generate 3.60% to 4.5% of income, leaving only 2.4% to 1.5% to come from the portfolio principal. Structure the cash reserves to be 3% to 5% of the overall portfolio and thereby allowing your equity investments to have two to three years to meet your target objectives.

(C) Some clients want an aggressive growth portfolio that generates little or no income and still want to withdraw 6% to 8% a year. The rationale is that the aggressive growth will more than make up for the withdrawals. With the right stocks in a bull market, this is a reasonable assumption. When the market turns bad, serious damage can be done to a portfolio and, in turn, to you the advisor.

Option A is the prudent way to set up a systematic withdrawal. It can be done for any client no matter the age or circumstances. Option B is an acceptable alternative since the total portfolio asset withdrawal over a full six-year market cycle will only be a net 9% to 14.4% and the retained growth over the same period should total more than that. A good market and good security selection should even improve on the retained growth numbers. Option C is a career ender for you. If you want to retain the client and protect yourself, you should write a letter to the client clearly spelling out the risks and the consequences. Meet with the client and go over the letter in detail having the client sign a copy of the letter acknowledging your warning. Place the letter in the client's compliance folder. If the client won't sign the letter, don't accept the account. Let the client be some competitor's future time bomb, not yours. There will eventually be a liquidity crisis and you don't want to be around when it happens.

FWIW # 163 .... *Mutual Funds*

Mutual funds are your competitors as well as a tool for you to use. The challenge is using mutual funds properly and understanding how they work best. A mutual fund is nothing more than a managed portfolio your client buys into. The difference between a mutual fund and your services is in some ways the difference between ready-to-wear clothes your clients can buy in a store and designer clothes which are tailored individually for the client. There are two differences, however: (a) you are giving designer portfolios for less money than the ready-to-wear mutual fund, and (b) the mutual fund you select for your client today may change completely in the next twelve to eighteen months as the asset turnover approaches 100% and the portfolio manager moves onto another style or job.

Your client will need to park uninvested assets somewhere and a Money Market Mutual Fund (MMF) is as good a place as any. Most MMF's have automatic sweeps of cash from a brokerage account and offer ready access to cash on a settlement date or when your client writes a check or uses a debit card. The fee is hidden because the MMF is expressed in terms of $1.00 at all times thereby having the yield quotation reflect the net of expense return. There are several ways yields are calculated, but the 30-day rate is probably the best way for you to compare one fund to another. Most of your clients will look strictly at the yield and pick the MMF offering the best interest. You might consider a different perspective.

A MMF should not take six nanoseconds of your thought time. It should be flawlessly safe in terms of the $1.00 principal value, it should automatically sweep into and out of the brokerage account, and the yield should be competitive in returns. The only MMF that meets all of these criteria all of the time without the slightest risk whatsoever is a U.S. Treasury Securities MMF. Notice, the term U.S. Government Securities was not used. U.S. Treasury Securities only is what you want. U.S. Government MMF will have some securities issued by what are called government agencies such as Ginnie Mae, Freddie Mac, Fannie Mae, and other government sponsored private corporations. Many of these securities are collateralized mortgage obligations (CMO's). The chance of default or illiquidity is slight but real. How can you explain in hindsight while you put at risk the cash reserves for a 1/4% to 1/8% more yield?

Regular MMF are a collection of securities both public and private with various maturities extending out as long as 270 days. If you find a MMF that pays more than its competitors, it will be worth your while to see what securities are in the fund. After looking over the portfolio, if you want to use the fund, that's fine. Just make sure you know what is causing the fund to pay more interest. Usually it means higher risk. There have been a few instances of MMF's almost "breaking the buck," that is having some securities go in default and the value of each MMF share being worth less than $1.00. In every case so far, government and industry pressure cause the sponsoring fund company to buy the defaulting paper out of the MMF thereby saving the shareholders from a loss. As more and more money pours into MMF's, there will be a point when this rescue operation will become too expensive. This is not a risk with U.S. Treasury MMF's.

Stock mutual funds come in all shapes and sizes. If you can't find one you like, wait a while and the industry will create one to cater to whatever is the investment fashion of the day. The fund industry has not only sliced and diced investment styles, but they have created several classes of funds with different fee structures. It's crucial that you understand the investment style and the fee structure for every class of fund your favorite mutual fund company offers. For example, Class A shares pay a commission up front but the Class B shares don't. The problem is the Class B shares usually have higher annual expense ratios and charge a fee if the client tries to sell in the first five to seven years. If the portfolio asset turnover is 80% to 100% a year, as many funds have, how does your client know they want to be in the fund five to seven years from now? A back end load fee is a tremendous psychological barrier to selling for most investors.

Some advisors decide to use only no-load funds. That's fine if the no-load mutual fund performs as well as the sales fee peer funds. The issue is challenging about sales fees as well as management fees and 12-B-1 fees. On top of these fees, you place your compensation for your expertise in deciding what fund or funds meet your clients' investment objectives and constraints.

Picking a fund by its label can be deceiving. Probably the only labels that come close to describing what's in a particular fund are pure sector funds and index funds. Even then, many managers take a great deal of latitude with what they put in a portfolio. An index fund usually gives you what you want which is performance in line with some designated market average or index. But you can forget about the rest of the equity funds. Some value funds have stocks with high P/E's, high price to book ratios, and high price to sales ratios. At times, some growth funds are full of REIT's and oil and gas shares.

How come? Simple. With mutual funds, the manager has to deliver performance every quarter or there is a real danger clients will pull out and go elsewhere with their money. Because of this simple mutual fund characteristic, the fund managers tend to demonstrate the herd instinct far more than any other group of investors. The overwhelming majority want to be right where everyone else in their style group is located. Because of this herd mentality, it's important for you, when building a particular portfolio of mutual funds, to examine what information you have on the holdings of the various funds you are considering. See if there is any overlap and try to build a group of funds that actually complement each other rather than duplicate each other.

While examining the funds, take time to see what provisions they have in the fine print for delaying return of client money or distributing securities rather than cash in times of serious market dislocation. See if the fund is allowed to use leverage. Find out if the fund has a line of credit at a bank to use if withdrawals become excessive and the fund can't or doesn't want to sell securities to meet withdrawal demands. These are minor issues in ordinary times, but you don't get sued in ordinary times, just when tough and challenging events change the risk of the game and your performance is reviewed with hindsight.

Mutual funds are in the business of investing in a certain style or market. If money comes in the door which it usually does when a sector or style is fashionable, the fund has to put the money to work no matter what the market level. This characteristic is somewhat a reinforcing event for the portfolio that is growing. The concept is similar to buying a stock when the pendulum is controlled by GREED rather than FEAR. You hope the momentum will continue moving to the GREED side. In other words, buy high expecting it to go higher. Conversely, when a style is out of favor, the investing public will withdraw money to go elsewhere forcing the fund manager to sell stocks to raise money. Selling low and, thereby, driving the price lower creating more FEAR when FEAR already controls the market's pendulum.

With the focus on quarter by quarter performance and the volatility inherent in the markets today, the portfolio turnover of most mutual funds has increased significantly. Portfolio turnover for taxable accounts means a sizeable tax bill each year for the dividend income, short term capital gains, and long term capital gains. Most investors have dividends and capital gains reinvested and pay these taxes from other monies. There is, however, a serious issue with the tax inefficiency of mutual funds. Your client's tax status is a critical factor in what type of stock mutual funds you use in their portfolio. A related tax characteristic can be troublesome as well. In a declining market, mutual funds will sell some of their overpriced securities to lock in a profit. At year's end, these funds can have negative annual performance, but report large capital gains. Tax deferred retirement portfolios do not worry about these tax implications, only the manager's investment success. It becomes a matter of matching your client's objectives with a mutual fund's stated objectives.

A rising risk today is when a mutual fund seeks to boost performance by using leverage. If a mutual fund wants to use margin loans, it must state the fact in its prospectus and that traditionally has not been attractive for funds to do. To use leverage without having to announce it to the world, a mutual fund will seek out approval from shareholders to use investment tools such as options, leaps, warrants, and, in some cases, futures. There is an active lobbying effort underway to create single stock futures contracts. All of these securities are derivatives and have embedded in them leverage since the security gives a holder the right to own a stock or basket of stocks at some point in the future at a certain price. The price does not have to be paid until the contract is closed, hence, the embedded leverage. Leverage can be the security holder's friend or foe (see FWIW # 161).

A related trend which comes along every generation is the use of private placement stocks or restricted shares. The mutual fund manager gets an opportunity to invest at an attractive price, usually has some way of placing an arbitrary value on the investment, and gets close to the company's management. Naturally, these private securities are part of the fastest growing most fashionable industry leaders. Private securities usually have a way of building in some "extra" capital gains for valuation purposes. As a financial advisor, you want to know if the fund you select for your clients uses any of these leverage and private security features. Once you know, you can decide if the practice is appropriate for your clients and which ones.

Bond mutual funds are a method of combining interest income

with potential capital gains. It doesn't make sense to buy most bond mutual funds just for the interest payment because your clients seeking the highest interest return will do better if you set up a bond portfolio with high coupons and leave it in place. Bond fund managers try to exploit the yield curve shifts, credit quality shifts, and bond type shifts in value to incrementally add to the interest payment some capital gains. The goal is to have a better total return than a bond portfolio index or fund without active management. In selecting a bond fund, it is critical to understand what securities are in the fund. Bond funds are more likely to use private issues of debt or illiquid issues which are non-rated to spice up the yield. This yield boosting is a major risk in owning a bond fund because it can backfire during economic recessions when one or more of the companies issuing the debt gets into trouble.

Bond funds will use leverage through derivatives just like stock funds. There is nothing inherently wrong with that as long as you know the leverage is being used and you place the fund with the clients able to accept the risk.

One bond fund feature that takes getting used to is the lack of a maturity. While there are some target maturity bond funds, most of them have no maturity. The manager moves assets up and down the yield curve at will. In times of rising interest rates, there isn't the opportunity to have bonds maturing for reinvesting at the appropriate point in the yield curve. There isn't the opportunity to build a maturity point which corresponds to some important life cycle event in the client's life such as children entering college, retirement, or even a known major expense such as a wedding, auto purchase, or second home purchase.

All of the management tools used to boost returns in stock funds are used by bond fund managers as well. Read two or three prospectuses to get a feel for how bond managers manipulate returns and lay out their strategy to be the most effective fund. Think about how these strategies fit your client's objectives and constraints. Find a bond fund family that gives you securities with more than one style of approaching the market so you have alternatives in different market environments.

Using mutual funds for your clients instead of developing unique portfolios is a decision you make as an advisor. If you choose to use funds, investigate the various fund families the same way you would a stock. Find quality management, a variety of investment styles, reasonable and competitive fees, and the ability to move from one fund to another with ease. Do this investigation with your composite clients' portfolios in mind. What you want to avoid is to have too many funds doing too many things and not giving your clients the opportunity to grow their portfolios with reasonable risk. It's not easy to monitor the portfolio holdings of a mutual fund, but make an effort to engage the fund wholesaler or investor relations department. By concentrating your investments in one fund family, you have the potential to develop good communications with the fund professionals and that should benefit your clients. Mutual funds are not an easy substitute for selecting stocks or bonds. They take work and effort to develop a coordinated strategy to meet your client's objectives.

There are times clients interfere with the portfolio development. They either have a neighbor who has made money in a stock or have watched someone on television recommend a stock or just decided it was a good company to own. When they call the first time asking you to look at the situation, look at it. If it's not a good investment, either tell them that or just don't call them back. If they call a second time and clearly want to own the company, buy it for them. If you don't buy it, the shares will go higher for sure and the client will hold you responsible for not following their suggestion. If it goes down, it will be your fault, but the client will probably not call again with a suggestion. Don't buy a lot of any company your client recommends and if it goes down, leave it in the portfolio as a constant reminder to the client that you don't need their assistance in building the portfolio. There is, however, one situation when you don't buy shares for the client. If the stock is clearly unsuitable for the client's objectives and constraints, you need to take the time to clearly explain the risks to the client and professionally decline to participate in buying the security. Follow up your refusal with a letter to their file. These clearly inappropriate circumstances are rare, so most of the time just swallow hard and buy a small amount of what your client wants. If the client calls more than once every couple of years, you will have to have a confrontation with the client (see FWIW # 55).

FWIW # 165 .... *Foolish Attitude*

Some advisors and their clients get caught up in the market's emotions and want their stocks to go up immediately after purchasing them. It's like they feel the particular security has been anointed and should sprout wings and fly to the sky. When this doesn't happen, they become restless and begin to make comments that they want to "make their money work harder" or the money invested is "dead money" and should be changed. These comments are a symptom that you haven't educated your client properly because they indicate your client is more interested in speculating than investing.

Real diversification and sustainable gains in share prices are your strategy for developing long term capital gains with a measured amount of risk. Sustainable gains come from buying shares when FEAR controls the pendulum and watching the pendulum move to the GREED side. It takes time for fundamental operating conditions to change and translate into earnings. The best securities to invest in are found when FEAR is in greatest control of the pendulum. By definition, extremes of FEAR will dissipate rapidly, but a lower amount of FEAR will continue until GREED takes over and the change takes time. As GREED assumes control of the pendulum, the price will move higher and precious, easy capital gains will slip away from your client if you have waited to buy the stock. The fallacy of returning and buying a stock when it starts to move is just that: fiction.

Keeping cash reserves is part of portfolio management. Some clients, however, want to be 100% invested 100% of the time. This is a regrettable position for everyone except the client who wants aggressive growth and has the where-with-all to accept the risk. Cash reserves are not dead money. They are the ability to seize a special opportunity or meet an emergency without disturbing the current investment strategy.

If a client begins to use these phrases while discussing the portfolio, it should be a warning to you to have an in-depth review of the investment strategy. Your client is trying to ask for higher returns. You have to help the client see the balance between risk and returns. Ask questions and get back in agreement with what the client expects.

FWIW # 166 .... *Rearview Mirror View*

The overwhelming majority of people active as investors and speculators look backwards in time to try to determine the future. This is similar to looking through a rearview mirror in a car instead of the front windshield.

The excuse for using this behavior is to see the trend of company operations, a share price, or where the economy is in its cycle. There is some validity to looking at the past, but it's important to make sure the past is not the only viewpoint you use. The three critical questions (FWIW # 122) are more important than past data, particularly when investigating a company where extremes of FEAR control the share price.

It's absolutely wrong to use past performance to pick a mutual fund or an investment manager unless a time series is used that encompasses at least a full market cycle of a market top, market bottom, and back again to the top. How many years did the mutual fund perform in a satisfactory manner over this time period? Did the investment manager have only one good year out of six or six acceptable years outperforming a benchmark a little each year for an accumulated above average return?

Are circumstances different now or will they be in the future due to some political, economic, or business condition that makes past data less reliable and helpful? A major challenge many investors and advisors have is to see a sector being a market leader for the last couple of years only to have fundamental shifts cause the shares in the companies within the sector to decline about the time they start buying them.

The rearview mirror is there to check up on where you have been and to make sure there isn't some danger rapidly approaching from the rear. The front windshield is for determining where you are going. Use both correctly, and your clients will gain in wealth and reward you.

FWIW # 167 .... *BB = TW*

Better Business = Thorough Work. If you want to succeed as an investment advisor, there are a number of different aspects to master. Developing a clientele is one. Conducting your business with impeccable ethics is another. Maintaining client confidence through successfully growing client portfolios is another. Doing all of this and keeping the business organized requires *Discipline, Confidence, and Organization.* The next section shows how KEEPING IT TOGETHER is possible if you run your business instead of it running you.

KEEPING IT TOGETHER

FWIW # 168 .... *Client Killer*

A financial advisor will lose more clients because of sloppiness in handling their money than will be lost in buying a security that goes down in price. Reread that sentence again because it is as true a statement as will ever be said about the financial advisory business. To be successful over the long term, an advisor must keep focused on the operational part of the client's account. FWIW # 30 discusses reviewing the monthly statements and how this necessary chore can become a major revenue generating function.

If you are an advisor at a firm that has custody of client funds, such as a bank or brokerage firm, make sure you have a tickler file for every security or check you or your staff receives from a client. Determine how long the deposit process takes and have the account checked to make sure the deposit was posted on time and correctly. When requesting a client be shipped securities or paid a check, use the same tickler system. Whenever possible, have the client use electronic withdrawals for regular payout of monies, or checks for optional and infrequent withdrawals.

For advisors who do not have custody of funds, urge your clients to let you know when they are depositing or withdrawing large sums of money, not an occasional withdrawal. Use a tickler file to make sure the transaction is handled correctly.

More and more today, the operational areas of large firms are in remote locations from financial advisors. Take the time to make an annual trip to that location and meet face to face with the operational people who handle your client accounts. This might seem like a daunting task, but it is worth the effort. Some firms use a team approach and others have just one or two individuals. Get to know these people as who they are, what type of family they have, what their ambitions are, and what their outlook on their career is. If you are unfortunate and have not spent any time in operations, call the manager of your operations center and ask for a tour. Begin to understand the stress these people have every day handling the massive amounts of challenges associated with doing their job.

Even better than your going to the operations center is to send your assistant so the people who talk daily will know each other better. Until you can go, take a picture of you and your staff and send the photo plus a disposable camera to the operations liaisons and ask them to take photos of their group and work space. Let them know they are more than a voice on the phone. At some point, you will have to ask them to help you be important to your client. They are more likely to assist if you have treated them as the important part of your team that they are.

FWIW # 169 .... *Responsibilities*

There are five areas of responsibilities financial advisors must manage no matter what size or type of firm they are part of:

1. ADMINISTRATIVE/COMPLIANCE - Advisors working with large firms have staffs responsible for the administrative, compliance

and operational areas of the business. The importance of these duties to building and maintaining a practice should be evident. Advisors with their own firm will rely on computers and software to be efficiently competent at a minimum of efforts. The advisor must have monitor points or systems that give early warnings if one area or another is not functioning, particularly when it comes to compliance issues.

2. BUSINESS DEVELOPMENT - This is your responsibility. Don't become so busy or important to lose the edge in securing new clients. Sure, you may have an assistant do some of the early screening of potential prospects, but you make sure you meet face to face with anyone who has the financial resources and interest to work with you and your firm.

3. PORTFOLIO MANAGEMENT - If you operate your business within a large financial services firm, you will have segmented your clients into those you will manage, clients who are appropriate for mutual funds, or clients wanting a larger outside money manager with a specialty you cannot deliver. The decision as to what is best for the client is yours to make, no one else. Jealously guard this role with your clients because even if a mutual fund or outside manager is appropriate, you want your client to know you made the decision and they can rely on your guidance as to what is in their best interest.

4. RESEARCH - There are two parts to research: (a) number crunching and (b) judgement making. In a large firm with a research department, you have the luxury of having professionals select the

universe of stocks and do the number crunching. Independent advisors or those at a small firm have a multitude of Internet resources that provide number crunching for free. This is an excellent place to use an assistant. Let them assemble all of the data necessary for you to make a decision. You determine how you want the data presented and prioritized so your maximum focus is on making a judgement decision as to the quality of the investment. Your client is doing business with you, not your firm's analysts, nor a newsletter writer, nor an outside manager you hired, so don't try to pawn off mistakes on someone else. That's why you need to be the sole decision-maker in your client's portfolio.

5. CLIENT RELATIONSHIP BUILDING - Clients want to talk to you, not your assistant or your firm's operations department. Don't be inaccessible at just the time they are the most frustrated with your services. You can't, however, spend your time on operational issues. A more satisfactory way to handle a client is to speak with them and have your assistant or operations person come in on a conference call with you and the client. You explain to the person who is going to handle the problem exactly what the problem is while the client is listening and request an appropriate time for the problem solver to respond to you and the client. The entire process will take less than five minutes, but your client will have immense satisfaction because you know how to get the job done and the client will be satisfied with talking to the operations assistant since you have been involved. Use your tickler file and administrative meetings (FWIW # 6) to make

sure the solution is reported back in the appropriate time.

Regular client contact, not just when there is a problem, is part of the relationship building process. What better time to ask for a referral or to get to know a client than when you call to update the portfolio's performance or just to say hello. While watching the news, perhaps you see there is a special weather situation in the client's town. Call to see if they are all right. Let them know they are important to you.

Every part of your business falls within one of these areas. Take the time to streamline each process. Reserve the crucial areas for yourself and delegate the others to assistants, but always remember the client looks to you for answers in every area.

FWIW # 170 .... *Team Spirit*

As your business grows, you will need to have some assistants. There will be a point when you will consider taking in a partner or training someone to eventually be your partner. One avenue is instant revenue generating and the other requires your carrying the financial burden until the new individual is productive. What road is the right road is hard to decide. There is an old saying that the hardest ship to keep afloat is a partnership. There is a huge amount of truth in that statement in the financial services business because there are different styles of success. Your methods may clash with someone else's even though the two of you are highly compatible in many ways. Taking in a partner is in every way the same as finding someone to marry for life. There are two strategies of finding a partner when deciding to take in an experienced person. The first strategy is to find someone who is equal to yourself in managing the five areas of responsibility. Each of you go about your business and place all of the clients under the same team umbrella where either of you can communicate with and make decisions for every client portfolio. This type of arrangement has two or more large egos moving around in the same space. This arrangement is probably the most dangerous of partnerships because all partners continue to compete with each other as to who brings in the most business, who works the hardest, or who has the strongest relationship with the most clients.

A second partnership structure between experienced advisors is where two or more advisors find that their individual strengths complement each other. One is excellent at administrative and operational management while only worth a C+ in business development and a B+ in portfolio management and research. The other partner gets a C+ in administration, an A+ in business development and client relationship development, as well as a B+ in portfolio management and research. Together, the team is A+ across the board. When mutual respect for each other and recognition of one's own weaknesses are combined with these complementing qualities, the team is unbeatable. There is no internal competition, just the desire to be good at the designated areas of responsibility.

Whatever structure is considered when putting together a team of experienced advisors, a clearly written and agreed upon method of unwinding the partnership should be incorporated in the partnership agreement. Yes, there should be a legal, clear, and concise partnership document that covers all aspects of responsibility, authority, and financial matters while the partnership is in existence including what happens if a partner dies or retires. Putting these issues in writing up front will solidify the partnership by giving everyone confidence in their position within the group.

An alternative to partnering with an experienced advisor is hiring someone and training them to fit your organization the way you want them to fit. The challenge here is to examine the raw talent and to be able to see that they will be willing to develop into what you are looking for as well as be stable enough to spend the years necessary to become successful in the financial services business. A successful financial advisor is, by nature, an impatient entrepreneur. The best way to help a potential partner focus is to lay out a five-year program with regular check points and incentives along the way. Use the same five areas of responsibility an advisor must deal with and add a sixth: The Chartered Financial Analyst Program (CFA). A model to start with might look like the following:

First year:
- Administrative duties
- Base salary + a year-end bonus if all areas mastered and a contribution to efficiency introduced

Second year:
- Assigned compliance duties (part of administrative package)
- Beginning of business development

- Beginning of research number crunching
- Base salary + percentage of new revenue above prior levels

Third year:
- Primarily business development – target new business goals
- Research number crunching
- Level One CFA – must pass
- Base salary + percent of new revenue over original target

Fourth year:
- Primary business development – target net new business goal
- Research number crunching
- Responsibility for part of equity universe coverage
- Participation on investment selection committee
- Level Two CFA – must pass
- Base salary + increased percentage of net revenue above original target

Fifth year:
- Primary business development – target net new business goal
- Increased responsibility for part of equity universe coverage
- Assign specific portfolio management client responsibilities
- Participation on investment selection committee
- Level Three CFA – must pass

- Base salary + same percent of net revenue above
  original target + right to buy a percentage of the
  business

Naturally, the individual entering this five-year associate program will be expected to sign a non-compete contract. The strength of this program is the person administering the process obtains real value for the large dollars being spent over the five years and is able to train the future partner the way the firm wants them trained. As the associate, the participant is able to understand the business completely, earn the respect of the entire staff by succeeding at each phase of training, and constantly sheds "the new person at the firm" image regularly as authority and responsibility is increased each year. Making sure the future partner can look at the entire program from beginning to end clearly laid out with the intermediate goals and rewards is important so the impatience that will naturally be felt is kept in check.

Whether an advisor works alone or in a group, there will be direct support assistance. In large firms, the operations and administrative areas will interface with the advisor's personal assistants. The major question is how to use the staff to maximize the advisor's and staff's efficiency. The advisor hiring an administrative assistant for the first time usually develops a list of all of the duties disliked the most and shifts them over to the new assistant. This is an utter waste of money (the assistant's salary) and the beginning of an administrative and compliance nightmare as the staff comes and goes in a steady progression. The correct concept is not to get rid of all of the unglamourous, hard-to-deal-with functions, but to increase the overall team efficiency so more clients can be served properly and more revenue generated by the team's clients by growing their portfolios faster. Stay involved with every area assigned to an assistant, just do it by monitoring rather than participating. In other words, learn the difference between delegating and dumping.

Dumping is commanding someone to solve a problem and walking away. Easy problems are solved, hard problems continue to fester, and eventually threaten the life of the business like gangrene does the body. Frustration builds in the administrative staff and finally the advisor becomes involved again as the client terminates the relationship. Whose fault is it? Clearly the advisor's because the client counted on the advisor, not the assistant. Never give any assistant a task to accomplish without discussing in detail the following: (a) the type of contact that will take place with other operation personnel, (b) what specifically needs to be done to fix the problem, (c) what type of interim client contact will take place, and (d) a definite date for the problem to be solved. That is delegating and it leads to an efficient operation. Focus your monitoring time at each of your staff meetings in the morning and evening. Allow the staff to tell you what is the best way to handle a problem. Allow them to recommend how you can help if an issue gets burdened with red tape. Let them be the chief operating officers while you are the chief executive of the team.

When it comes to building a staff, many advisors try to hire in their own image and that is a mistake. The best staff member is someone who wants to do the job as a team member, not use the position to become a team leader or advisor someday. Seek out a person who has demonstrated stability and loyalty. Find someone who is willing to learn no matter what their educational history. Pay the staff member well and expect top quality work for top pay. Understand what is important and not important in their position. Demonstrate your commitment to your clients and business and let them know you expect the same commitment from them. Every team member should be hired on a six-month probationary basis. At the end of the sixth month, you should have a formal review. If they are going to stay, they should get a raise. At the same meeting, you should lay out for the staff member what is expected in the way of job growth and additional duties between the current review and the next one. This is an important point. Your assistant should know in advance what new dimensions are expected over the next measurement period as part of the salary review process. The reviews do not have to come every year, but they should be frequent enough to have good feedback between you and the members of the team. Don't let a problem simmer. Take five minutes on a regular basis to just talk to your assistants about them and their job. Allow them to tell you of challenges they are confronting so you can assist in lowering the frustration level. Catch them doing something right and let them know you appreciate it. Staff loyalty is fleeting in the business world today, but it's the fault of both employers and employees. Make a work environment as positive as possible and the right employee will respond because they want to remain where they are appreciated.

Everybody wants to feel they have a certain amount of control over their daily work experience. No one wants to have someone hovering over them or interfering every ten minutes and breaking the smooth flow of accomplishing a task. You are always looking for ways to improve your efficiency. Well, there is a great way to allow your staff to work independently throughout the day and increase your communication with them at the same time. Use a micro tape recorder and manilla folder system. All of the tasks you give your assistant require you to speak to them and are usually client-focused. If you are working in the evening or early morning, dictate a letter or instructions and then place the tape and any supporting documents in a manilla folder keeping the folder in the same order as the messages on the tape. Using the transcription earphones, your assistant can move through the tasks putting any letters or documents that you must sign or review in each of the folders and returning them to you before the day is over for your approval or signatures.

This tape and folder system works. What you have to do is to keep a list of the folders given to your staff, when given, when discussed in a preliminary daily meeting, and when the staff indicated the task will be completed. The majority will be done the day given so the list should not grow. If it does, you have an early warning system about staff issues. Since a good amount of the work you assign to your assistant happens in an opportunistic fashion, that is when a client calls or the operations area calls, use an in/out basket system. Have on your desk the two trays, one you place all of the work going to your assistant; the other is for all of the work being returned to you for your signature or approval. Set up for your assistant to clear out the basket regularly each day. The tape and related folders are removed while the completed work of the prior time period is placed in your in basket. This might seem inefficient, however, it's not because you will not have something every time period since your time will be spent on business development, portfolio management, research, and client relationship building, as well as administrative and compliance duties. What the regular retrieving of new work does is avoid your going out with a new task and interrupting your assistant's steady work flow. The two of you can work out a system of prioritizing the task so you can routinely alert your assistant to a high priority item that comes in later in the day.

The two of you should agree to a cut-off time when everything given to the assistant before the cut-off must be finished that day by 5:00 p.m. Anything after the cut-off time may be finished or carried over to the next day depending upon its priority and your assistant's work schedule.

Small teams are easy to introduce to clients on a regular basis. When a large number of clients are involved or there are large distances so that clients infrequently come to the office, have a way of introducing your assistant to the clients when it becomes clear the assistant is going to remain a member of the team. It does not enhance your reputation if you give the appearance of losing support help on a regular basis. The point of introduction is a combination of job growth and tenure, not just one or the other. Since every business is unique, you have to establish the job growth criteria. Make it challenging but reachable. When the time comes to notify your clients of the assistant's role, make sure you do it professionally and carefully so the client clearly understands the areas of responsibility and authority for the assistant. Don't leave the impression you are giving up your responsibility or are taking on too many clients. Emphasize your assistant's role in facilitating a smooth relationship between the client and the administrative and compliance areas. Emphasize the fact that you will be aware of every communication the client has with the assistant and make sure the daily meetings keep you informed of the contacts.

The ideal situation has every operational issue handled and dealt with the day it surfaces. That doesn't happen, however. Your assistant should have an accordion file numbered 1-31 where every task to be followed up on, or waiting for a reply, will be placed. The 1-31 stands for the days of the month. Once your assistant has negotiated a follow-up date with operations or compliance, the paperwork is placed in the correct date file until the appropriate time. A master log keeps track of where the paperwork is in the time line. Each entry should have the original date the issue surfaced, the client's name, plus the date the client is expecting an update. For example, 2/15/00 Wilson 2/20/00.

Once the task has been completed, the paperwork should be filed in a client folder (FWIW # 171) or e-mail and notes maintained in a client file on the computer. When the client's statement arrives, if the task is clearly fixed on the statement, documentation can be destroyed with brief notes logged into the computer assuming regulatory requirements don't require the documents be kept for a multi-year period of time.

Having assistants puts more pressure on you and your time unless you set up the independent work routine with monitoring of pressure points by you. The objective is to allow you to service more clients professionally and to grow the portfolios in a reasonably steady and consistent manner. Obtaining these objectives means more time for business development, portfolio management, and research. Plan out how you are going to shift from administrative and compliance issues before you hire the first staff member.

FWIW # 171 .... *Client Folders*

Client folders are an excellent way to maintain a yearly history of your client relationships. The folder should have two sides with metal clasps. On the left, have the brokerage statements (if they are still paper and not on CD-rom) and a copy of every transaction confirmation. On the right, have all correspondence in chronological order with the latest information on the top. All correspondence means just that, birthday cards, notes, letters, quarterly reports, logs of phone calls, and anything else. If you meet with a client, place the notes of that meeting on the letter or report you discussed when together.

Set up a new file each calendar year. Place the old file in a box or destroy it depending upon your regulatory requirements. Registered investment advisors must keep records for six years while the record retention requirements for brokerage firms are different at the financial advisor level. Don't keep anything that you are not required to keep, but what you do have, make sure it is complete.

FWIW # 172 .... Regulatory Record Keeping

Depending on what part of the financial services business an advisor operates in, the controlling regulatory agency has very specific requirements for record keeping and retention. The requirements can be time-consuming and tedious. Large firms make it easier on the financial advisor while small firms place the burden squarely on the shoulders of the client relationship advisor. Become familiar with the rules and requirements. Make sure your assistant is up-to-date and responsible for the correct cataloging of what is needed. If you operate a small firm, engage an independent consultant, usually a retired regulatory staff member, to conduct a mock audit every few years. The cost is well worth the amount you spend. Smooth and complete record keeping is the price of admission into this wonderful field of endeavor. It is also your first line of defense in case of a client dispute.

FWIW # 173 .... *Window To World*

Thirty years ago, stock brokers had small terminals on their desks that gave the price of a stock and nothing else. Today, any financial advisor has access to substantial information about securities, economic data, and clientele. Some of this information is proprietary to the advisor's firm and other information is available over the Internet.

Advisors with large brokerage firms have a wealth of information at their fingertips, most of it tailored to the firm's research department and the advisor's clients. The concept of being able to cross reference your clients and their holdings is crucial to keeping on top of the business today. Being able to quickly find out who owns how many shares of a particular security, or who does not own the security, is helpful in placing buy and sell orders to maximize the potential of receiving the best execution. Having access to full information about the securities covered by the research analysts allows the large firm advisor to sit at the desk and quickly see if the fundamental and technical aspects of a stock are in sync or diverging. A quick entry to the Internet will give an outsider opinion as a backup to the firm's analyst's opinion. Some of the information terminals have a split screen allowing the advisor to watch business television while going through either client accounts or research data.

Small advisors have a greater challenge assembling the data necessary to operate their business even though they have access to the Internet. Financial information on the Internet is the second most sought after data (you can guess what is more interesting). Because there is so much information available, it's important for an advisor to take the time and find the sites that concisely present information needed. Financial sites offering fundamental research, technical analysis, and company web pages are just three categories important to advisors. Having an account at a brokerage firm usually gives access to the full research of that firm as well as such independent information as supplied by Standard & Poor's. The challenge is not in having enough information, it is having too much and not being able to digest it all or extract usable and timely facts from the enormous quantity of statistics.

Small advisors have to rely on one of two sources for client data. Most advisors use an internal operating system from one of the software companies. Some of these systems are highly sophisticated and allow the advisor to cross reference clients by a number of different characteristics as well as cross reference the securities in clients' portfolios. For advisors who choose to have only one custodian for all of their accounts, an Internet link with that custodian can take the place of an internal accounting system particularly if the advisor does not supply clients with extensive quarterly reporting. For those advisors who have the resources, there are business services supplying terminals for the professional advisor's desk that are extremely complicated and sophisticated resources of investment market data. These are the same terminals available at major Wall Street investment banks. While expensive, the value far outweighs the cost if used properly.

It does not matter whether your firm is a large brokerage house, a small regional boutique, an independent investment counseling firm, or a bank. What matters is taking the time to fully understand what services your information terminal can supply to you daily. This takes time. Find the time because it will make the difference between having the confidence to develop portfolios in times of extreme FEAR and missing the opportunity because you don't have the critical data necessary to make a decision.

The paper calendar, carried by an advisor like a Bible, is dead. The personal digital appliance (PDA) is here to stay and very important to the smooth flow of your business. Not just because it can fit in your pocket or briefcase better, but because of what it can do. The address file cannot only keep the name, address, and phone number of all of your clients, it can also keep their account numbers at the custodian as well. Have you ever wanted to make a trade for a client while away from the office and realized you didn't have their account number? That won't happen again. Ever sell a stock the day before an earning's announcement only to see it go up the next day on good news? With a PDA, you can put alerts as to when earning's announcements are due every quarter forever with one entry using the repeat function. The same action can tell you when dividends are due.

Ever get a thought while out of the office of something you want or need to do by next Friday? With the PDA, you can put it on the calendar and the to-do-list function all at one time. Ever wanted to send a quick message back to your office while you were out somewhere with a phone not available? Some PDA's, and probably all in the future, will allow you to have wireless e-mail through the Internet. The PDA is in its infancy for becoming an Internet connection. Eventually, you will not have stored memory, but a way for you to access the entire memory and functions back at your office or several sites on the Internet. Get one now and get used to it. Learn to write either using the shorthand code built into the machine or the pop-up keyboard. Above all, learn to pay attention to the battery power level and back up your data on a regular basis. Otherwise, you will have sweet memories of the bulky paper daily diary you used to carry that did not do as much, but was always there.

FWIW # 175 .... Today's Opportunities

On a regular basis, you should go through your universe of stocks and the industry groups you monitor to prioritize them as to whether the securities or sector should be bought, sold, or held. This doesn't mean you will take action daily, but it does mean you will develop a sense of where FEAR is dominating the share price or sector and where GREED is in control. Reviewing the prices will alert you when a security is starting to move. It gives you the ideas for portfolio changes and allows you to direct your daily research time to those areas that are the most beneficial.

FWIW # 176 .... *Paper Machine*

It must be a conspiracy. The more digital and online the world gets, the more paper seems to cross an advisor's desk. It's hard to understand why paper stocks aren't the growth stocks of the 21st century. All of the paper streaming across the advisor's desk falls into one of two categories: NICE TO KNOW and NEED TO KNOW (FWIW # 12). It only takes seconds to understand which category a particular report falls under. Don't read the nice to know. Pick out the important part of the need to know information. Shred both pieces of paper unless required by regulatory agencies to keep it. Don't fall into a trap of keeping the mounds of paper that will come across your desk.

FWIW # 177 .... *Time Control*

FWIW #35 discussed time management in context of being efficient and focused. No one, however, is 100% efficient 100% of the time. There is a way, however, to painlessly increase your productive time each year by one 50-hour week. How? By simply and deliberately finding ten minutes each day to be more productive. Here's the math: six days a week (remember you only need ten minutes extra each day) for 50 weeks (you have at least two weeks vacation) = 300 days. If you find ten minutes extra per day, you gain 3,000 minutes over the 50 weeks. At 60 minutes per hour, you pick up 50 hours more productive time.

Now, how can you increase your productive time by ten minutes per day without taking time away from your family, your rest, or your leisure? Easy. Here are some of the ways:

(1) Turn off the business television shows at the office for three hours.

(2) Take less personal phone calls from other professionals who want to talk about the markets.

(3) Pre-plan your outgoing phone calls and end them when your objective is met.

(4) Let your assistant open the mail and give you only what needs your attention.

(5) Segment your activities and don't allow any interference, other than clients, with the assigned task during the segmented period.

(6) Be aware of small distractions. When you recognize a recurring distraction, take steps to eliminate it, or, at best, control it until a particular segmented task is over.

Ten minutes a day is not much until you realize how quickly it mounts up. Find yours and find a *goal* mine of treasure.

FWIW # 178 .... *The Score*

If you aren't ambitious and goal-oriented, you won't be in the business for long. If you are, you want to measure what progress you are making daily. Transaction-based advisors keep track of commissions. Fee-based advisors keep track of assets under management. Either way, validating your hard work is not only acceptable, but a must. Demand results of your efforts within the constraints of ethical business. If you are right for the business, realizing a goal will not make you lazy or slack, it will only inspire you to set a new goal and build your business more efficiently to achieve the new summit.

FWIW # 179 .... *Time Out*

Being a financial advisor is challenging and stressful as well as exhilarating and rewarding. It is addictive in terms of being so complex that a lifetime can be spent improving and succeeding, but never mastering the markets. To be able to enhance this all consuming career, you should take time every day to do nothing but sit quietly and think. Think about whatever you want. Develop the discipline to not think about the markets except in context of your overall life. Make sure you are spiritually calm with who you are, where you are, and where you want to go. Think about what truly are the important aspects of life: relationships and health. Think about how fortunate you are to be where you want to be. Think about what you need to do to be at peace with yourself if you are not. Think about what you can do to bring happiness to someone who does not have it. Think about the fact that success in life is a journey and not a destination. Allow your subconscious to develop what you want to think about in this time out period. It will allow you to dream without becoming a dreamer. You will find that this time out will cleanse your mind, soul, and body and make you a better person and financial advisor.

Index

126, 130, 133, 136, 161, 170, 172,
178–180, 191, 202, 212, 213, 217,
220, 224–226, 230, 246, 248, 250,
251, 253, 255, 265, 303, 304, 306,
312, 314, 315, 317, 323, 330, 334,
337, 342, 354, 359, 362, 363
Balanced   119, 229
Equity   10, 11, 13, 30, 51, 86, 113,
226, 229, 236, 263, 265, 266, 272,
278, 286, 321–323, 325–328, 332,
352
Fixed income   29, 30, 85, 86, 88, 159,
194, 195, 212, 214, 224, 229, 248,
249, 255, 261, 262, 263, 265–267,
272, 291, 328
Positive attitude   24
Potholes   192, 320
PowerPoint   165
Practice   30–34, 91–93, 96, 98, 108, 131,
136, 147, 148, 151, 155, 163, 167,
168, 178, 183, 201, 202, 306, 335,
347
Presentation   32, 98, 110, 111, 123, 130,
143, 147, 161, 165–167, 172, 173,
177, 179, 181, 185
Price changes   36, 190, 208
Pricing power   195, 243
Private placement stocks   335
Probability weighting   242
Products   15, 53, 242, 273, 305
Professional attitude   38
Profile   14, 16, 34, 44, 78, 84, 93, 97,
119, 130, 176, 183, 215, 226, 228,
237, 243, 251, 263, 275, 277, 302,
328
Profit margins   195
Promoter   297, 299
Proposal   163, 166
Prospect   25, 37, 38, 44, 46, 47, 72, 96,
98, 100–103, 110–112, 114, 116,
118, 128, 129, 161–164, 166–171,
174, 177, 184, 202, 292
Prospect storage   171
Prospecting   27, 37, 38, 47, 49, 51, 95,
97, 98, 99, 108, 117, 170, 171, 173
Cold calling   97, 108
Community service   17, 48–51, 53, 98,

100, 108
Direct mail   97, 100, 108, 109, 111
Referrals   12, 98, 99, 100, 107, 108,
114–116, 170
Seminar   98, 104–107
Prudent investing   156
Pruning   131
Psychology   32, 113, 135, 136, 153, 199,
310, 319
Put   19, 21, 22, 31, 34, 37, 46, 52, 70, 85,
102, 108, 120, 127, 133, 141, 167,
193, 237, 248, 249, 250, 254, 259,
265, 270, 273, 285, 288, 290, 297,
302, 322, 324, 331–333, 363, 364

Q

Qualified investor offerings   298
Questionnaire   118, 119
   Why   118
Quote machines   36

R

Radio   282
Rapport   127, 130, 163
Ratios   120, 232, 275, 276, 278, 279, 286,
289, 332
Real estate   5, 30, 95, 159, 194, 197–200,
207, 261–264, 297, 305, 322
Recession   156, 207, 269, 272, 278
Recommendation   74, 76, 77, 145, 160,
202, 300
Referral   17, 99, 105, 113–116, 162, 173,
181, 349
Referrals   12, 98–100, 107, 108, 114–116,
170
   300 Club members   114
   Clients   12, 98, 114, 116
   Family and friends   114
   Other professionals   114, 115
Refinancing   182
Refund   134
Reinforcement   146
Reinvestment   70, 220
REIT   214, 223, 224, 263, 332
Relationship   11, 15, 19, 23, 39, 42, 43,
46, 57, 62–65, 67, 69, 75–77, 83, 84,

NOTES

NOTES

NOTES

NOTES

NOTES

NOTES